the
BOATYARD
BOOK

SIMON JOLLANDS

the BOATYARD BOOK

A boatowner's guide to yacht maintenance, repair and refitting

ADLARD
COLES

LONDON · OXFORD · NEW YORK · NEW DELHI · SYDNEY

ADLARD COLES
Bloomsbury Publishing Plc
50 Bedford Square, London, WC1B 3DP, UK
29 Earlsfort Terrace, Dublin 2, Ireland

BLOOMSBURY, ADLARD COLES and the Adlard Coles
logo are trademarks of
Bloomsbury Publishing Plc

First published in Great Britain 2021
This edition published 2021

Copyright © Simon Jollands, 2021
Illustrations © Simon Jollands, 2021

Simon Jollands has asserted his right under the
Copyright, Designs and Patents Act, 1988, to be
identified as Author of this work

For legal purposes the Acknowledgements on p. 219
constitute an extension of this copyright page

A catalogue record for this book is available from the
British Library

Library of Congress Cataloguing-in-Publication data
has been applied for

ISBN: PB: 978-1-4729-7710-6;
ePDF: 978-1-4729-7709-0;
ePUB: 978-1-4729-7708-3

2 4 6 8 10 9 7 5 3 1

Typeset in ITC Veljovic by Susan McIntyre
Printed and bound in India by Replika Press Pvt. Ltd

To find out more about our authors and books visit
www.bloomsbury.com and sign up for our newsletters

CONTENTS

It is October. I have just returned from a magnificent day's sailing down the Solent in near perfect conditions for the time of year, with a Force 4 northerly breeze and clear blue skies. Coming after a prolonged period of stormy weather and heavy rain, this sail was a real treat that raised the spirits big time. *Sulali*, my 40-year-old Contessa 26, behaved impeccably, coping well with the 20-knot gusts under full main and genoa. Turning back towards the entrance to Chichester harbour meant beating to windward. Now *Sulali* was almost sailing on its side as the wind continued to strengthen. Magic!

Back ashore there is an email from Tim Cath, owner of the Bosham Yacht Company, with a winter lay-up form attached. It is time to start planning *Sulali*'s winter lift out and storage ashore. Tim's boatyard still has availability, but I need to book a space soon before the boat park is full to capacity. Over the past five years Tim's network of contacts has helped me keep *Sulali* in good condition. Nothing can really compare with picking up advice from experts such as Tim, plus spending years gaining personal experience of boat ownership, if you want to build up a true understanding of how to look after a boat. However, I hope this book will provide boatowners with a useful practical resource and aide memoire to keep onboard and scribble notes over, not only while working on their boats in the yard but also when they are afloat.

Sulali does not need a serious amount of work this winter, but I won't be sure until I get the boat ashore.

WHO IS THIS BOOK FOR?

The word 'boat' is a relatively vague term that might apply to almost any vessel that floats. For the purpose of this book, 'boat' refers to sailing and motor yachts ranging from 6 to 20 metres in length. I hope all boatowners in this category will find this book useful, but more likely it will be enthusiastic boatowners with limited technical skills who get the most benefit.

When I bought my first yacht 20 years ago, it was a big leap from the Wayfarer dinghy I had owned for a good many years beforehand. Even though it was only 30 feet in length, my Etap 30 had complex electrics, plumbing and a Volvo Penta inboard diesel engine with saildrive transmission to get to grips with. Having almost non-existent engineering skills, my only sensible option was to turn to professionals for help with almost every task, which of course got very expensive. I needed to learn more practical skills.

Enthusiasm is one thing, but experience and expertise really count when it comes to looking after boats. I quickly realised that cutting corners was not an option and that a job was only worth doing if it was done properly. This means working to high standards and making a serious effort to learn new skills in order to begin doing more maintenance and repair tasks oneself. It also means being prepared to call in the professionals when necessary.

There are many tasks that seasoned boatowners do themselves. Most boatyards in my experience have no objections to owners donning overalls, provided they are not continually asking the boatyard staff for advice. The DIY ethic is strong throughout the boating

▲ Lowering a fin-keeled yacht and cradle onto a trailer at the beginning of a season. The hull has been treated with antifouling, the topsides polished and the yacht is ready for launching.

▲ Yachts being lifted ashore at the end of the season. The yacht in the slings is being pressure washed to remove as much marine growth as possible before it is transported to the yard.

▼ This small wooden yacht will be a joy to sail but requires much more work to keep in good condition than a fibreglass boat.

▲ My Etap 30 having its hull cleaned and sacrificial anodes replaced mid-season in Cowes. This was just a two-hour lift out and well worth doing.

community and there are many owners with practical skills who hardly ever call in the professionals. It also clearly makes a lot of sense for a boat skipper to be able to fix a problem at sea, especially offshore.

Going out to sea in a boat that has not been properly maintained increases the risk of equipment failure and can endanger the lives of those aboard. So the care and maintenance of a boat is a serious business, arguably more so than the care and maintenance of a car. However, it can also be great fun and very satisfying when you find you can fix a broken down engine yourself, without having to call out the rescue services.

This book is divided into two main parts. Part One covers some fundamentals about how to look after a boat, from keeping records, doing regular checks, knowing when to call in the professionals and how to stay on top of the costs and budgeting. As an owner, there is a lot to learn about boat care. How much of the work can you realistically do yourself? Do you know the differences between sealants, adhesives and adhesive sealants? Do you understand electrics and how to service an engine? How do you go about choosing a boatyard? Part Two gets down to the nitty gritty, the practical work of troubleshooting and getting jobs done in the boatyard. Starting with the hull, it then goes on to the deck, mast and rigging, followed by sails, engines and propulsion, dealing with electrics and interior work.

Understanding what needs to be done and when is as important as knowing how to do the work itself, but if you have the time and inclination to get your hands dirty and do the work yourself, then you will doubtless reap the benefits.

PART ONE

Owning a boat is a big commitment that should bring no end of satisfaction to the owner as well as their family and friends. In return for bringing all that joy, a boat deserves and needs a good deal of care and attention.

Caring for your boat is not just about scrubbing the decks and polishing the hull. It is also about getting to know your boat from stem to stern. This entails understanding as much as you possibly can about what goes on in every nook and cranny and how all the various systems of the boat work.

If you shy away from the prospect of keeping a boat well maintained and in good condition then perhaps boat ownership is not for you, unless you have the significant resources required to employ others to look after the boat on your behalf. Even then you run the risk of not being able to cope with equipment failure or a breakdown at sea as you lack the technical skills and know-how to fix the problem.

BOAT OWNERSHIP

Whether 'hands-on' or 'hands-off', an owner is the custodian of their boat in a similar way that a homeowner is a custodian of their house, with both responsible for the upkeep of their possession until they pass

it on to the next owner. However, a boatowner arguably needs to act much more responsibly than a homeowner. A neglected house might fall down, but at least it won't sink. A boatowner has to think about the safety of all those who are going to travel on it during their ownership. Ownership can become challenging occasionally, but as long as the rewards and benefits outweigh the effort and costs then you should live in harmony with your boat and get years of pleasure from it.

You should also end up with an asset with a good resale value, as it will have been well looked after. A neglected boat will not only quickly drop in value, but things can spiral downwards until it becomes unsafe to use. That said, it is no use pretending that the costs of boat ownership are negligible. It is better to be realistic and to budget for expenditure. Be prepared to be in it for the long haul as boats may be easy enough to buy, but invariably they are much more difficult to sell.

▲ Maintaining varnish is not too arduous provided that water is prevented from penetrating the wood. Here, a scraper is being used to remove the flaking varnish. The timber will be sanded smooth before new varnish is applied.

BOAT CARE FUNDAMENTALS

Leaving aside the costs for a few pages, it is worth thinking about a few fundamentals of what's involved with caring for a boat.

Firstly, there are major differences between the work involved with 'maintaining', 'repairing' and 'refitting' a boat. These terms are often used fairly loosely and can lead to confusion. For the purposes of this book and as generally accepted in boating circles, here are some definitions to consider:

- **Maintain** – to keep something in good condition.
- **Repair** – to restore something that is damaged, faulty or worn back to a good condition.
- **Refit** – to replace or repair machinery, equipment and fittings.

YOUR BOAT'S HISTORY

It helps to know as much about your boat's history as possible. Clearly, if you buy a brand new boat this won't apply. However, you will still need to do the checks and keep records for the future. All the various systems and equipment on board will need servicing according to the manufacturer's recommendations. There will be plenty to get your head around in the first year or two of ownership. For the rest of us who own older boats, knowing their history will be a help when looking after them and making plans for their future.

▲ A complete refit is needed before this boat can go afloat again.

▲ This abandoned boat's owner cannot be traced. Any takers?

I made the mistake of buying a boat some time ago that had virtually no records. I am ashamed to admit I also decided against commissioning a full survey, instead only having a lift out and hull inspection done by an engineer who was not a fully qualified surveyor. Huge mistake. I discovered after I bought it that it had been seriously damaged in the past and was no longer 100 per cent seaworthy. Although it had been repaired the hull was no longer sound and to have it stripped back and repaired properly was going to cost thousands. I decided to sell the poor old boat as soon as I could and lost money as a result. The two big lessons I learned were:

- Only ever buy a second-hand boat that comes with detailed records as you need to know what you are letting yourself in for.
- Always have a full survey done by a qualified surveyor.

KEEPING RECORDS

A boat's records should provide information about maintenance schedules, when major work was done and when equipment was replaced or added. Without this information you are left guessing when things are likely to need replacing and what the costs are likely to be.

Keeping detailed records will help you when it comes to ordering spare parts, buying new sails, knowing when equipment is likely to need replacing and being able to estimate what your future costs are going to be. For example, if the boat had two new batteries five years ago they are likely to need replacing within one or two years maximum. If you know the standing rigging was replaced eight years ago and it appears to still be in good condition, you can expect another couple of years' life from it, but not five or ten.

I have owned my current boat for seven years. Each year I make sure I keep every receipt spent on the boat and keep these in a draw. I also keep a record of invoices received and paid electronically as it can be easy to forget these. At the end of each year I go through the draw and file all the receipts. I then enter all the receipt details and expenditure into a spreadsheet, keeping a record of each item, the payee, the invoice date and the amount. This is usually a sobering experience but, even so, I would recommend this as the minimum level of record keeping you need

▲ A spotless, well cared for boat stands out a mile. You get the feeling no expense has been spared to keep this motor cruiser in such good condition.

to do. I certainly find it helps with budgeting and planning.

If you like being more organised, then you can sub-divide your expenditure into categories to really see where your money is going. To be honest I don't tend to do this but for those who prefer this level of detail then headings to consider could include Insurance, Mooring Fees, Haulout Fees, Boatyard Fees, Fuel, Maintenance Costs, Chandlery and so on.

See: **Viki's Maintenance Worksheet** on page 24.

If there are gaps in the records, contacting previous owners can help you build a more complete picture of what has happened in the past.

DOING REGULAR CHECKS

It is a good idea to get into the habit of checking over the boat on a regular basis throughout the boating season. It is also important to deal with any minor issues or obvious defects as soon as they appear, rather than allowing a situation to worsen.

These regular checks need not take up lots of time, and if you make them part of your routine each time you visit the boat then under normal circumstances a few minutes is all that's required if everything is in good order.

For example, all owners of boats with inboard engines that have raw-water cooling systems know that they need to check whether water is flowing out through the exhaust before setting off. They should also know that doing a slightly more thorough engine check might reveal that the alternator belt needs tightening, or the raw-water filter needs cleaning. Both can be fixed quickly and prevent a more serious situation from arising.

Likewise, a check on deck might reveal that a halyard is showing obvious signs of chafe, a hairline crack has appeared at the base of a deck fitting, or perhaps a sail's stitching is damaged. In such cases, a timely repair will be much easier to do than leaving a potentially more serious situation to occur. This approach applies to all vessels, whatever their age and type, and is really just a question of common sense.

See: **Viki's Maintenance Worksheet** on page 24.

MORE THOROUGH CHECKS

More thorough checks can be done less frequently, depending on how much the boat is being used and if, for example, it has been out in heavy seas, where things get shaken up and fittings can become loose (such as the connectivity between electrical components and circuitry).

At the end of the boating season, when the boat comes ashore and before it goes back in the water, is the time to do still more thorough checks. Rig and hull inspections can be carried out by professionals, where necessary. Engines need more thorough inspections: heat exchanger tube stacks can be cleaned and exhaust elbows checked for corrosion blocking the flow of the raw-water cooling.

See: **Viki's Maintenance Worksheet** on page 24.

RESEARCH AND ADVICE

There is plenty of information out there on boat maintenance. In fact, you could spend your entire life reading boating magazine articles, manuals, books and watching how-to videos about refitting boats on YouTube. The challenge is to find the specific piece of information relevant to your particular boat plus all its equipment and fittings. If you come across articles that are directly relevant, hold on to them. Examples of these might include how to service a winch, bleed a diesel engine fuel system, service a sea cock or troubleshoot a faulty VHF radio.

Operator manuals prove invaluable, and if your boat does not have copies aboard, it is normally possible to download and print PDFs for your files. Having the correct manuals will also be a help when ordering spare parts.

◀ *Sulali* having a bottom scrub against piles at low water. The antifouling is doing a reasonable but not perfect job; removing the slime and grime will increase the boat's performance.

Reading all the information is one thing, but when it comes to fixing and mending a boat, don't be afraid to ask for advice on how best to deal with a challenging job. Talking with others who have dealt with the same problem can help you to decide whether this will be something you can do yourself or not.

Being informed will also help when getting quotes to do the job and ensuring you're getting a fair deal.

CALLING IN THE PROFESSIONALS

Knowing when to call in the professionals is a case of knowing your limitations. If you are honest with yourself and know you can't do a job as well as a pro can, then don't be tempted to go it alone, as you might end up in a worse situation than you started with. Ask your boatyard and other boatowners for recommendations and make an effort to meet everyone who works on your boat. This is not always easy when work commitments get in the way, but do your level best.

OWNERS' ASSOCIATIONS

If you own a class of boat that has an owners' association, it is a good idea to join it. Most associations organise sailing rallies and social activities for their class, but with boat care in mind they also host forums to promote exchanges of information, experience and advice.

The forums can really help if you have a technical question you need an answer to, especially if the manufacturers of the boats are no longer in business. Many owners are more than happy to share their experiences with others and advise on the best course of action for you to take. This information exchange is especially useful when it comes to replacing specific parts, but more general questions can lead to conflicting answers that might leave you guessing as to what is the best way to proceed. When in doubt, speak to your boatyard manager or alternatively contact your surveyor if it is a structural issue. Keep any questions very specific, giving as much detail as possible.

WHAT DOES MAINTENANCE WORK INVOLVE?

Maintenance involves keeping something in good condition, as close to its manufactured state as possible. The maintenance of a boat involves things like cleaning, varnishing, painting, polishing, antifouling, servicing the engine, servicing the sea cocks, and maintaining the gas and plumbing systems. It amounts to a fairly considerable amount of work that can't be ignored if you are to keep your boat in a safe and good condition.

If you are prepared to do some or all of the comparatively low-skilled work yourself and can do so to a high standard, then you can save yourself a

good chunk of money. There are usually right and wrong ways to do all these tasks, as you'll see later in the book.

If you don't have the time or inclination to do the work yourself you will need to arrange to pay for the routine maintenance to be done by others. Most yards will have people on site who are able to do this work for you, and you can expect to pay a significant hourly rate for their time. It is always best to check with a yard before lifting out what maintenance work they are able to arrange for you and what their rates are going to be. There is no harm in asking other boatowners about their experiences with the standards of workmanship of local yards.

REPAIRING AND REFURBISHING

In the end, almost every part or piece of equipment on a boat either wears out or breaks and will need to be replaced. Certain items, for example running rigging, engine hoses and interior fittings, are easy enough to replace, while others, such as the standing rigging, cutless bearings or through-hull fittings, are not so straightforward, even when replacing like for like. While it may be tempting to tackle these more complex tasks yourself, for peace of mind most owners tend to have them carried out by professionals.

Much will depend on your experience and DIY skills, plus

▲ Viki Moore gets a helping hand rubbing back the hull of *Wildwood*, her Young 88 keelboat, prior to applying antifouling.

REFIT

A complete refit is usually a complex and lengthy process that requires a carefully planned project timeline, the drawing up of a realistic budget and experienced project management. Whether the project manager is the owner or a professional, their job is to ensure that both the project timeline and budget are kept on track. Some owners like to take on the role themselves, but in order to do this they need to have the time, resources and expertise to see the project through.

Some prospective boatowners go in search of old and neglected boats in need of complete refits in the hope that they will pick up a bargain. The market is swamped with such boats, which can take years to sell. Many of them are virtually worthless, as

whether you have the time available and, in some cases, access to specialist tools. Another issue is the matter of sourcing spares, especially those that are no longer manufactured. This can take a prohibitive amount of time, depending on the age and class of your boat.

▲ Preparing the topsides of a boat for repainting is a time consuming job. The old coatings need to be removed and surface chips and dings must be repaired. Then the entire surface has to be sanded back before painting can begin.

▲ Maintaining a classic wooden boat may be time consuming but certainly has its rewards. Any flaking paint or varnish has to be scraped away to prevent water ingress. Teak decking also needs regular maintenance.

the costs of refitting and making them seaworthy again will likely exceed the market value of the repaired boat. That said, there are bargains out there for those who have the experience, resources and desire to renovate an old boat. This is good news for boatyards, as these boats often remain ashore indefinitely as they are painstakingly restored.

ADVICE ON REFITTING

There are plenty of trained shipwrights who have the experience to advise on whether a neglected boat is worth refitting or not. Some offer a service to help prospective buyers investigate a boat's condition and to estimate what a refit would cost. While these services are not free, they are a safeguard against buying a boat that could turn into too big a project.

THE REWARDS OF BOAT OWNERSHIP

It is no secret that the costs of running a boat soon mount up and they need to be factored in from the outset.

Not wanting to end this chapter on a downer (hard work, costs, more hard work, more costs), caring for your own boat brings a great deal of satisfaction. While being able to stand back and admire a well-looked-after boat in all its sparkling glory in the boatyard is one thing, I hope you will agree that the real rewards are to be enjoyed out on the water.

▲ All the hard work pays off once you are back on the water and the boat comes alive.

3 PLANNING, COSTS AND BUDGETING

This chapter looks at some specifics to do with planning a boat's routine annual maintenance in the boatyard. It includes tips on choosing a boatyard, surveys, how to plan both minor and major repairs, how to plan a major refit. It also looks at costs and budgeting.

CHOOSING A BOATYARD

There are a number of considerations to take into account when choosing a boatyard. These include the type of vessel, its size, current location and any work that needs to be done. It makes sense not to rush into making decisions until you are fully satisfied. Here are three key factors to consider:

1. Recommendation

Arguably the number one factor that will influence your choice is being recommended a yard by someone you trust. If you know someone who has had work done by a yard and was satisfied with the result, this is a good starting point. If the work was of a similar nature to the work you need doing, even better. Double-check with others to get second opinions. Perhaps even ask your surveyor about the yard you have in mind.

2. Location

If you are looking for winter storage where you can do routine maintenance yourself, the yards closest to you are going to be

▲ If you can, choose a yard where the boats are not packed in too tightly and there is an orderly feel about the place. Check out all the facilities and talk to the staff to get a feel for the place before committing.

the first place to look. It is not that helpful to be recommended a yard hundreds of miles away, which would necessitate staying over every time you wanted to visit the boat. That is unless you have been recommended a specialist yard for exactly the type of work you need to have done.

3. Specialisation

If you are looking for specialist work to be done, for instance major hull repairs, a complete interior refit or new teak decks,

you will want to know that the yard has specialists on site to do this type of work. Knowing about your boat's history and previous routine maintenance schedules is a good place to start. If your boat has a well-kept maintenance log, this will help you organise and manage your boat's future maintenance and the boating budget. If you don't have a maintenance log yet, the example on pages 26–33 should help get you started.

BOAT SURVEY

If you have recently purchased a used boat, presumably you had a survey done. The surveyor will have advised you of any faults that needed rectifying, potential problems that might need dealing with in the near future and even an itemised list of how the boat might be improved over time.

In the early days, therefore, a survey can provide the basis for a list of work to be carried out over the first two or three winters of your ownership, in addition to normal routine maintenance and boat care.

A full survey assesses the condition of the hull, mechanical gear and means of propulsion. The full survey is carried out with the boat ashore in order to be able to properly inspect the hull and rudder. The following is an example of a typical inspection of a glass reinforced plastic (GRP) yacht:

- The hull will be inspected for voids, delamination and damage. The surveyor will comment on the under hull condition, whether the hull has been gelshielded, antifouled and well maintained.
- The surveyor will take moisture readings above and below the waterline and report whether these are at an acceptable level for the age and type of vessel.
- All structural bulkheads and internal hull members will be checked.
- The topsides will be checked

▲ Some repair work has to be done under cover. This will mean increased storage costs so be prepared to shop around and go further afield if necessary.

and any repairs that need to be done will be listed.

- The keel will be inspected for any defects and grounding damage.
- The rudder and steering gear will be inspected, and the condition of the rudder mountings, bearings and pintles noted.
- The stern gear will be checked, including the propeller, stern tube, stern gland and the prop anode.
- Deck hardware such as winches, cleats and stanchions will be inspected, and the condition of the spars and rigging will also be recorded.
- All skin fittings will be checked, including the speed and depth transducers and the condition of the sea cocks.
- All sea cock-related pipework and the condition of the sea toilet will be checked.

- The shroud anchorage points will all be inspected, including the forestay fitting, inner forestay fitting and backstay fitting.
- The engine beds and general condition of the engine will be checked.
- The deck and superstructure will be examined by tapping with a small hammer over the outer surface. This is done to check for any voids or delamination.
- Windows and hatches will be checked for any signs of leakage.
- The stanchions, pushpit, pulpit and guardrails will be examined for the quality of fixings and whether they are all in a serviceable condition.
- The deck gear will be checked.
- The hull–deck joint will be inspected for soundness.
- The mast base will be checked.

▶ When buying a boat, it is always advisable to commission a survey, whatever the age.

Any defects will be recorded by the surveyor in their report. It is normal practice to have a boat survey carried out every five years or so, possibly longer. Quite a bit can happen in the intervening years and this is where it can be very helpful for boatowners to learn how to inspect and troubleshoot defects and potential faults themselves. Waiting for something to break before fixing it is generally not advisable.

DIY SURVEYING

Doing your own boat inspections should not be considered a substitute for having a professional survey done every five years, which is a highly skilled process and a necessary part of your boat's long-term care. However, carrying out a DIY survey will help you identify and monitor potential problems at an early stage and remedy them before they develop into a major issue.

For example, this might be knowing how to identify if there is excessive movement in the propeller shaft. How would you know if this is excessive movement if you had never checked the propeller shaft for movement in the past? If you are able to identify for yourself that this is excessive movement and has developed quite rapidly then you will know that it needs fixing and should be a high priority. If it has been the same for years maybe it is not such a high priority but just needs regular monitoring.

DIY survey tools

Surveyors can often be found in boatyards tapping on the hulls and decks of boats with small hammers, listening carefully for sounds that indicate there could be a problem beneath the surface. While professional surveyors still do this, they also have all kinds

Surveyor's tips (TiP)

• Make sure that your surveyor has proper liability insurance (they will be able to show you this) and is accredited by at least one well-known marine body.

• For an insurance survey, it is helpful to empty bilge storage areas of 'clutter'. There is nothing worse than spending a lot of the survey simply moving items in and out of compartments.

◄ Older boats need surveying at least every five years. Most insurers will require boatowners to do this as a condition of cover. Focus will be on such features as fuel and gas systems, skin fittings, safety appliances and the general condition of the yacht.

of expensive, hi-tech moisture meters, ultrasound equipment, corrosion meters and various other testing gadgets. The good news is that carrying out a DIY survey requires little in the way of tools. These include:

- **Lightweight tack hammer:** Surveyors use hammers to search for signs of delamination in the hull. Note they tap rather than whack the hull with the hammer. If in doubt about what you are listening for, then asking a friendly surveyor for a quick demonstration should soon clarify things. This is what they listen for:
  • As the hammer taps a GRP hull in good condition, a clear crisp sound should be heard and the hammer should bounce back.
  • A hammer tapping a GRP hull that has a wet core will make a dull, deeper sounding

tone and will not bounce back.
- **Bradawl:** A thin pointed tool like a bradawl is useful for prodding into cracks in a gelcoat and testing whether timbers might be rotten.
- **Scraper:** A small scraper is handy for scraping away small areas of antifouling or flaking paint where necessary.
- **Duct tape** for marking spots or places that require attention.
- **Tape measure.**
- **Notebook** for recording measurements and observations.
- **Small mirror:** An old dentist's mirror is useful as it helps you to see into awkward places and around corners.
- **Magnifying glass** for taking a close look for hairline cracks.
- **Head torch.**
- **Smartphone** for taking photos. Also very useful as an additional torch.

Tack hammer

Bradawl

Scraper

Duct tape

Tape measure

Notebook

Mirror

Magnifying glass

Head torch

Smartphone

MAINTENANCE LOG

Keeping a maintenance log is an ideal way of reminding yourself what needs to be done to the boat and when. There are some excellent downloadable maintenance log spreadsheets available. One I would recommend in particular is produced by Viki Moore of Astrolabe Sailing (https://astrolabesailing. com/2017/11/27/the-ultimate-boating-spreadsheet). This Excel spreadsheet collates all kinds of boating-related information, including maintenance, boat details, spare parts, annual budget, personal inventory, passage log and more.

Viki's Maintenance Worksheet is designed to work as a reminder of work to be done, as well as a record of what has been done in the past. There are columns to add the parts required, their part number, measurements and other details to make life easier when you need to place orders and plan the work.

ROUTINE MAINTENANCE

Should you decide not to keep a computer-based maintenance log, it would still be a good idea to make a plan of what routine maintenance needs to be done through the year and noting the jobs that can be done only when the boat is hauled out.

Who will be doing the work?

Planning routine maintenance will really help you in the long run. If you are thinking of doing the bulk of the work yourself, you need to be realistic about how much work needs to be done and approximately how long it is going to take you.

However keen you may be to do everything yourself, organising yourself can be challenging on occasions. Boat maintenance can take up a considerable amount of time. Can all your other commitments really be forgotten in favour of the boat? The winter weather often puts a spanner in the works so you may need to build

▲ Having a maintenance plan worked out as soon as a boat comes ashore will help ensure the essential tasks are not overlooked and can be done before the new season gets underway.

in some flexibility. If you are fortunate enough to have friends or family who are happy to give you a hand, then the sooner you can firm up the dates in your diary for doing this work the better. If you would like others to help you with specific tasks, it is better to give them plenty of advance warning, preferably when the sun is still shining.

If you are not going to be doing the routine maintenance work yourself due to the pressure of other commitments, physical impediment, or because you can afford not to, you still need to do some planning well ahead of time. This means speaking to your boatyard early on and explaining what tasks need to be done and when. It is a little foolhardy just to take the boat ashore at the end of the season and three months later ask the yard to do all the maintenance just before you plan to go afloat in the spring.

▲ Servicing a yacht's engine is not too challenging as long as you have the right tools, spares and an engine manual.

Doing the work yourself

Begin by checking through the boat's maintenance history, noting when work was done in previous years, how much it cost and estimating how long each task took.

Make a list of the materials and tools you will need for each task coming up and remember to keep a note of what you spent on materials and where you bought them. It always pays to shop around to get the best price for parts.

While your local chandlery might be your favourite shop in the world to browse in, if you are after non-specialist products, such as sponges, brushes, paint rollers, thinners, solvents and tape, you will most likely find similar items in large hardware stores at a fraction of the price. If you are really organised, buy enough materials to last a whole season and you will save yourself both time and money in the long run.

Overview plan

Here are some extracts taken from Viki Moore's maintenance log that give an overview plan of the routine maintenance to be carried out annually on a typical mid-size cruising yacht.

▲ Viki Moore of Astrolabe Sailing.

Part of the boat	Things to check	Date done	Date done	Date done	Date done	Date done	Date done
Engine	Oil level						
	Coolant level						
	Battery fluid						
	Drive belt tension						
	Check raw-water inlet strainer is clear						
	Stern gland lubrication						
	Fuel water separator – drain water						
	Change engine lubricating oil						
	Change lubricating oil filter						
	Transmission oil level						
	Air cleaner element						
	Raw-water pump impeller						
	Wasting anode – replace when necessary						
	Remove heat exchanger tube stack, clean. Replace rubber O rings						
	Lubricate key switch with WD40						
	Check all external nuts, bolts and fastenings are tight						
	Check ball joint nyloc nuts for tightness on gearbox and speed control levers						
	Grease control cable joints and end fittings						
	Grease exposed parts of gear shift mechanism						
	Check for leaks in fuel system						
	Drain water off fuel filter						
	Check engine mounts						
	Change engine oil and oil filter at end of season						
	Top up fuel tanks to prevent condensation						
	Protect the sealed cooling circuit with antifreeze						
	Protect the raw-water cooling circuit with antifreeze						
	Disconnect the batteries and take ashore						

Part of the boat	Things to check	Date done	Date done	Date done	Date done	Date done	Date done
Engine	Ensure cockpit engine instrument panel is protected						
	Spray engine instrument panel key switch with WD40 or equivalent						
	Clean engine space						
Outboard	Check fuel lines						
	Replace fuel filter						
	Spray electrical connections						
	Flush cooling system with fresh water						
	Check for external corrosion						
	Check gear oil level						
	Replace sheer pin						
	Replace spark plug						
Stern gear	Stern tube						
	Stern gland – requires annual maintenance						
	Propeller – grease moving parts as required						
	Prop anode						
Hull and keel	Pressure wash immediately after lift out						
	Check hull–deck joint						
	Inspect for chips and dings in the gelcoat						
	Check for signs of osmosis – mark any blisters						
	Check bulkheads and internal hull members for signs of movement						
	Check keel bolts						
	Check keel for rust spots						
	Check for signs of grounding damage						
Rudder	Check rudder is in line with keel						
	Check rudder bearings for excessive play						
	Check rudder mountings and pintles are in good condition						

Part of the boat	Things to check	Date done	Date done	Date done	Date done	Date done	Date done
Rudder	Check tiller and tiller head for condition						
Steering	Check steering cables						
	Lubricate steering cables						
	Check adjustment nuts are tight						
	Check sheave supports are firmly mounted						
	Ensure area is free from gear and tangles						
	Examine rudder shaft						
	Test emergency steering						
Deck	Check for signs of delamination or damage						
	Check hatches for signs of leaks						
	Check windows for signs of leaks						
	Check star crazing in the gelcoat						
	Check the toerail is properly fixed and in good condition						
	Check stanchions, pushpit, pulpit and guardrails are all well fixed and serviceable						
	Check all deck gear is in a serviceable condition						
	Check the mast base is sound and well fixed						
Electrical	Clean battery tops and terminals						
	Lubricate terminals with petroleum jelly						
	Check electrolyte levels in wet cell batteries						
	Check all electrical connections are clean and secure						
	Check fuses						
	Check light bulbs						
	Check shore power connections						
	Check for any loose connections						

Part of the boat	Things to check	Date done	Date done	Date done	Date done	Date done	Date done
Electrical	Check wiring for signs of chafe						
	Use cable ties to tidy loose wires						
Gas system	Check gas lines and pipes						
	Check hose clips						
	Check CO_2 alarm is working						
Plumbing	Clean bilges						
	Check sea cocks						
	Ensure all through-hulls are in sound condition and have wooden plugs						
	Check bilge pumps are working						
	Check and clean water tanks						
	Check water pumps are working						
	Check sea toilets are working. Service where necessary						
	Check all taps are working correctly						
	Check shower sump and drain						
	Inspect all hoses for leaks and kinks						
	Ensure all hose clamps are tight						
Anchoring	Lubricate bow roller						
	Clean and inspect anchor chain						
	Check anchor shackles						
	Clean and inspect anchor						
	Check mooring lines						
	Check and clean fenders						
	Check line and buoy for emergency ditching						
Navigation and communications	Check GPS is working						
	Check chart plotter is working						
	Do VHF radio check						
	Swing compass						
	Check compass light						
	Check handheld VHF						

Part of the boat	Things to check	Date done	Date done	Date done	Date done	Date done	Date done
Navigation and communications	Look for signs of water ingress or corrosion						
Deck gear	Replace any bent or corroded fastenings						
	Check lifelines						
	Ensure stanchions are secure						
	Service winches						
	Check cleats – ensure back plates and nuts are secure						
	Check jammers						
	Check sheets						
	Check grab rails are secure						
	Check all blocks and shackles are in good condition						
	Wash blocks with detergent to remove salt and dirt						
	Polish stainless steel deck fittings						
	Wash traveller cars with detergent						
Sails	Remove sails for storage ashore						
	Wash and dry sails in fresh water/ send to be laundered						
	Wash sheets and halyards						
	Check for any tears and chafing						
	Check seam stitching						
	Check condition of eyes and cringles						
	Lubricate sail track						
	Check battens and pockets						
	Inspect head, tack and reef points						
	Replace tell tales if required						
	Examine all halyards						
Galley	Clean cupboards						
	Check gimbals on stove work						
	Clean stove						
	Check and clean fridge						

Part of the boat	Things to check	Date done	Date done	Date done	Date done	Date done	Date done
Rig	**Safety first**						
	Check halyards used for rig inspection are not damaged						
	Check the bosun's chair is in good condition						
	Attach two halyards to the chair using knots						
	Attach tools by a lanyard						
	Have two capable people operating the winches						
	Deck check						
	Split pins are not broken or missing						
	No broken strands of wire						
	No visible signs of cracking along swage						
	No visible signs of rust streaking, indicating broken strands or cracks						
	Halyards lead correctly to exit slots. Chafe guards if fitted are secure and in good condition						
	No visible signs of damage to forestay from anchor						
	Masthead						
	Halyard sheaves rotate freely						
	Split pins are not broken or missing						
	Sideways movement of sheaves not too excessive						
	No sharp edges of sheaves able to cause wear to halyards						
	Electrical wires are clamped correctly and no signs of chafing						
	Windex and wind instrument gear correctly aligned and operating freely						
	Forestay and furler						
	Roller furler headstay is not damaged from halyard wrap						
	Halyard leads at the correct angle to the swivel car (see furler manual)						
	Slacken genoa halyard and inspect wear on sheaves, fairlead and top swivel						
	Mast tang pin hole has not elongated						

Part of the boat	Things to check	Date done	Date done	Date done	Date done	Date done	Date done
Rig	**Forestay and furler**						
	Split pins are not broken or missing						
	No signs of corrosion around mast tangs						
	Fastenings are all secure						
	No visible signs of cracking along length of swage						
	No visible signs of rust streaking, indicating broken strands or cracks						
	Inner forestay/cap shrouds						
	Mast tang pin hole has not elongated						
	No signs of corrosion around mast tangs						
	Fastenings are all secure						
	No visible signs of cracking along length of swage						
	No visible signs of rust streaking, indicating broken strands or cracks						
	Split pins are not broken or missing						
	Spreader root						
	No signs of cracking or movement						
	Fastenings are all secure						
	Spreader ends						
	Remove covers for inspection and replace afterwards						
	Wire is securely seized or clamped in spreader end						
	No broken strands or wear						
	Spinnaker pole ring and car						
	Attachment points are secure						
	Pole ring is sized correctly for pole end						
	Deck collar						
	Collar is secure in position						
	Watertight shield is secure and not perished						
	Mast step						
	No evidence of excessive corrosion						
	Mast step is secure to hull						
	Chain plates						
	No sign of elongation in pin holes						

Part of the boat	Things to check	Date done	Date done	Date done	Date done	Date done	Date done
Rig	Split pins are not broken or missing						
	Chain plates align with stay angles						
	No evidence of fracture in chain plate at deck level						
	Chain plates are fastened securely below deck to hull integrity						
	Gooseneck/vang knuckles						
	No signs of corrosion around mast tangs						
	Split pins are covered and well protected to avoid damage to sails						
	Fastenings are all secure						
	No signs of excessive wear on spacers or bushes						
	No signs of elongation in fittings						
Dinghy	Clean						
	Check painter						
	Check anchor						
	Ensure there is a bailer						
Safety gear	Check fire extinguishers						
	Inflate lifejackets						
	Check lifejacket cylinders						
	Service liferaft						
	Check liferings						
	Check safety harnesses						
	Check lifelines						
	Replace batteries in grab bag						
	Replace batteries in EPIRB						
	Check expiry date of PLB						
	Test bilge pumps and alarm						
	Check first-aid kit						
	Check grab bag						
	Check flares and replace as necessary						
	Check jack lines and pad eyes						
	Check fog horn						
	Check wire cutters						

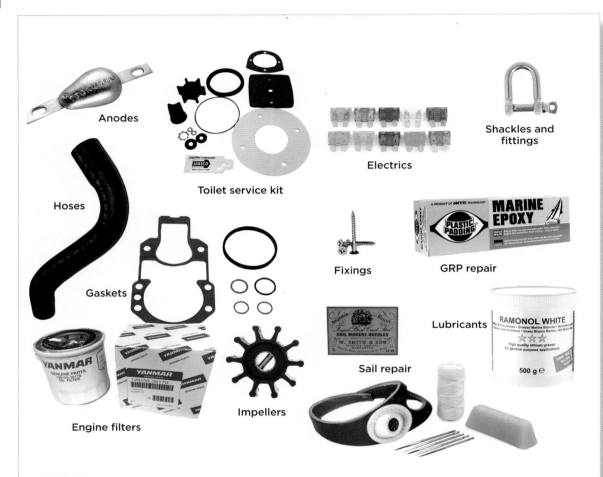

Anodes

Toilet service kit

Electrics

Shackles and fittings

Hoses

GRP repair

Fixings

MARINE EPOXY

Gaskets

Lubricants

RAMONOL WHITE

High quality lithium grease for general purpose applications

500 g ℮

Sail repair

YANMAR

Engine filters

Impellers

SPARE PARTS

Carrying spare parts aboard a cruising boat is clearly advisable as this will make life a lot easier in the event of a breakdown, although racing sailors might not necessarily agree with this as saving weight is going to be high up their list of priorities.

A basic spares kit might include filters, hoses, impellers, gaskets, alternator belts, engine oil and anodes. Where you draw the line after that is debatable.

Items like shackles, blocks, nuts and bolts, fuses, bulbs, jubilee clips, tapes, toilet service kits, epoxy resin, gelcoat filler and various repair kits all merit a place aboard. Some owners might choose to keep some if not all of these ashore to avoid cluttering up their boat, which is fine until you need them when you are out at sea.

For routine maintenance purposes, I have tried to get into the habit of keeping at least

one of everything that needs replacing annually in reserve. I then buy new spares and keep these in reserve. Sometimes I am loathe to throw something away that could be used as back-up in an emergency, but you do have to be careful here because there is a tendency to build up far too much stuff. So what I do is to store these at home in boxes that never get opened. This is a bad, fairly pointless habit.

REPAIRS AND UPDATES

It is a good idea to think about any repairs or updates well in advance of bringing your boat ashore, unless of course it has suffered something like collision damage that needs fixing immediately, which is another matter altogether.

One of the first things to consider is whether your regular boatyard is the right place to carry out the work. Does the yard have the necessary facilities and workshops for the job? If not, ask them if they can recommend somewhere more suitable.

Talking with your boatyard sooner rather than later is important because organising repairs will entail sourcing the parts, lining up specialists, getting quotes and booking everyone's time. The earlier you can do this the better, as the busiest time of year for boatyards is over the winter months, building up to a crescendo in the spring when most owners want to get their boats in the water.

Marine engineers don't like to turn down work and if you find yourself at the back of a queue you might well end up having to keep the boat ashore for much longer than you previously intended (as has happened to me). This can lead to higher storage costs and mounting frustration all round.

Forward thinking can save you thousands. When you leave things too late, there are a number of catchphrases in conversations with potential suppliers that can cause the

alarm bells to ring: 'We will do our best to fit you in, but we've got some big jobs on right now', 'Those parts need to come from Sweden', 'That was a design fault with that particular engine' and 'We could knock you up a new one for eight grand but not before April'. Give yourself time to get second opinions and ask around. You might well find that by doing some research and buying some specialist tools you could fix a problem yourself for a fraction of the cost you have been quoted, which is always a good outcome providing the repair is 100 per cent effective.

CONTACTING INSURERS

If your boat has been damaged, whether by a collision, a storm or a fire, the first thing to do is to contact your insurers. They will send you a claim form, and the usual practice is that they will ask for photos of the damage, how it happened and request an estimate for the repair costs. They sometimes ask for two or three estimates.

In the case of minor damage such as a splintered toerail or a scrape in the topsides, the insurers may give the go-ahead to have the repair done based on the information you supplied and an approved estimate. If the damage is more substantial, for example a hole caused by a collision, they will normally appoint a surveyor to assess the damage and provide a report and estimation of the likely repair cost.

REFITS

A refit involves major work covering a multitude of large and small jobs that need to be done to both old and newer yachts. This might follow extended cruising or a change of ownership.

A typical refit may entail a job list that includes osmosis treatment, repainting the topsides, new rigging, mast renovation, replacing teak decks, rewiring and electronics replacement and complete interior refurbishment. The list could go on to the bottom of the page and beyond. A major refit of a yacht can entail months of work.

Owners of larger yachts contemplating a refit normally appoint a single yard that will manage the entire process for them. This doesn't mean that the work is done without the owner's involvement. Instead, it ensures that the process is handled professionally and that all specialists working on the project report into the yard's project manager rather than direct to the owner.

While this approach is logical and in many ways desirable, there are owners who want to have a much more hands-on approach to a refit, possibly even wanting to manage the whole process themselves. This could be partly a question of trying to save money and partly because the owner wants to have a complete understanding of all the boat's systems, which could prove invaluable if they are contemplating long-distance offshore cruising.

It is worth considering some critical questions if you are contemplating project managing a refit yourself (note that there is no mention of whether you have the financial resources):

- Have you managed a similar project before?
- If so, did the project keep within its budget?
- Was the project completed on time?
- Did you have any unexpected issues along the way?
- Are you good at managing people with a range of skill sets and experience?
- How about contractors? Are you used to handling negotiations?
- Are you confident that you could draw up the detailed specifications required when briefing contractors?
- How good are you at making decisions?
- How good are you at dealing with unexpected problems that occur at inconvenient times?
- Do you have sufficient time to devote to it?
- Have you considered taking out project insurance?
- How much contingency time will you allow?
- Where will the vessel be based during the refit?
- What specialist skills do you have?

It is also worth thinking back to any smaller projects you may have done on your boat and ask yourself these questions:

- How many estimates for work were exceeded because of 'unforeseen issues'?
- Did you ever have any difficulties sourcing parts?
- How many times were you held up because contractors did not complete their work on time?
- Did you get stressed out by the experience or was it stimulating and enjoyable?

I think it is fair to say that almost all of these questions could apply to managing a whole range of trade and business activities. However, as far as boats are concerned, the risks of escalating costs and overruns are particularly high.

Refit for the long haul (TiP)

Refitting an old boat only makes financial sense if you plan to keep the boat for a long time (at least ten years). There is little point refitting a boat and then selling it as you will not recoup the time and money you put into the project.

Project management

Whoever is going to be responsible for the project management of a refit, before any work can begin a comprehensive survey of the vessel needs to be carried out. A comprehensive survey is critical as it will flag up the true structural condition of the vessel. The hull, deck, mast and rigging, engine and propulsion system, electronics and hydraulic systems all need to be thoroughly surveyed before going ahead with any work. Any hull defects found will need to be dealt with before any of the interior refurbishment can begin.

On larger vessels, this survey assessment alone can run into weeks of time before a proposed plan can be put into place. Assuming the refit is going to be handled professionally, the plan will be produced by a refit manager and include a detailed breakdown of the work to be carried out. The plan will then be presented to the owner and if it meets with their approval the work can start.

Once the plan is completed, the work that needs doing can be arranged into a logical sequence of priority tasks.

A word of warning TiP

As boatowners, we need to be brave when contemplating our boating budgets, but if we choose to ignore these hard realities then boat ownership could become a burden rather than a pleasure.

Restoring a neglected wooden boat requires woodworking skills. If these are lacking then doing a boatbuilding course would be a good idea before embarking on a project.

COSTS AND BUDGETING

Let's leave aside the capital cost of buying the boat in the first place as the initial outlay required for buying the range of boats we are covering in this book will vary enormously, anything from the equivalent cost of buying a small second-hand car to the cost of buying a large house.

A commonly used rule of thumb is that annual boating costs of a second-hand boat are usually the equivalent of about 20 per cent of the purchase price. I wish the same could be said of my current boat. I have just calculated that in six years of ownership the average annual spend has been over 30 per cent of the original cost. This means that in six years my total costs for the boat have been near enough three times the purchase price.

Granted, I have done my best to keep the boat maintained to a high standard, but all the work I have done on it I have considered to be necessary. I have also done all the engine servicing, lower skilled and manual work myself, so these costs could have been quite a bit higher. So in today's market I think 30 per cent would be a fairer estimate.

Many boatowners choose not to discuss the running costs of their boats because they simply do not know how much they spend. This might sound incredulous to people with

Marina costs are normally charged on a price per foot or metre. These can vary quite considerably depending on location and length of stay.

limited disposable incomes, but this is part of boating folklore. There are unavoidable costs that have to be faced each year, but inevitably there will be unexpected costs that take you completely by surprise.

To help deal with both the nasty surprises and known running costs it makes sense to draw up a boating budget and consider opening a boat bank account to cover all your boating expenses.

It is generally accepted by boatowners and yacht brokers that a well-looked-after second-hand boat will hold its value. The rate of depreciation of a well-kept boat will be far less than that of a car, and the lifespan of a typical boat is far greater than that of a typical car. On a less positive note, as soon as a boat becomes neglected, the value will drop and the costs of restoring it back into a usable condition are likely to be considerable.

COST BREAKDOWN
Annual maintenance costs

- **Marina/mooring fees:** These are usually the biggest individual annual cost, with marina fees costing considerably more than swing moorings.
- **Winter storage:** This is normally charged on a monthly basis. Allow three to four months ashore.
- **Haul out/launching fees:** These will be added to the winter storage bills.
- **Insurance:** Prices vary, so it is worth shopping around.
- **Essential maintenance:** This includes antifouling, hull cleaning and polishing, varnishing, paint, sacrificial anodes, sail laundering, spares.
- **Engine servicing:** Routine servicing of a yacht diesel engine is not too challenging, especially after completing a two-day diesel engine maintenance course. For motor vessels, this is much more significant.
- **Fuel:** For yachts, this is not such a serious item. For motor vessels, it is much more significant.

Associated costs

- **Clothing:** all weather gear, boating footwear, lifejackets.
- **Equipment:** items such as Personal Locator Beacons (PLBs), rope, tools, charts, first-aid equipment.
- **Visitor berths:** charges incurred when visiting marinas, plus harbour dues.
- **Yacht club membership fees.**

Repair and upgrade costs

This is the unknown factor when it comes to budgeting. However, the chances are that repairs and upgrades will be necessary every year and some of these may be substantial. It is sensible therefore to make an annual allowance for repairs and upgrades in your boating budget.

With your plans made for the lift out and winter storage arrangements, it is worth setting aside some time a couple of weeks beforehand to prepare the boat while it is still in the water.

When your boat is still in the water, there are a number of tasks worth doing before the lift out:

- If you plan to keep the mast up while the boat is ashore, it is a good idea to check the rig as it is safer to do this when the boat is in the water. You may discover that the mast needs to be unstepped to have some work done and it is better to find out now so you can warn the boatyard (see also Chapter 9: Mast and rigging).

- Remove as much from the boat as possible as it will be easier and safer to do this when the boat is alongside in the water rather than having to climb up and down ladders with bulky objects over your shoulder. This includes bunk cushions, soft furnishings, books, galley equipment, gas cylinders and, in truth, as much as you are prepared to transport back home.

- Remove the sails for laundering and checking. If you have some dry days ahead, then washing them in fresh water at home and drying them may suffice for storage ashore, if you are confident they are in good condition and have somewhere dry to keep them. Otherwise, for peace of mind, have them laundered and stored by your local sailmakers.

▲ It is best to have the rig checked when the boat is in the water.

▲ Removing cushions, bedding, clothing and books will help reduce damp down below.

- Empty the water tanks. If you have flexible ones they can be removed easily and cleaned and stored at home over the winter. Make sure the hot and cold water systems are drained.
- If you have a holding tank, don't forget to make sure this is pumped out.
- Finally, the last thing I do before the boat is lifted is to change the engine oil and replace the oil filter when the engine is warm after motoring to the lift out point. The new oil will help protect the engine over the winter and is the first step towards winterising the engine.

LIFT OUT

It is important to know where the lift points are for your boat so the crane operators can adjust the slings into the right position. Some boats have the lifting points marked on the hull, but if yours does not, you could mark the correct positions with tape. Another idea is to show the yard photos or a side profile plan of your boat out of the water so they can be sure how the keel is configured.

The lift out is usually quite an exciting time. Most yards are happy to do this without the owner around as they simply want to focus on the job with the minimum of interruption. However, this moment always presents a photo opportunity as your pride and joy dangles beneath a crane.

▲ Most yards will pressure wash a boat's hull as soon as it is lifted from the water.

- Be aware that you will not have access to the boat until the yard team has finished securing it in its storage cradle.
- Make sure you have a tall enough ladder standing by that you can tie safely to the side of the boat. Most yards prefer owners to supply their own ladders.
- Securing the ladder to the boat's storage cradle with a padlock and chain is a good idea when you are not there, in case it is 'borrowed' and not returned.
- Keep an old rug or doormat at the foot of the ladder to prevent grit and dirt from making its way on to the deck.

▶ Larger yards have mobile travel lifts that can lift and transport large yachts from the water to their storage location.

Before you hand the boat over to the lift operators, make sure the batteries are switched off and all the hatches and cockpit lockers are closed. Leave the sea cocks open.

▶ Remove the engine's rubber water pump impeller to prevent it seizing in one place over the winter.

AFTER LIFT OUT

Once the boat is ashore there are a few tasks to be done shortly afterwards to protect the boat before you start on any maintenance work and winter projects:

ENGINE WINTERISATION

Winterising the engine is all about protecting it from corrosion and damage from freezing temperatures. Engines like to be used and not to be left in damp, cold environments for months on end, so making them as comfortable as possible is only fair.

With the oil already changed, the first essential thing to do is drain the raw-water cooling system, flush it through with fresh water and fill it with antifreeze. It is a good idea to check the yard are happy for you to do this. They might understandably ask you to place a tarpaulin and buckets under the exhaust and dispose of any messy discharge. With the engine flushed through with fresh water, you can then fill the cooling system with antifreeze. This is how to go about things:

Step 1
Close the inlet sea cock to the engine.

Step 2
Disconnect the sea water inlet pipe and dip it into a bucket containing 50/50 antifreeze solution.

Step 3
Start the engine, keeping it out of gear, and run it for ten seconds or so until the antifreeze has been used up and can be seen coming out of the exhaust outlet.

Step 4
Shut the engine off and reconnect the inlet pipe to the sea cock.

Step 5
The raw-water circuit is now protected by antifreeze.

Once you have winterised the raw-water system, check the antifreeze level of the closed-

Refer to your engine maintenance manual for the correct type of antifreeze to use.

▲ Loosening the tension of drive belts over the winter will help them last longer.

circuit cooling system if the engine has one and top it up if necessary.

▲ Removing the batteries and storing away from the damp and cold will help prolong their life.

OTHER ESSENTIALS

The main objectives at this stage are to make sure that the interior of the boat does not become damp and mouldy over the winter and to protect any items that might be damaged by the cold. If you haven't already done so, now is the time to remove as many items from the boat as possible and take them home for winter storage. Here are some checklists of other things to do:

Down below

- Disconnect the batteries and take them home to protect them from the cold. If this is not possible, leave them on board on a trickle charge supplied by a solar panel.
- Clean the bilges with fresh water and make sure they are dry.
- Any salty residue around the boat will attract moisture, so it is a good idea to wipe clean all interior surfaces, galley cupboards, cool box and fridge if applicable and then dry them.
- Drain the cold and hot water systems.
- Clean the heads, making sure no foul water is left in the system.
- Allow air to circulate around the interior, leaving doors and cupboards open. This will help to prevent damp and keep the interior dry.
- If the boat will be connected to shore power, consider leaving a dehumidifier on board or possibly a low wattage heater. If you do not have shore power, another

▲ Clean the heads with mild bleach solution.

▲ Ensure marine toilets are flushed thoroughly and pumped dry.

▲ Plug the exhaust with an oily rag.

option is to leave disposable dehumidifiers on board that use hydrophilic crystals to absorb airborne moisture.
- Flush the sea cocks with fresh water and service these with fresh grease to ensure they do not seize up over the winter (see page 196).

On deck
- Make sure the cockpit drains are left clear and open.
- Remove all sails and take ashore for laundering and storage.
- Remove sail covers, dodgers and spray hood, wash in fresh water, then store in a dry place.
- Remove the running rigging, wash in fresh water and store in a dry place.
- Sailing vessels with masts left stepped should have halyards tied well away from the mast to prevent slatting, which can get noisy in windy conditions and lead to chafing. Wrapping a bungee around a sidestay

▲ Hulls should be checked thoroughly after pressure washing.

and hooking it to a halyard can help keep a halyard away from the mast.
- Check the fuel tank is topped up with diesel and fuel treatment is added to prevent diesel bug.
- Check all hatches and ports are watertight.
- Once the decks are clear, wash the decks with fresh water. Use a pressure washer if you have access to one for best results.

Hull
- After the hull has been jet washed, check for any damage or signs of osmosis below the waterline.
- Check the hull–deck joints are sound.
- Check all through-hulls are clear, giving them a poke and clean from below with a bottle brush.

▶ Check the rudder for signs of damage as soon as the boat is ashore.

▼ Some yards allow owners to construct a frame around a boat and cover this with tarpaulin, enabling work to be carried out in all weathers.

Boat covers

If you look around a boatyard, you may see an assortment of different kinds of tarpaulins being used to protect boats over the winter. A good-quality cover will protect paint and varnish from the elements and prevent leaking decks and hatches from causing problems before these can be fixed.

A purpose-built cover made of breathable fabric such as poly-cotton is the ideal arrangement, but understandably this will come at a cost. Breathable fabric is best for a boat where ventilation is needed and there is no dehumidifier on board. However, if you do have a dehumidifier it is best for the cabin to be sealed from draughts altogether. In this case, a non-breathable polyvinyl chloride (PVC) cover would be best.

A simpler, lower cost alternative is to adapt an off-the-shelf tarpaulin into an over-boom cover, using bungee cord to hold it in place. This arrangement works pretty well but is a little more tricky to sort out if you have lowered the mast.

Another glance around the boatyard after a gale will reveal a lot of these low-cost cover options flapping about in tatters, making the owner unpopular with the locals and the boat no longer protected. So whatever boat cover arrangement you go for, the cover needs to be very securely fastened.

A cover ideally needs to be wide enough to reach below the rubbing strake and long enough to partially wrap around the stern. If the cover does not come below the rubbing strake, tie-down ropes can chafe grooves in it. Another tip is to remove side deck stanchions, which will allow a cover to form a pitched roof.

A comprehensive and well-organised toolkit and supply of spares is essential, both for routine maintenance and to deal with unexpected breakages and equipment failure.

TOOLS

You can get by with very few tools aboard a boat, as long as nothing breaks and someone else does all the maintenance for you. The previous owner of my boat used it mainly for inshore racing and in order to save weight made do with a small ratcheting screwdriver with six double-ended bits, a large rusty hammer and very little else.

For cruising boats this is not a good plan.

Good hand tools will last a lifetime with proper care. The marine environment shows no mercy on cheap tools which can corrode in next to no time, so it pays in the long run to buy good quality and to look after them. It is a good idea to build up a collection of specialist toolkits for rigging, sail repairs, engine and electrics.

Tool tips

Only buy tools that will withstand the marine environment.

• Organise the storage of your tools wisely and make sure you know where they are kept.

• If you plan to head offshore and go cruising, take a comprehensive toolkit to cover every eventuality, plus plenty of spares.

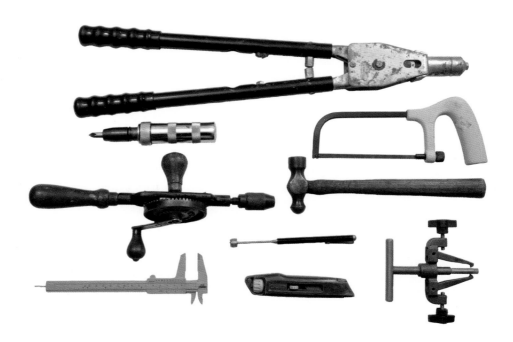

POWER TOOLS

A selection of cordless power tools are also useful. Cordless tools with lithium-ion batteries are the best, as their batteries retain charge almost indefinitely when stored. Potentially useful items include drill/drivers, saws, soldering irons, Dremels and angle grinders.

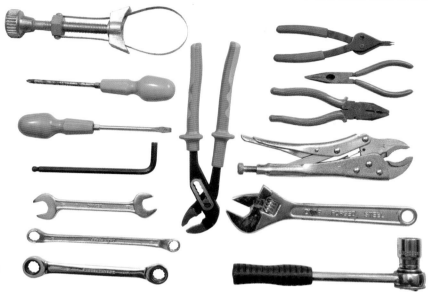

GENERAL TOOLS

- Allen keys.
- Bolt cutters.
- Bradawl.
- Centre punch.
- Chisels.
- Drills: hand and powered, plus drill bits for wood and metal, including stainless steel.
- Files: wood and metal.
- Hacksaws: large, small and spare tungsten carbide blades.
- Hammers: 2lb lump and plastic mallet.
- Hole cutters.

- Knives: craft, palette and spare blades.
- Mallets: wooden mallets are kinder to a boat than hammers.
- Mastic gun.

- Mole wrench.
- Multitool.
- Oilstone for sharpening blades.
- Paint scrapers.
- Pliers: various sizes and types, including circlip pliers.
- Screwdrivers: various sizes and types.
- Screwdriver bits: various sizes and types, including Torx bits.
- Socket sets: both half-inch and quarter-inch drives with metric and imperial sockets as appropriate.
- Spanners: open ended, ring and adjustable types.
- Tap and die set.
- Torches, including a head torch.
- Vernier gauge.
- Vice: the type designed to fit on top of a winch is ideal.
- Wire brush.
- Wood saws.

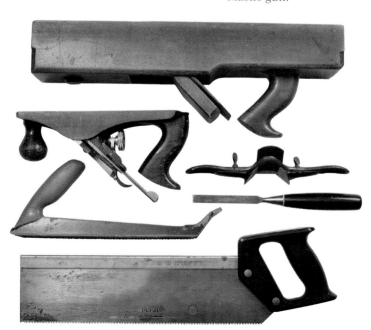

ELECTRICAL TOOLS

- Crimping tool.
- Electrical pliers.
- Multimeter.
- Precision (small) screwdriver set.
- Soldering iron.
- Wire cutters.

ENGINE TOOLS

- Feeler gauge.
- Filter wrench.
- Injector spanners.
- Oil change pump.
- Spark plug spanner for outboard motor.
- Torque wrench.

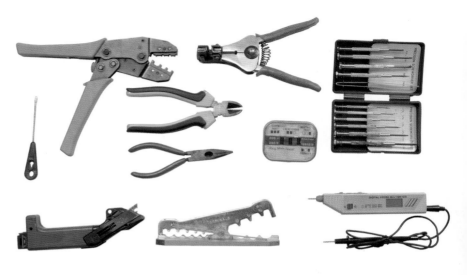

RIGGING AND SAIL REPAIR TOOLS

- Cutting board.
- Hot knife.
- Rigging cutters.
- Sailmaker's needles: It's worth noting that many of these are sized for rope work and only the smallest sizes tend to be suitable for sail repairs.
- Sailmaker's palm.
- Sharp knife: Consider a ceramic one as these maintain an edge for longer.
- Splicing fids.
- Swedish fid.

SPARES

GENERAL SPARES

- Adhesives.
- Abrasive paper (in various grades).
- Duct tape.
- Hose clips in a range of sizes.
- Marine grade sealant.
- Masking tape.
- Petroleum jelly (Vaseline).

- PTFE tape.
- Spray can of lubricant.
- Stainless steel nuts, bolts and screws in a range of sizes.
- Washers (including large penny washers).

ELECTRICAL SPARES

- Cable ties.
- Electrical tape.
- Fuses.
- Heat shrink tubing.
- Light bulbs, including navigation lights.
- Solder.
- Spare battery terminals.
- Torch batteries.
- Wire terminals and connectors.
- Wire of different sizes.

RIGGING AND SAIL MAKING SUPPLIES

- Blocks, including a snatch block.
- Dyneema line: 2mm and 4mm.
- Electrical tape.
- Sailmaker's thread.
- Self-adhesive sail repair patches.
- Self-amalgamating tape.
- Shackles in a range of sizes.
- Spinnaker repair tape.
- Whipping twine.

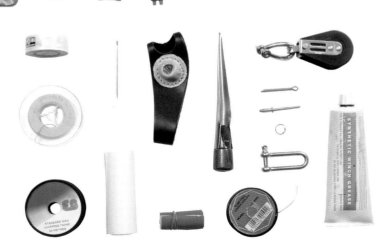

SEALANTS, ADHESIVES AND ADHESIVE SEALANTS

There is a bewildering variety of sealants, adhesives and adhesive sealants available for marine use. When making a choice it helps to understand some fundamentals about all the chemical wizardry that has created this vast range of products, often misunderstood by boatowners.

While your local chandlery or boatyard manager might be helpful and knowledgeable and happy to help you choose the best product for a specific job, learning the basics of this yourself will make life a lot easier. It should avoid that unpleasant feeling when you discover you have bought and used a product that was not the right one for the job. So what are the differences between a sealant, an adhesive and an adhesive sealant? Here are some fundamentals to consider:

- A sealant essentially does a similar job as a washer or gasket. Its function is to provide an airtight or watertight seal. Sealants are not adhesive and require fittings to be fastened with screws or bolts to create watertight seals.
- An adhesive is a glue that binds two materials together.
- An adhesive sealant is a sealant with adhesive qualities added.
- Only marine grade sealants should be used on a boat. This is partly because of the curing agents they use, partly because they are designed to withstand

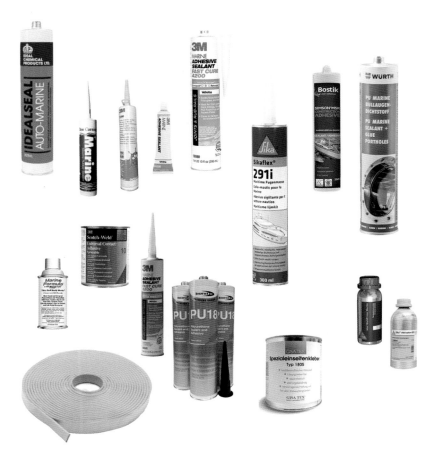

the marine environment and partly because you want them to be waterproof.

CHOOSING THE RIGHT SEALANT

When it comes to choosing a marine sealant, you need to be clear about the purpose you are using it for, then consider the options and work out the best sealant for your specific task. For example, is it for sealing a deck fitting, is it for use below the waterline, is it going to be exposed to plastics or solvents,

do you need a permanent seal or one that will be removable? Other things to consider are how long is the cure time, how long will it last and whether you can paint over it.

Types of sealants are subdivided into polysulphides, polyurethanes, silicones, polyethers (also known as hybrids) and butyl rubbers:

Polysulphide

Polysulphide is a synthetic rubber with good adhesive characteristics. It is a good bedding compound, grips well to surfaces and allows for some movement caused by stresses and changes in temperature. It is used for caulking teak decks and bedding teak rails. It is resistant to UV, oil and fuel. It also makes a good electrical insulator and can be painted.

Polysulphide should not be used on plastic surfaces (especially acrylics such as Plexiglass and Perspex) as it causes many types of plastic to harden and split.

Polyurethane

Polyurethane is a very strong adhesive and creates a permanent bond. It can be used below the waterline and is UV resistant. It is used for skin fittings, GRP hull–deck joints, bedding keels to hulls and bedding toerails.

Polyurethane should not be used on most types of plastic – therefore like polysulphide it is no good for sealing plastic windows and Perspex. It should not be used where sealing is the main objective, rather than permanent bonding, for example on items which you may want to take apart in the future.

Also, polyurethane is affected by cleaning solvents, teak oil and diesel oil so is not suitable for bedding deck hardware.

Silicone

Silicone is ideal for creating gaskets – it is best to think of it as a gasket material. It is stretchy and compatible with plastics. Silicone is used for bedding windows and is a good

insulation between metals, so it is particularly useful when fixing stainless steel fittings to aluminium masts, reducing the risk of galvanic corrosion. It is heat and UV resistant, non-shrinking and a good insulator.

Silicone should not be used below the waterline and is a very weak adhesive. Marine-grade silicones use alcohol or water cure agents. Silicone sealants that use acidic cure agents, which have a distinctive vinegary smell, are not suitable for marine use. These are widely used domestically. Silicone sealant cannot be painted over as it resists paint.

Polyether

Polyethers are better known as hybrid adhesive sealants, that is, part silicone, part polyurethane or sometimes part polysulphide. The aim is to combine the flexibility and elasticity of a sealant with the strength of an adhesive, resulting in a durable product that seals, bonds and fills. Their list of properties sounds almost too good to be true – claiming to be fast-curing, low odour, high adhesion, non-sagging, non-corrosive and non-yellowing. They provide durable, permanent watertight seals for joints subject to structural movement. They adhere to metal, glass and wood and are mildew resistant and acid free. Added to this impressive list of attributes, most can be used above and below the waterline and they are environmentally friendly.

Butyl

Butyl is a gasket-type sealant, with virtually no adhesive properties, which makes a good alternative to silicone sealant. It is a synthetic rubber, impermeable to air and its first major application was for tyre inner tubes. For marine purposes, butyl is usually manufactured in tape form with paper backing. It is malleable, does not harden and is considerably less messy than silicone to use. It is useful for small jobs as you simply cut off a bit of tape from the roll and use what you need – you can even put any excess back with the tape and keep it for future use. Butyl works well as a bedding compound, is ideal for bedding deck hardware and sealing windows. It never hardens but stays soft indefinitely.

Butyl should not be used below the waterline. It has low resistance to chemical solvents, particularly petroleum.

In summary, consider the following when choosing a sealant:
- Bonding versus sealing
- Flexibility and stretch
- Suitability for above or below the waterline
- Compatibility with other materials
- Resistance to ultraviolet, weathering and chemicals
- How long it will last.

Boat storage facilities are potentially hazardous environments and it is the responsibility of both boatowners and boatyards to ensure that the safety of those working on boats and those nearby are given top priority.

The most common boatyard accidents include people falling from ladders, tripping up over wet or uneven surfaces and equipment malfunction. Always tie ladders to the toerail of a boat to stop them slipping.

Some boatyards may not allow certain work to be carried out on boats that they feel could put people at an unacceptable risk, particularly those that might cause a fire hazard. Welding is an obvious example of work that might cause a fire hazard. It is always worth checking with your boatyard that the work you are planning to do is allowed in their yard. This also applies to any specialist contractors you may wish to appoint, who may be unfamiliar with the particular boatyard and will need to get permission from the yard to bring specialist equipment and vehicles.

Tim Cath has attached a useful Environmental and Health & Safety Regulations document with his yard booking form, and with his permission I have included details from it here.

▲ Antifouling paint is toxic, so wearing a respirator mask and protective clothing is essential to prevent nasty headaches and worse.

PROTECTIVE CLOTHING

- Always wear non-slip shoes or boots when working on the deck of a vessel, even when it is stored ashore.
- Wear appropriate personal protection equipment for specific tasks, including coveralls, gloves, eye protection and face masks as recommended.

DUST CREATION

Any operation that uses power sanders or grinders is likely to release dust into the atmosphere. During operations that cause significant dust or debris, appropriate measures should be taken to contain the dust and debris by using vacuum extraction and/or the use of dust sheeting to tent off the area.

▲ Tenting off an area protects the spread of dust and debris and is obligatory in some yards.

Sanding painted surfaces and GRP can be necessary during annual maintenance. It is important when carrying out such operations that consideration is given to containing the dust that may be produced in the process.

ANTIFOULING

ANTIFOULING REMOVAL

Antifouling is notoriously toxic. Dry sanding of antifouling should be avoided whenever possible. If this is unavoidable, only sanding tools with vacuum extraction should be used or the vessel should be appropriately sheeted in to contain dust. The debris should be sealed in bags and disposed of in hazardous waste bins.

- The preferred methods for the removal of antifouling are manual scraping or chemical removal, using ground sheets beneath the hull to collect the waste.
- Workers must use appropriate personal protective equipment including coveralls, gloves, eye protection and breathing masks.

PROTECTION FROM ANTIFOULING PAINT

The preparation of existing antifouled surfaces should be carried out taking into account the toxic dust created.

- Existing antifouled surfaces should be prepared only by wet sanding.
- Follow the safety instructions on the antifouling paint tin.
- If antifouling is spilt on the ground, this should be cleaned up. Dispose of empty paint tins and used masking tape in hazardous waste bins.
- Appropriate personal protective equipment should be used, including eye protection, coveralls, gloves and face masks.

▲ Take special care with ladders.

SHOT/SANDBLASTING

Most boatyards only allow shot or sandblasting to be carried out by fully insured contractors, in areas fully sheeted in to contain any waste material.

ENGINE WORK AND SERVICING

When carrying work out on engines, care must be taken to avoid the spillage of fuels, oils or other lubricants into the bilges or on to the ground. If a spillage does occur it must be properly cleaned up.

- If there is a spillage of fuel or oil into the bilges, this must not be pumped out on to the ground and automatic bilge pumps must be switched off.
- Use absorbent rags to clean up fuel spills and dispose of them in sealed bags.
- Waste oil, oil filters and fuel must be suitably contained and removed from the site for appropriate disposal.

▲ Take used engine oil and filters to recycling centres.

PART TWO

Many different materials have been used to build boats through the ages, but broadly speaking there are three main types of material used in hull construction: wood, metal and composite. Whatever the construction method, an annual inspection of a boat's hull is needed to check if deterioration is taking place.

Hull design is a complex subject involving three basic criteria:
- Shape and size of the hull
- Variables involving chemistry, physics and engineering
- Materials used in a hull's construction.

A boat designer will think of all these elements, whether designing a heavy displacement fishing vessel, a high performance speedboat or a sailing boat.

When caring for your boat's hull it is worth trying to find out as much as possible about its design and construction. A copy of the plans used for building your type of boat will provide useful information about how the hull is constructed, including information on where the bulkheads are, how the framing works or where the stringers are.

COMPOSITE HULLS

Composite is a term used to describe a material made from two or more constituent materials with different chemical properties. Importantly, when the constituent materials

are combined they give characteristics that differ from their individual components.

In the case of boatbuilding this may be a resin combined with a reinforcing material such as glass fibre to create glass reinforced plastic (GRP). There are other types of composite, including carbon fibre, ferro-cement and ones that combine wood with epoxy resin. In boatbuilding the big advantages of composites over metal and wood are their lightness, strength and durability.

Many composite hulls are strengthened with frames and stringers that help to provide rigidity. If your boat's hull has these, it is good to know where they are so their condition can be checked. It is important that they remain firmly attached to the interior of the hull and that there has been no flexing of the hull to weaken or break the bond between the stiffeners and the hull.

Another method of composite hull construction is known as sandwich construction where

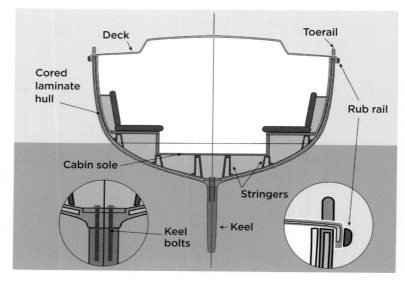

A few of the many different hull designs used for sail and powerboats. *Above* A planing hull powerboat. *Above right* A fin-keeled GRP sailing yacht. *Right* A semi-displacement hull powerboat. *Below left* A clinker-built long keel sailing yacht. *Below right* A long-keel GRP sailing yacht.

materials such as balsa or foam are added as core layers sandwiched between two outer skins of GRP. Two ranges of yachts constructed using the foam sandwich method are Etap and Sadler yachts. Their hulls have the benefits of being well insulated and unsinkable, as their foam cores act as buoyancy.

GELCOAT

The thin outer skin of GRP hulls is known as the gelcoat and it protects the underlying layers of fibreglass and composite materials that make up the hull. Gelcoat is made from polyester resin and acts as a moisture barrier, as well as providing a smooth, glossy finish to the exterior of a hull. Note that gelcoat is not used on wooden or metal hulls.

COMPOSITE HULL INSPECTION

Surveyors generally start a hull inspection by standing well back and looking for signs of distortion and unevenness. They will check from behind to see whether a sailing boat's mast, hull, rudder and keel are in line and then from the sides to check the hull is even and smooth. Do this yourself and if you notice any uneven bulges or bumps in the hull surface, these will need to be checked out by a professional. Then take a closer look as follows:

- Look at the joint between the keel and the hull. On sailing boats, check along it for any corrosion or signs

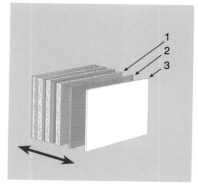

▲ Solid GRP construction has multiple layers of fibreglass (1) soaked in resin (2) with an outer skin of gelcoat (3).

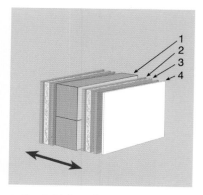

▲ Sandwich (cored) type construction has a core of balsa, foam or similar material (1) applied after the outer layer of GRP is laid to the mould (2 and 3) with an outer skin of gelcoat (4).

▲ The hull of this Etap 30 is of sandwich construction with a foam core.

of disturbance. If you find any such signs, seek a professional's opinion. On motorboats, check the keel band for any signs of stress or movement.

- Check whether the gelcoat is intact and whether there are any chips that might need filling. If you find any imperfections, mark them with a piece of tape so that you can find them later as they will need to be repaired. Surface scratches are not quite as important, but if they are really noticeable make a note that you will need to attend to them.
- Check if there are any cracks in the gelcoat. These indicate that there might be impact damage beneath the gelcoat or that there has been stress damage, possibly caused by a deck fitting.
- Check for blisters on the hull. These are a sign of osmosis, so mark where they are and then if in doubt get some advice as to how to proceed. If you have owned the boat for a number of years, are they now more evident or much the same as when you last checked? This will help you decide whether you need to do something about them. If there are only a few blisters, they can be dealt with by grinding them out, leaving the laminate to dry and then filling them. If there are loads, then the situation is more serious and it would be wise to seek a professional's opinion.

GRP HULL MAINTENANCE

Some owners of GRP boats can get a reputation for being obsessed with cleaning, polishing and waxing their boats' hulls. After all, if gelcoat is just a very thin outer skin with virtually no structural value, do we really need to keep it polished to a high gloss all the time? While polishing and waxing your hull does not need to become a weekly chore, gelcoat does need looking after. It is to some extent porous and can become stained, dull and chalky over time. The causes for this include exposure to ultraviolet light, oxidisation and pollutants in the air and water. Hosing regularly with fresh water is a good idea, as is sponging along and just above the waterline to remove any algae and pollutants. If neglected, a yellow or brown stain will soon begin to appear along the waterline.

When it comes to gelcoat care, note that polishing and waxing are two different processes. The polishing process removes the oxidisation and restores the colour and lustre, which no amount of washing can do. The waxing process then adds a layer of protective wax over the top which will slow down further, fading and prevent haziness developing.

◀ The hull of this GRP yacht has been polished, waxed, had antifouling applied and is ready to be launched.

CLEANING AND POLISHING GELCOATS

With the boat ashore, the gelcoat can be pampered and restored to its former glory relatively easily. It is important to remember that gelcoat is only a very thin outer layer of the hull, often less than 1mm thick, so you should avoid cleaning it with highly abrasive cleaners, or anything that could potentially damage its surface. As ever, if in doubt, ask around the boatyard for advice from other boaters and the pros.

This is how to go about keeping your topsides in good condition:

Step 1

Cleaning: The first step is to clean the hull thoroughly with fresh water to remove any loose dirt and grit.

Step 2

Shampoo: If there are some obvious marks that won't come off using water, try a boat shampoo before resorting to stain removal products. Don't be tempted to use a domestic cream cleaner as these are very abrasive, even if they cost a fraction of the price. Wear protective gloves if advised by the manufacturer.

Step 3

Stain removal: Stains can be formed by fouling and environmental pollutants. These tend to build up along the waterline if a boat is left unattended. Such chemical stains can be treated using a variety of products, most of which contain acids, including oxalic, phosphoric, sulphuric and even hydrochloric acid, which is very strong and caustic and perhaps best avoided. These products include liquid cleaners, sprays, powders and gels. Gel products containing oxalic acid are generally the most popular and considered the most effective and safest to use, as they are easy to apply and do not drip. You simply brush the gel over the stain, leave it for ten minutes and then rinse it off thoroughly with fresh water. However, oxalic acid is harmful to humans and wildlife in concentrated forms, so it should be used with caution in the boatyard. Wear rubber gloves and safety goggles when using any of these stain remover products.

Step 4

Degreasing: Once the gelcoat is clean, it should be degreased before polishing. Use a soft rag soaked in acetone, but go carefully as you don't want acetone flying all over the place, especially if working above your head. Wear rubber gloves.

Step 5

Polishing: There are many brands of hull polish available, but broadly speaking they all do the same job, which is to remove surface imperfections and oxidisation (note that polish is not a coating). The critical difference is how abrasive they are. If your hull is in pretty good shape there is little point in using a highly abrasive, coarse grade polishing compound, when a fine grade polish will do the job perfectly well and not wear away the gelcoat. Hulls in poor condition may require two or three polishing compound treatments, using different grades. If in doubt, test a small area of the hull with a fine grade rubbing compound first and see how it looks. Hull polishes are applied using a soft cloth or foam pad and allowed to dry. Then buff with a soft cloth using a circular motion until you have a high gloss shine.

If this sounds like too much hard work, there are electric-powered polishing machines that make the task easier. The pros tend to use these. The good machines are usually quite pricey but are better than cheaper alternatives as they are lighter, vibrate less and generally easier to use. Those with variable speed settings and orbital type movement are best, as they will leave fewer swirl marks on the surface. High-speed machines produce too much friction and can damage the gelcoat. Once the polish is applied, start the machine at a low speed and keep it moving slowly from side to side and then up and down but not in a circular motion.

Step 6

Waxing: The last all-important step is applying the wax, which needs to be done to protect the gelcoat and provide a lasting gloss finish. Waxes can be in liquid or paste forms – which

▲ Pressure washing removes antifouling but not stains that build up along the topsides. These will need to be removed by hull cleaner or polish.

is best really comes down to personal choice. Paste waxes are a bit more physically demanding to use, but they tend to leave a harder protection and last longer than liquid waxes. But if you are hand polishing your boat, a good-quality liquid wax is much kinder on the wrists and elbows. Mechanical polishers can also be used with paste or liquid waxes, using the same up-and-down, side-to-side slow movements as with compound polishing.

CARE OF PAINTED TOPSIDES

There are a number of dos and don'ts that paint manufacturers recommend for the maintenance of painted topsides:

Do wash the surface regularly with fresh water using soft, non-abrasive cloths and sponges. This will prevent build-up of dirt and algae that can degrade the surface of the paint.

Do use cleaning solvents recommended by the paint manufacturer of your hull's topcoat. If you don't have a record of what type of paint it is, then ask a professional for their opinion on the best solvent to use. Some paint manufacturers, such as Awlgrip, produce their own surface cleaners.

Do rinse painted surfaces with fresh water after using cleaning solvents or detergents.

Do use distilled white vinegar and hot water to remove stains. Rinse with fresh water after use.

Don't use traditional waxes for gelcoat protection. These can cause discolouration of the paint and attract dirt. Instead, use protective polymer sealers which will protect the paint, leaving a gloss finish.

Don't use abrasives, scratch pads or polishing compounds as these will reduce the life of the paint.

Don't allow teak cleaners or metal polishes to come into contact with the paint as they contain acids that will discolour the paint.

Don't use strong solvents such as acetone to clean paintwork.

STEP-BY-STEP

REPAIRING CHIPS AND DINGS IN GELCOAT

Sooner or later a GRP boat will receive the odd knock, chip or ding in its gelcoat. This might be caused by a minor bump against a dock, an object in the water or even another vessel. When this happens it is usually not critical to repair it immediately, but it is wise to put it on the to-do list of jobs for when the boat is next in the boatyard. However, if the ding has gone through the gelcoat, exposing the laminate beneath, then it does need filling with a temporary repair to stop water ingress, normally by using gelcoat filler.

When the boat is ashore, you need to decide if this is a job for a professional or is something you can tackle yourself. Gelcoat repairs need to be done in temperatures of at least 16°C otherwise the gelcoat will not harden off, so this is not a mid-winter job unless you can do it under cover in the warmth.

It is perfectly possible to do a decent-looking minor repair yourself. This will save you a chunk of money and be satisfying to do. First try a small gelcoat repair, to get the hang of what is involved and then move on to doing more challenging repairs. This is how to go about it:

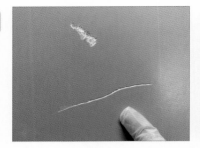

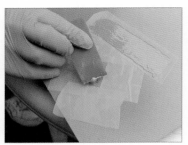

1. Wipe down the area needing repair with acetone to remove surface dirt, wax and any contamination.

2. Remove any loose or flaking material with a sharp, V-shaped tool or a small grinding tool such as a Dremel with a burr bit. Be careful not to cut into the laminate.

3. Remove the dust and wipe with the acetone rag again. Then mask up the repair, leaving about 4cm all around it.

4. Mix the gelcoat filler following the manufacturer's instructions and apply it with a spatula, making sure there are no air bubbles. Build up the repair so that it stands proud of the surface.

5. Leave the gelcoat filler to cure, carefully peeling the masking tape away before it hardens completely. This may take several hours.

6. When the gelcoat has cured, rub it back using wet fine grade abrasive waterproof paper.

7. When the gelcoat is flush, cut it back with cutting paste until it is glossy.

8. Finish it off with a layer of wax polish.

Done? The problem with this quick fix is that the colour of the repair will most likely not match its surroundings.

HOW TO COLOUR MATCH GELCOAT

You may have heard that colour matching a gelcoat is very difficult to do and best left to the professionals, but don't be put off by this if you want to do a minor repair yourself. With a bit of practice at colour mixing, you should be able to get a satisfactory match. However, to get a 100 per cent colour match takes years of experience and it is not realistic to expect that the first time you try it. It is better to try to get somewhere close and then blend the two colours using polish and wax.

Gelcoat as a base comes in three different colours: white, black and neutral.

- **Black:** Use a black base if you want to match a dark colour such as a deep blue.
- **White:** Use a white base for all lighter colours, not only different shades of white but also creams, pale yellows or pale blues.
- **Neutral:** The neutral base is almost clear and takes up the pure colour of the pigments you add to it, so it is used for strong, vivid colours such as a bright red, bright blue or green.

Gelcoat pigments

A basic gelcoat pigment set is all you will need and this should include a red, blue, black, brown and yellow. You will need these even if your boat has a white hull. There's no such colour as pure white, but there are countless colours that come close.

Remember that gelcoat changes colour as it ages due to oxidisation. Consequently, as you walk around a boat the gelcoat colour will vary according to how much exposure different parts have had to sunlight and the elements.

Colour matching an off-white gelcoat

Here are some basic steps to doing a colour match of an off-white gelcoat. Off-whites usually have tiny amounts of brown, yellow or black added.

1. Wet sand some of the gelcoat close to the repair with 1500-grit paper to get rid of dirt, grime and oxidisation.

2. Wipe the surface clean and add a thin layer of wax to bring the colour back.

3. Stir the base white gelcoat, uncatalysed. Measure some out into a mixing pot, enough to cover the repair. Keep giving it a stir every now and again.

4. Use wooden mixing sticks, one for each of the three pigments. Spread some pigment on to each mixing stick.

5. Add a tiny bit of black from its mixing stick to the base gelcoat and stir it well in. Dab a small spot of the mix on the clean gelcoat.

6. Little by little, add more colour to the mixing pot, testing as you go by dabbing a small spot of the mix near the repair. Think of this as an artist's palette. Add tiny amounts of the other colours, each time mixing thoroughly. Keep doing this until you are satisfied you have the best colour match you can get. Be prepared for some trial and error and, if it all goes seriously pear-shaped, start again with a fresh pot.

7. Wipe the test swatches off using acetone.

You now have some coloured gelcoat that should be miles closer to the colour of your boat's gelcoat than the base white colour.

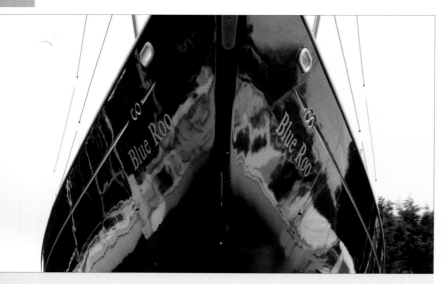

Applying gelcoat

The next step is to apply the gelcoat, which entails adding catalyst to it and painting it on.

1. Use 150-grit paper and wet sand a few centimetres all around the repair so that the new gelcoat can blend in with the existing one. Then wipe clean.

2. Give the gelcoat mix a good stir and add the catalyst according to the manufacturer's recommendations. This is usually in the order of 1 per cent catalyst to gelcoat mix. Mix this very thoroughly.

3. Apply the gelcoat using a brush. Note that spray guns are used for major repairs, mostly under cover in controlled conditions.

4. Paint the gelcoat on in thin layers, alternating up-and-down brush strokes for one layer with side-to-side brush strokes for the next.

5. Build the gelcoat up so that it is just proud above the surrounding gelcoat.

6. Leave the gelcoat to harden. The gelcoat may take several hours to harden, so ideally leave it overnight and come back to finish things off the next day.

7. Start by using 400-grit paper to wet sand the cured gelcoat from side to side, then top to bottom.

8. Then gradually use finer grits papers all the way to 600, 800, 1200 and 1500.

9. Wipe all the residue off and buff with a compound polish at a slow speed.

10. Finally add a layer of wax and buff by hand for the perfect finish.

There are manufacturers that supply a large range of coloured gelcoats and you might be lucky enough to find a close match and save yourself a lot of time and effort. The likely downside of this solution is that the minimum quantities you can buy are going to be far more than you need, plus the cost will be prohibitive.

REPAIRING A HOLE IN GLASS FIBRE

Repairing a hole in a fibreglass boat is a relatively straightforward thing to do, at least to a level where the repair will be watertight and sound. However, making a repair that will be as good as new will be more challenging and more likely entail calling in a professional. This will depend on the complexity of the job and your own DIY skills.

Before launching into a repair, it helps to know something about the chemical make-up of the two types of material you need to make a glass fibre repair: glass fibre and resin.

Polyester and epoxy resins

The two main types of resin used for making fibreglass repairs are epoxy and polyester. Most fibreglass boats are made using polyester resin as it works particularly well when building up multiple layers of glass fibre cloth that bond together in the cured resin. It is easy to use: you simply add a small amount of catalyst to the resin, mix it up and it will immediately begin to cure, although it will not go

Safety (TiP)

Wear protective clothing including gloves and a respirator (if using polyester resin).

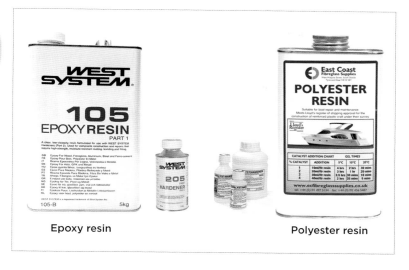

Epoxy resin   Polyester resin

rock solid for several hours. As it cures the mix shrinks a little, which can result in problems when using it for repair purposes. One of polyester resin's advantages over epoxy is that a polyester gelcoat will not adhere well to epoxy resin, so if a repair is to be finished with a gelcoat it is best to use polyester resin. Polyester resin is also much cheaper than epoxy.

While epoxy resin is a lot more expensive, it has a few advantages over polyester resin: it does not shrink, it bonds to other materials such as wood and it is a very strong adhesive. A repair needs to bond well with the existing structure, so in most cases epoxy is the better choice. Expert advice will help you decide the best route to take when contemplating a specific repair. Hopefully, being aware that there are these differences between the two types of resin should help you decide which is best for your particular job.

Glass fibre cloth

There are several types of glass fibre cloth and tape that can be used to make a repair. These provide strength and come in various thicknesses and weaves. Cloth consists of thin strands or fibres of glass that are woven together in various patterns to suit specific requirements such as strength and flexibility. This includes chopped strand mat (CSM), which comes in sheets of woven glass glued in layers that form the lay-up. Chopped strand mat is very flexible so it can be easily shaped as the layers are built up. Due to its composition,

CSM should only be used with polyester resin, not with epoxy.

Other types of cloth are woven roving and stitched cloth. Since both of them can be used with both types of resin, they are normally the ideal cloths to use when making a small repair. Woven roving is more flexible, but stitched cloth is stronger.

Glass fibre tape comes in rolls and is made from woven glass fibre cloth. It has a strong edge that prevents the cloth from coming apart. Tape is useful for strengthening edges and seams and comes in various widths and thicknesses.

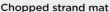

Chopped strand mat   Woven roving cloth   Fibreglass tape

STEP-BY-STEP

GLASS FIBRE REPAIR

Here are the steps involved in making a repair. Note this example assumes that you will have access to both sides of the repair.

1. Begin by preparing the damaged area around the hole using a jigsaw or a Dremel tool.

2. Use an angle grinder to chamfer the lay-up a few centimetres all around the inside of the hole.

3. Clean inside and outside the hole with acetone.

4. Cover the outside of the hole with some firm material that will resist resin. A scrap piece of waxed plastic, taped to the outside, would be ideal.

5. Cut a series of fabric patches to go over the repair. You will need more to go over the hole itself and a few more to cover right up to the edges of the repair.

6. Mix up some resin with hardener in the ratio recommended by the manufacturer.

7. Lay up some glass cloth on the inside of the repair, beginning with the widest patches. Use a disposable brush to work the resin into the cloth and follow with a metal roller to remove any air bubbles.

8. When these first layers have cured, lay up some more layers over the inside of the hole using the smaller patches until the lay-up is all even. Leave to cure.

9. Remove the outer face plate. Using a straight edge to check there is a smooth finish and that none of the reinforcing cloth is proud of the outer gelcoat surface. Grind away any if there is.

10. Fill the outer surface of the repair with epoxy so that it is just proud of the surface. Allow to cure and then sand it back just far enough for a gelcoat layer to be added.

11. Fill the outside now with gelcoat mixed with a wax drying agent.

12. Rub back the cured gelcoat with wet sandpaper, compound polish it, then wax polish to finish the repair to the outside.

13. The inside of the repair can be left as it is if out of sight. If a gelcoat finish is required the inside surface will need fairing back until it is smooth, then more epoxy and gelcoat added as needed.

OSMOSIS

Many owners of old GRP boats live in fear of osmosis, but what exactly is osmosis and what can be done about it?

Osmosis comes about when water molecules make their way into the laminate of a GRP hull. Water molecules can pass through gelcoat and into the laminate, condensing into liquid water when they reach voids or small air pockets. The water then reacts with uncured chemicals in the polyester resin, known as hydrolysis, causing it to decompose. This forms a water-absorbing solution that then attracts more water into the laminate. This process continues and the chemical reactions cause a build-up of pressure that results in blisters being formed. These become visible in the gelcoat.

The build-up of water in the hull can take many years to become a problem and it can be challenging for surveyors, let along boatowners, to determine exactly where the water is. The question is whether water is permeating the gelcoat or the CSM layers or whether it is in

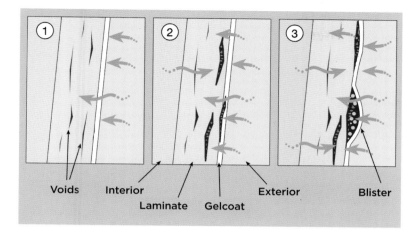

Voids Interior Exterior Blister
Laminate Gelcoat

the structural laminates made of marine ply, or whether it has penetrated a balsa core.

In severe cases, large areas of the hull can become rotten. This can lead to structural failure if the situation is not dealt with. In less advanced cases, the hull can be sand- or pellet-blasted in the affected area. It is then allowed to dry out and a gelcoat filler is applied in the small cavities left where the blisters had been. Surveyors will also advise that the affected boat is stored ashore for several months over the winter each year to help the hull to dry out.

MOISTURE METERS

The first visual signs of osmosis are blisters and by then the osmosis is already advanced. Early warnings of osmosis developing in a hull can be diagnosed by taking moisture readings using moisture meters. While high moisture readings of the hull produced by moisture meters can indicate the presence of osmosis, surveyors usually warn that meters do not always produce infallible results. Readings will be affected by the atmospheric conditions on the day and how long the boat has been hauled out for.

In ideal circumstances, therefore, the most reliable method to determine if hull cores are wet is to take the moisture readings from the inside of the hull, on a dry day, after the boat has been ashore for at least a few weeks in the summer months. Clearly this is not always possible.

TREATING OSMOSIS: PROFESSIONAL CURES

Professional cures of osmosis can be expensive because of the labour and materials involved. The process involves removing the underwater gelcoat and any delaminated lay-up beneath. The exposed hull is then dried out thoroughly, often using infra-red heaters to speed up the drying process. Once the hull is completely dry, new epoxy resin and an epoxy gelcoat are applied to form a long-lasting impermeable layer.

The end result usually produces a stronger hull than the boat had to begin with. It should never need treating again, provided the repair is done to professional standards.

▲ A surveyor taking moisture readings.

Surveyor's osmosis tips

Osmosis is one of the issues that I spend most of my time discussing with owners and purchasers of older vessels. Here are a number of useful tips for determining how bad your osmosis blistering is:

Tiny blisters forming on the hull aren't a sign that osmosis has just begun. Osmosis will have been occurring a long period before this. Even tiny blisters are seen as quite far along in the osmosis process.

Is your blistering localised? If the blistering on your hull is localised to a specific area, e.g. around a bow thruster, this does not mean that your whole hull would need osmosis treatment. Localised, and considerably cheaper, osmosis treatment can be undertaken on specific areas of a hull with relative ease.

How big are your blisters? As a rough guide, blisters of up to a ten-pence piece size would not be seen as a serious structural issue. Blisters of this size or over may have started to form within the fibreglass matting of the vessel. This will begin to weaken the structure of the vessel.

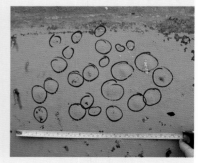

Does your blistering need addressing? In my opinion, the sooner that a boat with osmosis blistering is treated, the better. Even if the blistering found is not yet affecting the structure of the vessel, there is no way of telling how long it will be before this does become the case. Treating a boat with minor osmosis is also a lot cheaper than treating a boat covered in large blisters. Large blisters can seriously affect the resale value of your vessel. I would strongly recommend having a surveyor check over your hull as soon as you start to see signs of blistering. They will be able to advise on the best course of action.

Storing your vessel ashore each year for four to five months will give the hull time to dry out properly. This will help to reduce the rate of osmosis within your hull, and the likelihood of developing osmosis blisters in the first place.

TREATING OSMOSIS: THE DIY SOLUTION

There are ways for a resourceful DIY boatowner on a tight budget to deal with osmosis themselves, depending on the severity of the case and the extent of the blistering. This will entail plenty of hard work. It will help to have a sheltered spot ashore where the boat can be properly dried out under cover.

Check where you might access the various bits of kit mentioned in the following step-by-steps before launching ahead.

How to treat mild cases with localised blistering

1. Remove the antifouling from the affected area to expose the gelcoat. This can be done by hand using scrapers. If the area warrants it, consider hiring a professional to blast the hull for you.

2. Grind out the blisters and wash the area thoroughly with fresh water to remove all the impurities. Steam cleaners are sometimes used for this.

3. Check there is no delamination taking place and grind back further if necessary to expose sound lay-up.

4. Leave to dry inside and out as thoroughly as possible, using infra-red heaters and fans if necessary. One or two weeks' drying in warm weather should be sufficient.

5. Once the area is dry, mix up epoxy filler and fill the craters where the blisters were.

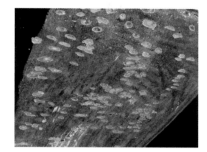

6. Sand back the filler, ensuring the hull surface is smooth.

7. Finish off with primer before applying antifouling.

How to treat more advanced cases with widespread blistering

1. Remove the gelcoat from the affected areas. This is best done using an electric gel-plane. Consider having this done professionally as it is a tricky job.

2. Grind back the blisters and areas of delamination to sound lay-up.

3. If there has been serious delamination, consider having a new lay-up done professionally. Taking professional advice on this would be a sound plan.

4. Steam clean all the ground back areas to remove all residues of impurities.

5. Leave the hull to dry inside and out. Fans and infra-red heaters can be used. Drying can take a few weeks, depending on conditions. Remember that moving air evaporates water more quickly than anything else.

6. Use a moisture meter to check the old lay-up is dry. Compare readings with those taken in an area of the hull that is always dry, such as the topsides.

7. Prime the area with two coats of epoxy barrier paint, carefully following the manufacturer's instructions.

8. Fill all holes with epoxy filler and fair back when dry.

9. Apply more coats of epoxy paint according to instructions.

10. Coat with antifouling primer before finishing off with antifouling.

Further steps can be taken to slow down the osmosis process. Given that water moisture can permeate a GRP hull from the inside as well as the outside, it is advisable to keep the bilges dry and the interior well ventilated. In addition, GRP hulls with high moisture readings should be dried out ashore for several months each year as a preventative measure.

STEEL AND ALUMINIUM HULLS

The two metals used for hull construction are steel and aluminium. These are both very strong materials and will last a long time as long as they are cared for, which primarily means protecting steel boats from rust and aluminium boats from electrolytic action.

Steel hulls are constructed of a frame with steel plates welded to it. As soon as steel is exposed to the air it begins to rust (the steel reacts with oxygen to form iron oxide). If sea water is added into the mix the process accelerates rapidly. Steel boats built before the introduction of epoxy coating systems in the 1980s are more prone to rust and their hulls

▲ This steel fishing boat is waiting to be grit blasted, before layers of primer, undercoat and top coats can be applied.

need to be closely monitored and repainted frequently. Those with epoxy paint systems tend to be far more resilient, as long as the paintwork is not damaged. If it is, rust will very soon begin to appear.

Aluminium hulls are constructed in a similar way to steel hulls, but the two metals are quite different from each other. If you leave aluminium exposed to the air it will not rust, which gives it a big advantage over steel. However, aluminium suffers from electrolysis, which is a form of corrosion caused by different metals coming into contact with each other. The telltale sign, the equivalent to rust with steel, is a white powder that literally crumbles the aluminium away as you touch it. The two main preventative measures taken by builders of aluminium boats are firstly to ensure that different metals, such as aluminium and stainless steel, are very well insulated from each other and secondly through the use of sacrificial anodes.

METAL HULL INSPECTION

- Check for any distortion in the hull that might have been caused by an impact or collision.
- Check the outside of steel hulls for any signs of rust. If the rust is only on the surface it can be rubbed down and treated. If the surface is pitted it indicates a deeper level of corrosion and this will need to be taken back to the bare steel and treated.
- Check for corrosion around the stern gear and through-hull fittings, which could be caused by electrolytic action. Pay particular attention to where the head's through-hulls are located as this is a known problem area.
- Check that the paintwork is in good condition and the surfaces are all sound. Look for any signs of the paint bubbling, which could indicate rust is about to break through.
- Check all the anodes and replace if necessary.
- Check the inside of the hull for any signs of corrosion, which will most likely entail reaching into inaccessible places using lights, mirrors and cameras. For a thorough hull inspection it helps to know where specific areas of vulnerability are. These include beneath fresh water, black water and fuel tanks. This is not necessarily due to the tanks leaking, but because of the condensation build-up in these areas that can lead to pools of water forming. Another obvious place to inspect is the hull areas beneath where the shower or heads and galley are located. Seepage of water can work its way to these inaccessible areas, collecting along the frames with nowhere to go.
- Look inside all the bilge areas and make sure they are dry. If water is allowed to sit in the bilges of a steel boat it will soon cause problems.

- Check along the welding that joins the frame to the plating, as this is a common place for rust to start inside the hull.
- Look carefully at the edges of any timber that is fastened to the steel. Check for signs of rust, as timber is notorious for taking up moisture which works its way between the timber and the steel, which then rusts.

STEEL HULL MAINTENANCE

Steel boatowners' biggest enemy is corrosion. They don't have to worry about osmosis or rotting timbers; instead, rust is the number one issue that will keep them awake at night.

Steel hull maintenance mainly involves checking inside and outside the hull for rust and then dealing with it. This means sanding, chipping, scraping, grinding or blasting rust out until the metal beneath is shining. The metal then needs to be covered up as soon as possible with multiple layers of rust converter, primer and paint.

It is just as important to deal with any corrosion that may be present on the inside of the hull as on the outside. It is a widely acknowledged fact that steel hulls generally decay from the inside out, so it requires dedication from both the builder and owner of a steel boat to ensure that every nook and cranny inside the hull is cared for almost to the point of fanaticism.

It is worth noting that with modern painting systems, if a well-built steel hull is backed up

▲ A steel boat's hull is being restored and is now nearly ready for painting. The interior of the hull has been thoroughly checked for damaged paintwork.

by being properly prepped and painted at the build stage, then it need not be too arduous to maintain. Rigorous attention does need to be given to prevent rust from forming. The time spent doing regular checks and dealing with rust as soon as it appears will reap benefits in the long term.

Stripping back larger areas

For larger areas, there are a number of options. Check with your boatyard which of these options they will allow. For all these options the use of full protective clothing and eye protection is recommended as they all generate a lot of dust and dirt:

- **Needle guns:** These tools use compressed air and are very noisy. They have vibrating needles that chip away at

the rust and paint and are particularly good for getting into tight corners inside the hull. Good-quality ear defenders and eye protection are essential.

- **Shot blasting:** There are several types of shot blasters, including dry and wet variations; some use sand or grit, others soda. They all require a compressor to work. As well as getting rid of the rust, shot blasting prepares the surface very well for painting as it scratches the surface, which helps paint to adhere to it.
- **Rotary blaster:** These come in various forms from drill-mountable rotating discs to dedicated machines complete with guard and dust extractors. They are all designed for the removal of rust, paint, tar and

other materials, which leaves the equivalent of a sand-blasted surface with a texture suitable for applying protective coatings. For DIY purposes, the rotary blaster is well worth considering as it can be used on most types of electric drill.

- **Polycarbide abrasive discs:** These are fitted to a standard angle grinder. They are effective at cutting through paint without damaging the steel. They work best over smooth areas but are not as good dealing with deeply pitted areas.

Rust converter and preventer

Apply a rust converter and preventer to the freshly blasted steel surface. Rust preventer is basically phosphoric acid and converts rust to iron phosphate. Leave the rust converter for an hour or two and then brush it over with a hard bristle brush to remove the residue left on the surface. The rust converter provides an insoluble, non-conductive and oxide-free surface over which paint can be applied. The surface will now be ready for priming and painting.

HOW TO REPAIR RUST SPOTS

1. Begin by chipping out the rust using a chipping hammer or a grinder with a very coarse 16-grit grinding wheel. Remove any loose paint with a putty knife.

2. Use a wire brush to clean the surface thoroughly.

3. Sand and feather the surrounding paint surface so that it has a smooth edge.

4. Clean and degrease the surface before applying a metal primer.

5. Apply the epoxy primer and leave it to dry.

6. If there are any deep spots these can be filled using an epoxy filler. Apply the filler with a putty knife, smooth it back and leave it to cure.

7. Sand the surface smooth using a 200-grit paper.

8. Wipe clean with acetone and apply another coat of primer. Leave to cure.

9. Apply the topcoats.

Fairing: sanding and filling

Boat hulls of all kinds will require filling and fairing from time to time. Fairing is a time consuming and arduous process but can substantially enhance a boat's appearance, as well as providing additional protection for the hull. While the appearance above the waterline is one consideration, beneath the waterline the priority is to ensure that the hull is as smooth as possible in order to offer the least resistance through the water.

Fairing compounds use either polyester- or epoxy-based systems. In the case of polyester, using a small amount of catalyst results in a hard plastic finish. With epoxy, the resin reacts with a hardener and they form a chemical bond that also results in a hard plastic material. The big difference between the two is that epoxy systems are inherently more water resistant, shrink less when cured and are more adhesive and stronger than polyester resin. Hence epoxy fillers are generally recommended for marine use.

STEP-BY-STEP

REPLACING A SECTION OF STEEL PLATE

Steel hulls can be repaired comparatively easily, provided a skilled welder does the job and the work is done to a high standard. A section of the hull may need to be replaced because it has been weakened by corrosion to the point that it is unsafe, or it may even have rusted through completely.

Each situation will be different and some patches will be easier to do than others, but the principles broadly remain the same:

1. Before you cut a large hole in the hull you need to ensure that the surrounding steel around the hole will be well supported to prevent the hull buckling and becoming distorted. This may entail adding some temporary structural steel bars, for example, inside the hull to support it.

2. It may be obvious, but the inside of the hull needs to be stripped out before the fireworks can begin to prevent a fire from breaking out.

3. As with repairing rust spots, all the rust in the area of the repair needs to be removed, using a chipping hammer and wire brush.

4. Put a thin coat of red oxide etch primer over the repair area to prevent further rusting.

5. Cut out the weakened area using an angle grinder, oxy-acetylene torch or plasma cutter.

6. With the hole cut, a new patch can now be welded in place. This is done by tack welding the patch in place, starting with the corners, followed by short tacks midway along the edges.

7. After the patch has been secured the welder welds a seam all around the edge.

8. The raised seam can be ground flat using a small angle grinder.

It may sound daunting, but replacing a larger area can sometimes be easier than smaller patches in order to create a uniform shape. Much will be down to the skill of the welder and the specific circumstances. Welders advise it is best to take your time when welding and grinding, in order to let the heat disperse and to avoid distortion.

Applying the filler

- On sandblasted metal, first wipe with a solvent, then apply a pre-coat with a thin solvent-free epoxy resin mix. Apply the filler mix while the pre-coat is still tacky.
- On primed metal, the surface needs to be sanded and then wiped with quick evaporating solvent to ensure the epoxy filler has a good key.
- For small areas, apply the filler with a plastic spatula or a metal straight edge. Aim for a slight overfill so the repair

can be sanded back flush with the surrounding surface.

- On larger areas, apply the filler using a flexible metal applicator that enables you to spread the filler over the surface.
- On larger areas, it usually requires two people to work together with a fairing batten, spreading the fairing compound evenly and smoothly over the surface. The aim is to apply no more than 3–4mm at a time and end up with a slight overfill that

can be faired back when the filler is cured.

Sanding

Once the filler is fully cured, the objective is for the excess filler to be sanded back to leave an even, smooth surface. This usually needs to be done in a number of stages, beginning with coarser grit paper and finishing off with a finer 200- or 240-grit paper.

Getting this right in one go is not always possible. The solution is to apply fresh fairing compound over any remaining uneven or pitted areas. Once again, after the filler has cured you can sand it back until you are satisfied with the finish.

And then it will be time to begin the painting process.

PAINTING A STEEL HULL

When it is time to paint a hull, it is also time to ask yourself whether this is a job for you or the professionals. The people who know best about marine quality paint are the paint manufacturers. They have advisors who will talk things through with you and recommend what is best for your boat. There are a few paint options to consider including two-pack polyurethane, single-pack polyurethane and epoxy. Paint is expensive and the last thing you want is a botched job.

To get the best results, preparation needs to be the top priority and that entails a lot of hard work. Only after all the corrosion and fairing have been dealt with completely (see pages 70–74) can the actual painting begin – after a final clean with degreasing solution of all surfaces has been allowed to dry, that is.

As with many boatyard jobs, safety is paramount. High-quality respirators, eye protection, gloves and all-over paint suits are needed.

▶ Every blemish has to be dealt with before repainting can begin, both outside and inside the hull.

The three-part painting process

This is what is involved in the three-part painting process:

Step 1

The first coating to apply is the epoxy primer. Several coats of primer are normally recommended. It is always best to check with the manufacturers and follow their advice. Sand between primer coats with a fine sandpaper (320–400 grit). The primer coats can be applied using rollers. Smaller rollers are often the preferred option for epoxy primer as it is quite a thick, sticky paint and bigger rollers can become heavy going.

Use a paintbrush to apply the primer to areas where the rollers can't reach. It is a good idea to tint the colour of the primer between coats to ensure you are covering the surface evenly.

Step 2

The second coating is the undercoat. Epoxy primers are best overcoated with two-pack polyurethane paints. At least two coats of this are usually recommended.

Step 3

The third stage is the topcoat. Two coats of this are usually recommended.

GALVANIC AND ELECTROLYTIC CORROSION

If sacrificial anodes are disappearing very quickly this can indicate there is a galvanic or electrolytic problem caused by electrical currents, which means an electrical circuit is being made for some reason. In order to understand what could be going on, it is worth trying to get to grips with the differences between these two forms of corrosion.

Galvanic corrosion

Galvanic corrosion is an electrochemical reaction between two or more different metals, in the presence of an electrolyte (such as salt water). In other words, one piece of metal (known as the anode) will be corroded, and the other piece of metal (known as the cathode) will be unaffected. Common examples of galvanic corrosion are where an aluminium outdrive comes into contact with a stainless steel propeller, causing the aluminium to corrode, or where aluminium comes into contact with copper or bronze fittings. The first signs of galvanic corrosion is blistering of paint below the waterline and the formation of a white powdery substance on exposed metal. The exposed metal areas become deeply pitted as the metal is eaten away by the corrosion. (See diagram.)

Electrolytic corrosion

Electrolytic corrosion, also known as stray current corrosion, is an electrochemical process where a metallic surface is corroded

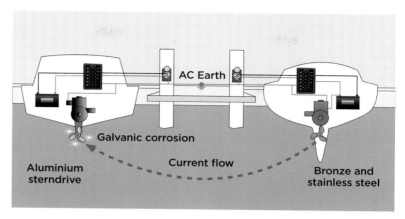

Galvanic corrosion
Aluminium sterndrive
Current flow
AC Earth
Bronze and stainless steel

▲ A partly wasted sacrificial anode needs monitoring as it may soon need replacing.

▲ A newly fitted anode should last at least six months.

by another metal it is in contact with, due to an electrolyte and the flow of an electrical current between the two metals, caused from an external source of electromotive force (EMF). In other words, electrolytic corrosion is caused by a current such as a boat's battery or a shore supply. Metal hull boats are particularly at risk because their hulls are good conductors and stray wires or connections use the hull as a ground.

Preventing electrolytic corrosion requires good electrical installation where marine-grade wiring should be insulated return with two wires rather than earth return. Metal hulls must never be used as the earth return.

ALUMINIUM HULLS: SOME PROS AND CONS

Aluminium is very lightweight and strong, hence why it is widely used in aircraft construction. Aluminium is not so widely used in the leisure marine industry, which is perhaps surprising given the advantages it has over other materials. This is mostly due to cost, not only of aluminium itself, which is more expensive than steel, but also labour costs. Aluminium hulls are welded together by skilled labour and not cast from moulds as GRP hulls are, which is a far quicker process.

Aluminium hulls form their own protective oxide surface, which means that the topsides do not have to be painted.

◀ Despite being strong and lightweight, aluminium hulls need careful maintenance to prevent electrolytic and galvanic corrosion.

Left to its own devices, an aluminium hull takes on a dull patina as it self-anodises, creating a self-protecting surface. In a sense, therefore, aluminium has a remarkable natural resistance to corrosion, quite unlike steel.

As well as being strong, an aluminium hull will not split open like a fibreglass one if it hits a submerged rock. However, welding aluminium requires a lot of skill, so when repairs are necessary they can be very expensive.

Aluminium hulls do require careful looking after, all the same. Beneath the waterline, there have been some issues in the past with producing an antifouling coating compatible with aluminium that is not toxic to marine life. Tributyltin fluoride (TBTF) paints are now banned in most parts of the world. Instead a new system using high-quality barrier coats is used: one acts as an anode and is then covered with a less reactive form of copper that is not harmful to marine life. Read more about antifouling for aluminium on page 92.

Aluminium is very prone to corrosion if it is in contact with other metals, so much so that aluminium is itself used as an anode material. It is important therefore that an aluminium hull is not allowed to come into direct contact with other metals, such as stainless steel, bronze or copper.

RISKS FROM ELECTROLYTIC AND GALVANIC CORROSION

Aluminium boats are at risk from electrolytic and galvanic corrosion. Aluminium boatowners need to take precautions that would not be of concern to owners of GRP boats. For example, it is wise not to stay too long berthed next to a steel-hulled boat in a marina, where both vessels are connected to shore power. The reason for this is that an electric circuit can form between the two vessels with the aluminium hull acting as an anode and the steel hull acting as a cathode, resulting in galvanic corrosion of the aluminium hull.

Owners need to make sure that the shore power polarity is

correctly wired in marinas as this can also lead to corrosion. They have to pay particular attention to the condition of their wiring and electrical systems, to protect the boat from electrolytic corrosion.

Some aluminium boats are equipped with current leakage meters which display real-time corrosion potential that warns of problems with electrolytic and galvanic corrosion.

PROTECTING AN ALUMINIUM HULL

- **Electrolytic action:** All stray currents must be removed from the boat's electrical system.
- **Anodes:** Zinc anodes should be positioned on the outside of the hull and replaced when 80 per cent consumed.
- **Stern gear:** To protect the stern gear, the propeller shaft should be fitted with an electro-eliminator brush and earthed to the hull.
- **Insulation:** Insert plastic seals between aluminium and other metals. For example, ensure gaskets are fitted between aluminium and the flange of a stainless steel or brass valve. The same applies to lead or iron keels, where insulating washers and gaskets should be placed between the hull and keel.
- **Painting:** While aluminium topsides do not need to be painted, antifouling coating beneath the waterline does need to be applied. Only use coatings that are designed for use with aluminium.

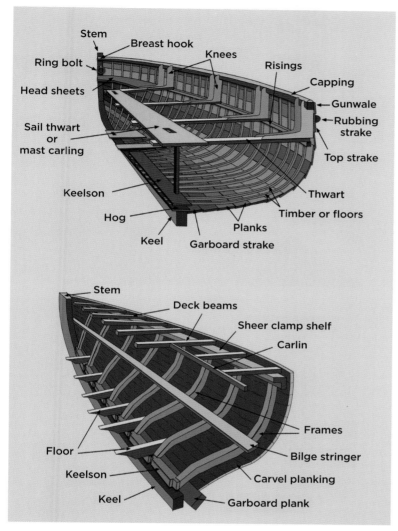

Stem
Breast hook
Knees
Risings
Ring bolt
Capping
Head sheets
Gunwale
Rubbing strake
Sail thwart
or
mast carling
Top strake
Keelson
Thwart
Timber or floors
Hog
Planks
Keel
Garboard strake

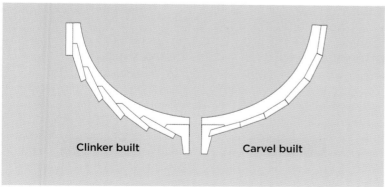

Stem
Deck beams
Sheer clamp shelf
Carlin
Frames
Floor
Bilge stringer
Keelson
Carvel planking
Keel
Garboard plank

Clinker built   Carvel built

WOODEN HULLS

Traditional wooden boats have a plank on frame construction, a centuries old boat building method that is still in use today. The hull of a wooden boat usually has a keel and frame made from a hardwood such as oak, with planking made of softwood, such as pine or cedar. Variations of the traditional method include carvel, clinker and strip planking, which all relate to the way the planking is attached to the frame.

Top left a clinker-built wooden boat. *Bottom left* a carvel-built wooden boat. Diagrams based on illustrations from *Basic Seamanship* by Peter Clissold, published by Brown, Son & Ferguson, Glasgow (1936).

▼ A carvel-built wooden boat in immaculate condition.

CARVEL HULLS

The frames of carvel-built hulls are put in place first and then the planks are fastened to the frames. The frames provide most of the strength of these boats and the planks are thinner than on clinker-built boats.

▶ A well cared for carvel-built motorboat. The planks of a carvel-built hull are not glued; instead there is flexible sealing between the planks which keeps the hull waterproof.

STRIP PLANKING

Strip planking is a type of construction used for smaller, lighter boats. The edges of thin strips of planking are glued and fastened together, similar to the carvel method but needing no caulking between the planks.

CLINKER HULLS

The construction method of clinker-built hulls, also known as lapstrake, is different from carvel-built hulls. The bottom and sides of clinker-built hulls are made first, after which the ribs are fitted. Then the planks are fastened to each other through the overlap between one plank (also known as a strake) and the one running along beneath it. The strength of clinker-built hulls comes from their wide, thick planks.

OTHER WOODEN HULL CONSTRUCTION METHODS

More recently, since the mid-20th century, marine plywood has been used for hull construction. Marine ply is very durable and less prone to rot than ordinary plywood, offering high resistance to water and fungus, the causes of wet and dry rot. Plywood panels are either fixed to a frame, known as ply-on-frame construction, or alternatively the panels are edge-glued together and reinforced with fibreglass, which is known as the stitch-and-glue method (as used by the popular Mirror dinghy). This method does not use a frame and is a little more straightforward to build.

Another modern type of wooden construction is cold moulding, which is similar to strip planking but uses several multiple layers of thin wood or veneers. Layers of veneer are laid at criss-cross angles to one another, resulting in a strong, flexible and lightweight hull.

BOAT COVERS

If you look around a boatyard one of the first things you might notice is that some boats have some serious covers over them, while others don't. Is that just excessive love and attention by some of the boatowners? Or is there more to it than that?

▲ A clinker-built wooden boat being repaired. To achieve a smooth finish with a plane, layers of fine shavings are removed and the plane is kept flat and level.

If you were to look under many of those covers you would probably find that most of the boats are wooden. Covers prevent rain (fresh water) from penetrating the inside of the hull through deck leaks, which can lead to wet rot. Note that salt water is not such an issue, as salt water prevents rot from developing, while rain water does the reverse.

Covers also prevent the sun from harming wood and will therefore make a big difference to a boat that is left ashore for several months.

▲ Wooden hulls will dry out if left ashore for long periods. A sheltered spot like this in a tidal estuary alongside a yard is ideal.

PREVENTING A WOODEN HULL FROM DRYING OUT

At the same time, allowing a wooden hull to dry out completely is not desirable as the timbers will shrink. It is important that wooden boats have just enough air circulating around them to ward off mould and mildew, but not so much that they dry out completely. The trick is to keep the boat's moisture content constant, allowing enough moisture in to prevent it from drying out. That means taking the covers off from time to time when the sun is not too strong and there is a gentle breeze blowing, rather than a howling gale.

WOODEN HULL CARE AND MAINTENANCE

It is important to ensure the essential hull maintenance of a wooden boat is done, even if you are paying others to look after your boat for you. The priority is to prevent rot from taking hold. The protective layers of paint and varnish over wood are far more critical than on GRP boats, where the topsides are painted more for cosmetic reasons.

One of the fundamental things to understand is the nature of wood itself. If wood becomes soaking wet, it swells. As it dries, it shrinks. The proper care of a wooden hull is down to keeping a balance between the cycle of wet (i.e. afloat) and dry (i.e. ashore) periods. Dry weather dries out wood, causing it to shrink. Salt water is good for wood as it not only protects

the wood from fungus but also moistens the wood, which stops it from shrinking.

WOODEN HULL INSPECTION

- Check the condition of the paintwork. If there is any cracking of the paint along the grain of the wood this indicates there might be rot developing beneath. To be sure, cracks need to be scraped out to check for rot.
- To check for rot, tap along the hull using a small wooden mallet, or the wooden handle of a tool. Listen out for the sounds the tapping makes. A high, metallic or slight ringing sound indicates the planking is in good condition. If there

is a dull, soft sound, this indicates there is rot. Mark the area and if in doubt have it checked thoroughly by a surveyor. Note the tapping will sound different as you pass over the ribs.

- If the timbers themselves show signs of splitting along the grain this indicates the hull has dried out.
- Check the plank edges and seams are in good condition. If these are proud in places this can indicate the planking has moved.
- Check the caulking is in good condition and remains well bedded in the seams.
- Inspect the plank fastenings for signs of corrosion – green

▲ Wooden boat hulls rely on layers of paint to prevent water ingress. Paintwork needs regular inspection and any imperfections dealt with to keep the hull in sound condition. The same applies to the decks and brightwork.

coloured stains indicate corrosion of copper fastenings, rust stains indicate corrosion of steel fastenings and white stains indicate corrosion of galvanised fastenings.

- Pay particular attention to the fastenings where the planks attach to the transom. Also check for splits in the ends of the planking where it joins the transom.
- Likewise, check the fastenings of the planking at the stem. This is where the planking is under considerable stress.
- Make sure none of the frame ribs are broken, especially near the tops where most damage can occur.
- Check there is no gap or signs of corrosion along the joint between the keel and the hull.
- Check the keel band of motorboats is in good condition.
- Check the keel bolts are in good condition.

STANDARD WOODEN HULL CARE

If your boat passes the hull inspection with flying colours, then the care and maintenance of the hull when it is hauled out entails the following:

- Fitting a cover that comes down to the waterline.
- Priming any bare timber that may have been exposed by the pressure washer.
- Rubbing down the topsides, patching with undercoat as necessary, applying topcoat as required.
- Below the waterline, rubbing back, patching undercoat where required and then applying antifouling.

HULL STRIPPING

For wooden hulls, the two main methods to consider for removing paint are a chemical paint stripper or a heat gun. The heat gun is generally recommended as it will be cheaper and less messy to use.

These are the steps involved in stripping the paint from a wooden hull:

Step 1

Heat gun: Use a heat shrink gun and a putty knife to scrape the old paint layers off. Take special care not to scorch the wood. If you have not used a heat gun before, practise on some scrap of painted wood, an old painted wooden door for example, until you are confident you can work the machine correctly. Wet the bare wood using salt water to make a wet barrier to protect it from the heat gun.

Step 2

Electric plane: When you have removed as much paint as possible with the heat gun and putty knife, use an electric planer to take off any remaining paint, being careful only to remove a tiny bit of the wood if necessary at the same time. Again, practise using this machine before diving into planing your hull.

Step 3

Rotary sander: Go over the surface of the wood with 40-grit sandpaper using a rotary sander at low speed. Keep the sander flat against the hull with an even pressure, moving at all times in order not to leave sanding marks. Never stop the machine when it is against the wood as it will leave a nasty mark.

▲ Flaking paint should be scraped away, then sanded back with medium grit paper. Layers of primer, undercoat and topcoat can then be applied.

WOODEN HULL REPAIRS

While wooden boat hull maintenance is pretty straightforward, it is always a good idea to take expert advice on any repair job needed on a wooden boat. Carrying out minor repairs requires some good basic woodworking skills, including knowing how to use chisels, planes and saws correctly, which is all within the grasp of the average DIY boatowner. When carrying out more major repairs, assessing exactly what needs doing, the materials required and how to carry out the repair invariably calls for some expert advice and advanced skills. Very few boatowners are shipwrights with decades of experience and our DIY skills might only be based on woodworking courses in the distant past. Your boatyard and/or your surveyor should point you in the right direction.

◄ Corroded chain plates have been removed to expose rotten timbers beneath.
▼ Almost any wooden boat that is worth saving can be. Assessing the viability of a project is best done by professional advisers.

WET AND DRY ROT

Wooden boats are at risk from two types of rot: wet rot and dry rot. Both are types of fungal decay and can easily spread throughout a boat if it is not looked after. Wet rot develops when unprotected wood remains continually in contact with moisture. Dry rot develops when unprotected wood is in contact with moisture, then dries out, then gets wet again, then dries and so on.

The only proper remedy for rot is to remove it completely and then patch in a new piece of timber or fill the void, if appropriate and small enough, with a suitable epoxy putty.

The early warning signs for rot are blistering or flaking paint and a dull, soft sound produced when tapping along the hull with a plastic mallet.

▶ A small area of rotten wood can be repaired using a graving piece, traditionally diamond-shaped. 1. Begin by removing the rotten wood with a chisel. 2. Cut and plane a piece of timber slightly bigger than the rotten area. 3. Chisel out the rotten wood to create a straight-sided recess. 4. Glue the graving piece, then tap it in place. Screws are sometimes used to fix the piece in place but can be removed once the glue is set. 5. Use a smoothing plane to make a flush finish.

REMOVING AND REPLACING A BROKEN OR ROTTEN PLANK

The thought of replacing a broken or rotten plank may seem daunting at first, but this should be within the capabilities of a savvy DIY boatowner.

It will pay to plan the task out carefully, checking out exactly what needs to be removed and how you are going to do it. You will need to source suitable replacement timber and ensure you have all the right tools for the job, including decent planes and saws. This includes checking where the old planking is fastened, marking the fastenings and making sure you can access the planking from inside the hull.

I came across these fishermen mending their boat in Myanmar. The bottom of their boat had been holed on some rocks.

First, they removed the damaged planking and pulled out some of the caulking that needed replacing.

Then they took measurements, cut some new planking and planed the new planks smooth.

The fishermen made some adjustments to ensure the new planks fitted precisely, then fixed them in place with copper nails.

Once all the new planks were fitted and nailed in place they primed the new timbers and left for the day.

The next day they applied undercoat to the hull and tapped in new caulking along the seams. More coats of paint followed which quickly dried in the hot sun. They lost out on two days' fishing but were soon back out on the water.

◄ The traditional way to make a template for new planking. A template known as a spiling board is tacked to the frames. Each frame is numbered and their positions are marked along the spiling board.

SPILING

Before removing the old planking, thought needs to be given to creating either a pattern or template for the new planking. If the old plank is in a very bad shape it is unlikely to be of use as a template. The traditional method for making a pattern is spiling. This involves generating a number of points to determine the perimeter of a plank, using a strip of batten known as a spiling board. The spiling board is narrower than the planking. It is tacked to the frame along the centreline of where the new plank will run in order to hold it in place.

Another way of creating a template is to tape a length of paper over the hull before removing the old planking and tracing the line of the seams. This can avoid doing lots of measurements later, but it does need to be accurate. The tracing is transferred to stiff card or thin ply and this can be used as the template, offering it up over the gap left behind when the old plank has been removed. Other methods are used, but the key objective here is to be able to cut and plane a new replacement plank into a shape that will fit as well as possible.

► The outer edge of a short strip of wood, known as a dummy stick, is placed up against the adjoining plank. Marks are made on the spiling board along the bottom edge of the dummy stick to record the shape, repeating at each frame.

The spiling board is removed and placed on the new plank. The dummy stick is placed on the lines drawn on the spiling board and a pencil is drawn along the outer edge of the dummy stick to mark the shape required.

Plank replacement on a carvel-built hull

Here are the basic steps involved with removing and replacing a plank on a carvel-planked hull. Note these steps are a summary of what needs to be done and the specific circumstances of every individual case will need to be factored in to complete a satisfactory end result.

Step 1

Begin by raking out the seam compound and the old caulking in order to free up the old plank.

Step 2

Expose the fastenings, be they nail heads or screws, by chipping out the dowels or putty. Remove as many screw fastenings as possible.

Step 3

Use a hole saw to cut around the fastenings that won't move or have broken. Be very careful not to cut into the frame beneath. Double-check the thickness of the planking before you begin cutting.

Step 4

Once all the fastenings are removed or cut around, you should be able to spring the plank by tapping it from inside the hull.

Step 5

With the old plank removed, it will be easier to remove all the remaining old fastenings and clean up the frames.

Step 6

If using a spiling board, nail it to the frame after removing the old plank. Then, using a small strip of wood known as a dummy stick, make a series of marks along the spiling board at regular intervals. To do this, place the outer edge of the dummy stick against the upper and lower planks in turn, marking along the edge to record the perimeter for the new planking.

Step 7

Alternatively, offer up your template to check that it will fit correctly. If needs be make some further adjustments by adding extra small strips of card to make the template as accurate as possible.

Step 8

The next thing to do is transfer the template or marked-up spiling board to the new timber and then draw out the shape for the new planking prior to cutting.

Step 9

Once the new plank has been cut, it can be offered up in place over the frames, holding or clamping it in place to check the fit. This is really where the expert's skill comes into its own, as the last thing you want is a replacement plank that is a bad fit.

Step 10

It is usually advised to use the same type of metal fastenings as the existing ones, especially below the waterline where there may be risk of galvanic corrosion.

WOODEN HULL LEAKS CAUSED BY FAILED FASTENINGS

Wooden planking is fixed to the frame of a hull using metal screws or nails. The screws may be bronze or stainless steel. Note that boat nails can be either galvanised, also referred to as flat point nails, which are cut from sheet steel or copper boat nails. These are the flat countersunk, square shank variety. Over time all fastenings corrode and need to be replaced. Failed fastenings will result in the planks becoming loose, causing leaks to develop.

Replacing the fastenings is a labour-intensive job. While this may appear to be a simple repetitive task, it is best done by experienced, talented people as problems can develop. Removing the old fastenings can be challenging, especially if the old screws refuse to budge or break as they are removed.

There are a number of different ways to refasten and it is a good idea to ask others in the know about your specific circumstances. An easy method is to leave the old fastenings in place and add new ones between the old ones. Care needs to be taken to place the new ones through the centre of the frame beneath the planking and to prevent damage to both the planking and the frames. The disadvantage of this method is that you end up drilling more holes into the frames. This can lead to more problems in the future, as the frames will need to be replaced or sistered, where new frames are added alongside the old ones.

A better method, which is generally more expensive because of the additional labour costs, is to remove the old fastenings and replace these with slightly bigger ones. Much will depend on the scale of the problem, which needs to be assessed carefully by those in the know.

Assessing the condition of the fastenings

There are several telltale signs of failed fastenings, including cracks in the paintwork, streaks of rust running down the hull and the wooden plugs covering the screws protruding above the surface of the hull. The plugs begin to protrude because the fastenings expand as they rust, forcing the wooden plugs to move.

The only way to be absolutely sure of the state of the fastenings is to remove a number of them from different places around the hull, including those where leaks commonly occur in wooden hulls, such as the stem, where the garboard meets the rabbet and along the waterline. If the screw heads are found to be deteriorating, or the threads are worn or obviously corroding, they need to be replaced. A trained eye will be looking out for fastenings that may have been replaced recently in which case they will most likely still be in good condition.

A general rule to be considered is that fastenings can easily outlast the wood they are in. If a plank becomes loose it does not necessarily mean the fastening itself has failed, only that it is no longer holding the plank in place, which could mean either the plank or frame has become rotten.

REPLACING OLD FASTENINGS

- The first thing to do is expose the plug that covers the fastening by scraping away the paint.
- The plug can be tricky to remove and care needs to be taken not to damage the surrounding wood and screw head. Use a small chisel or awl to chip out the plug.

- Clean out the screw slots before trying to remove the screw.
- Place a correct-sized screwdriver that fits the slot well and give it a tap with a mallet. This will help loosen the screw.
- Use the screwdriver to rotate the screw back and forth a little to get it moving. Once again, take care not to damage the surrounding wood with the screwdriver or screw head as you begin to remove the screw. If you meet resistance, try rotating the screw backwards and forwards again, keeping a steady pressure on the screwdriver as you do so.
- If the screw breaks, it may be possible to drill it out by using a small diameter drill bit. If this fails, your best option is to reseal what's left of the screw hole with epoxy filler, plug it and drill a new hole. Alternatively, you could end up going from a bad situation to a worse one as you struggle to remove an old broken fastening.
- Old nails can also be difficult to remove. As with a broken screw, drilling into head of the nail and then driving in a gripfast nail can work, using a claw hammer to remove it.
- Once the old fastening has been removed a new one can be screwed into place, taking care to choose the right size and length of fastening, slightly bigger than the old one. Silicon bronze screws are normally recommended, protected either by a wooden dowel or a red lead putty plug.

▲ The planks of traditional wooden hulls are fastened by nails or screws. In time these fail and the planks become loose.

STEP-BY-STEP

ADDING FASTENINGS

If it is decided to add extra fastenings, the process is a little more straightforward than doing a replacement as there is less to go wrong:

1. First check that the plank and frame beneath it are both sound and free of rot. This can be done by drilling a small hole into the wood.

2. Mark where the new fastening will go, being sure that it will be as close to the centre of the frame as possible and away from any weak spots.

3. Drill the new hole with a drill bit that matches the size of the fastening.

4. Countersink the hole so that the new screw will be well below the surface.

5. Screw the new fastening in and cover with a dowel or red lead putty plug.

CAULKING

Caulking is the process of sealing between the timber planks of a carvel hull to make it watertight. The traditional technique involves using special tools and methods to fill the seams with natural fibres, cord and pitch, resulting in a flexible seal that makes allowance for movement in the timbers. It also has a structural role as it tightens up the hull and reduces the longitudinal movement of planks, preventing them from rubbing against each other as a boat moves through the waves at sea. Caulking lasts a long time, but it does need to be inspected regularly and repaired occasionally to prevent seams from opening up and causing leaks, which can also lead to the timbers rotting.

Recaulking can be undertaken by an amateur, but it takes some training and practice to be able to do this well. Either cotton or oakum can be used for the caulking, oakum being better suited for larger vessels with wider seams. Using purpose-made tools rather than improvised ones is best practice.

▲ Caulking hammers used for re-caulking.

STEP-BY-STEP

CAULKING

The job will require caulking hammers, irons and a raking tool. As with all woodworking jobs, great care needs to be taken to protect the wood from being damaged by the misuse of tools – practice makes perfect.

1. Remove the old caulking from the seam that has been leaking, using a raking tool. Allow the seam to dry out.

2. Twist a length of cotton to fill the seam being worked on, tapping it into place with a making iron and mallet.

3. Care needs to be taken with the amount of force used; enough to pack the caulking well in but not so much that the planking may become damaged. Use a hardening iron, which has a groove in its tip, to drive the caulking deep into the seam, with a to-and-fro rocking motion. The caulking needs to fill about half the depth of the seam.

4. Apply a coat of primer along the repaired area.

5. Apply a stopping compound, traditionally red lead putty, using a putty knife. Finish the seam off by rubbing it with linseed oil.

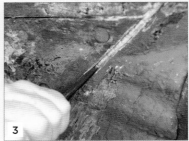

SEAM SPLINES

Splines are long, thin strips of wood that are glued into old seams in poor condition. They are an alternative to replacing old caulking and red lead putty. The old caulking is removed and the seams are normally prepared using a router. Although this entails widening the seam, which might seem like making a bad situation worse, it is important to ensure the prepared seam is of uniform thickness before the spline is glued in place.

▲ Loose splines should be replaced.

ANTIFOULING

Boats that are kept afloat can very quickly become a home for small marine organisms such as barnacles, weed and slime. Applying an antifouling paint to your hull is necessary to protect it from these micro-organisms, as a fouled hull can cause problems and will slow down a boat's speed considerably if left unchecked.

There has been much controversy over the years about antifouling products due to their detrimental effects on marine life, especially in marinas and crowded anchorages in estuaries. The big challenge for the paint manufacturers is to develop products that will keep hulls free of foul without harming the environment.

There are two main types of antifouling paint used for leisure boats, normally referred to as hard and eroding. Both contain biocides that kill and deter fouling organisms, but they work in different ways and are designed for different types of boat. The basis of most biocides found in antifouling are copper (Cu) and cuprous oxide (CuO). These are effective at deterring the growth of molluscs, larvae and some types of weed, but there needs to be high concentrations of copper in the paint for them to work. To be completely effective, some antifouling also contains zinc-based biocides or organic algaecides.

When choosing antifouling for your boat, it is advisable to talk to your local chandleries as they should be able to tell you what antifouling is best for your type of boat, its location and the environment. It is important to know the type of antifouling currently on your boat, as not all types of antifouling are compatible with each other.

HARD ANTIFOULING

Hard antifouling slowly releases biocide that prevents foul from settling on the hull. The biocide can last a whole year and, if several layers are applied, even longer. However, the leaching rate reduces over time and the paint loses its efficiency. This type of paint has a hard finish, which enables it to be scrubbed or wet sanded through the season to keep the bottom in good condition.

Hard antifouling is popular with boats where maximum performance is required – racing yachts and fast powerboats for example. It is also used for boats kept in fresh water as the alternative, eroding antifouling, is designed to be used in salt water and does not perform as well in fresh water.

There are some types of hard antifouling with a very high copper content, where tiny particles of copper are suspended in epoxy resin.

▲ Two coats of antifouling have been applied to this yacht prior to launching for the season.

Several layers of this copper resin have to be applied very carefully to a pristine hull. This process is normally done by a small professional team under controlled conditions. The final coat is sanded, leaving a layer of copper oxide that is effective, very hard-wearing and can last up to ten years or so. Copper resins are expensive to buy and apply in the first place, but after a few years they become a viable option as there is very little maintenance required.

ERODING ANTIFOULING

Eroding antifouling is also known as soft antifouling and, like hard antifouling, slowly releases biocide. The big difference between the two is that the paint itself erodes into salt water, leaving very little residue on the hull itself. This is ideal in many ways for the cruising boatowner as it reduces the build-up of successive layers of antifouling and makes maintenance much easier. However, this is not so ideal for those who want to keep their boat's bottom in pristine condition through the boating season as scrubbing or sanding it smooth takes off the paint.

Therefore, eroding antifouling is more widely used for cruising yachts and displacement motorboats where speed is not the absolute priority.

NON-TOXIC ANTIFOULING

Recent developments in antifouling technology have concentrated on finding non-toxic solutions that are environmentally safe. There have been some significant breakthroughs.

For example, several silicon-based products available now form a very slippery surface that prevents micro-organisms from gripping on to the hull.

While these developments have generally been well received by the leisure marine community, they perform best on hulls that regularly move through the water at speeds of ten knots or more. A great idea for powerboats, but not so good for most sailing yachts which rarely, if ever, exceed ten knots through the water.

Another option is electronic antifouling, which uses ultrasound technology to deter fouling organisms. These systems are easy to install and can be undertaken by competent DIY boatowners. You do have to swallow hard when it comes to the price, but hopefully in the future these will become commonplace and more affordable.

ANTIFOULING FOR METAL COMPONENTS AND HULLS

Outdrives, sterndrives, saildrives and propellers need special treatment. There are types of hard antifouling designed for them, but before choosing these paints you need to be sure what the components on your boat are made from.
- Most outdrives and sterndrives and some trim tabs are made from aluminium.
- Propellers are made from bronze, aluminium or stainless steel.
- Drive shafts, trim tabs and other fittings may be made from stainless steel, steel or bronze.
- Keels are normally made from cast iron or lead.

Bronze needs very thorough preparation and should be primed before applying antifouling. My boat has a bronze FeatherStream propeller and the manufacturers recommend that regular antifouling should not be used. There are many propeller antifouling products available and most can be used provided the product states that it is safe to use with bronze. Some owners send their propellers off to machine shops to be polished to a gloss finish and then coated in a thin layer of grease. As ever, it is worth checking your manufacturer's recommendations before doing this.

Aluminium needs to be painted with purpose-made antifouling. Standard copper-based antifouling is not suitable as it will lead to serious corrosion from the aluminium reacting with the copper.

ANTIFOULING FOR ALUMINIUM HULLS

Antifouling with high copper content is not compatible with aluminium, so it is crucial for aluminium hulls to have several layers of primer to create a barrier between the antifouling and the hull itself. Antifouling that is made from cuprous thiocyanate is a good option, but it still needs the correct type of

▲ Aluminium trim tabs should be painted with purpose-made antifouling.

▲ Check with the manufacturer before applying antifouling to a propeller.

primer beneath to protect the aluminium.

INSPECTION

It is a good idea to carry out an inspection of your boat's existing antifouling as soon as possible after it has been lifted out and pressure washed. Check it all over and remove any signs of remaining barnacles using a scraper. The pressure wash might not have dislodged them all and you don't want any of them gluing themselves to the hull as it dries out.

You also need to check for blisters. These may be caused by water being trapped under the paint or they could be signs of osmosis. If in doubt, then have an expert check them out for you.

Antifouling is one of the least pleasant boat maintenance jobs to

do, but it has to be done. The very worst job of all is removing the old antifouling as this can get seriously messy and is very hard work.

The easiest way to reduce the build-up of antifouling is by using

eroding antifouling and making sure that the hull is always pressure washed as soon as it comes out of the water. Much of the remaining antifouling will be removed this way.

Health and safety precautions

As antifouling is toxic and messy stuff, you must use suitable protective clothing. The biocides in antifouling can be absorbed through the skin so you need to protect yourself against this as well as any dust particles that you could breathe in. Wear a good-quality breathing mask that protects you from solvents, rubber gloves, safety goggles and overalls.

I normally wear an old hat for additional protection.

Lay down appropriate sheeting beneath the hull to collect any old paint and residue. You should check with your boatyard what the local regulations stipulate about removing and applying antifouling. You may need to use suitable tenting to protect others nearby.

ANTIFOULING IN GOOD CONDITION

If the existing antifouling surface is even and there are few or no imperfections, you can safely say it is in good condition. This means that preparing the hull before applying new antifouling will be comparatively easy, whether you opt to go down the DIY route or ask professionals to do the antifouling for you.

Preparation

Use 80-grit wet and dry abrasive paper to sand back the old antifouling. Be careful not to abrade too much as you want to keep the primer coat beneath intact. If in doubt, use 120-grit paper as it will be less abrasive. You need to keep the paper wet, so have a bucket of fresh water beside you to rinse in as you work.

When you have finished sanding, thoroughly rinse the surface with fresh water and allow to dry before applying the antifouling.

ANTIFOULING IN POOR CONDITION

If the surface is uneven and cratered, caused by patches of old paint that have flaked away and been progressively overpainted, then it is time to get your boat's bottom back into shape. All the old antifouling layers need to be completely removed before new antifouling can be applied.

You may decide to employ a professional to do all this work for you and if you have the budget for this it will be money very well spent. Although this is the expensive option, it will save you considerable time, hassle and

back pain. Remember also that applying antifouling in future seasons will be much more easy going afterwards.

REMOVING OLD ANTIFOULING

There are a number of options available for removing layers of old antifouling:

Option 1: Scraping method

For boatowners choosing the DIY route, scraping is the budget option. This method is also the most arduous, taking a lot of time and considerable effort. I have done it quite a few times. The last time I did so I promised myself that I wouldn't do it again. It can be OK for an hour or two, but the novelty soon wears off and you need to be prepared to be bent over double for a few days to scrape a whole hull. The only compensation here is that you are not paying someone else to do the work. Otherwise there is zero satisfaction gained from doing this particular boat job.

There are various types of scraper to choose from: flat-bladed types that you push, triangular-shaped ones that you pull and double-handed ones with very sharp carbide scrapers that you also pull towards you. You need to keep the blades sharp, but at the same time you have to be careful they do not dig into the gelcoat, which can leave a nasty gash that you will need to fill. It helps to round off the edges of the blades to avoid such mishaps.

▲ A mid-season gentle scrub will remove slime and grime from the hull and improve performance.

Avoid scraping old antifouling on a windy day as the scrapings can be blown all over the place. It is best to collect them up as you go, into a refuse bag.

Eventually you will reach the point when you decide you cannot do any more scraping. If you have any energy left, you will then need to wet sand the whole surface with 80-grit paper and rinse it off ready for painting. Alternatively, stagger home and come back the next day to do the sanding.

Option 2: Chemical stripper

There are several types of paint stripper specially formulated for the removal of old antifouling. These products can make antifouling removal easier as they soften the old paint, making it less labour-intensive. However, this method increases the amount of toxic waste to dispose of and can get very messy. If you are removing several layers you may have to repeat the process two or three times. Some paint stripping chemicals are more environmentally friendly than others and biodegradable, so it is worth shopping around.

Your boatyard or local chandlery should be able to advise you on which product to choose for your boat. Make sure the antifouling stripper you choose will not harm gelcoat if your boat has a GRP hull.

Most antifouling strippers can be applied with an old brush, using a stippling action to help the stripper work through the old layers. It is a good idea to then cover the treated area with clingfilm to prevent the stripper from drying out as it slowly softens the old paint. Some chemical strippers are faster acting than others so it pays to check before you buy.

After the stripper has done its job, the old antifouling can be removed with a wooden or plastic scraper while the old paint is still soft.

You will then need to wet sand. If the primer is still intact rinse the hull with fresh water, leave it to dry and it will be ready for painting.

Option 3: Blasting

There are a number of methods used for blasting a boat's hull to remove antifouling. These include using either dry ice, sand or soda. They do require costly equipment and usually a team of two or more people to do the work, which will include tenting off the boat to protect everything else in the immediate vicinity.

A compressor is needed, so for DIY purposes this method of paint removal is really a non-starter unless you can hire suitable equipment and have some assistance to do the work, as well as the permission from your boatyard to use a blaster.

It will pay to ask around for the most cost-effective method for your hull. Soda blasting is definitely worth investigating. It is a 'non-abrasive' blasting that uses a type of sodium bicarbonate (baking soda). It does no damage to sub-surfaces, so soft materials like aluminium and timber can be blasted without damage. Soda crystals exit a jet nozzle at high speed, and as each crystal explodes on impact the sudden release of energy blasts away the coating on whatever is being blasted.

Soda is harmless to the environment and washes away with water. However, soda blasting is normally done by tenting the blasting area, using plastic sheeting to form a tent and more sheeting on the ground to catch the old antifouling and residue.

HOW MUCH ANTIFOULING PAINT?

When buying antifouling, you need to buy enough paint for two coats. Most paint manufacturers can advise how much antifouling is required for different lengths and hull shapes.

A quick way to work out the surface area of a fin-keeled yacht beneath the waterline is to use this handy formula: (boat length × (beam ÷ draught)) × 0.6.

ANTIFOULING PRIMER AND EPOXY PRIME

If you have removed all the layers back to the gelcoat, it will be necessary to apply a coat of primer before painting on the antifouling. The reason for doing this is that the antifouling will not adhere properly to the gelcoat.

If a GRP hull is stripped back to the gelcoat you should consider applying an epoxy coating to seal the hull and protect it against osmosis. If your boat's hull has high moisture readings it is best not to seal in the moisture with a layer of epoxy so it is worth getting professional advice about this. You should dry a hull out as much as possible before applying the epoxy. It is tricky stuff to use and to be fully effective the hull needs to be very well prepared. Two or three epoxy layers are applied, and overcoating times vary according to the conditions. Each layer has to be allowed to dry to the point that it is touch dry rather than completely hard and then the next layer can be applied. Preparation is key, as is following the manufacturer's instructions.

APPLYING ANTIFOULING

Choose a dry, calm day. It is best to apply the antifouling in the middle of the day to ensure the hull is dry and as warm as possible. Minimum application temperatures vary so check what your paint manufacturer recommends. A common minimum is 5°C, but note this would need to be the temperature of the hull. If the paint is applied in too low temperatures, it may not flow over or adhere to the existing paint. Likewise, painting on a windy day is not advised as the paint will more likely become sticky and dry too quickly.

Make sure you have everything you need, including:
- Antifouling for two coats.
- Paint stirring stick.
- Protective clothing – goggles, gloves, respirator/breathing mask for solvents (not a dust mask) and overalls.
- Plastic sheeting to protect ground from spillages.
- Masking tape.
- Thinners as recommended by the paint manufacturers.
- Long- and short-handled rollers and a pack of gloss roller pads (not emulsion ones).
- Roller trays.
- Brushes.
- Paper towels and/or rags.
- Rubbish bag for disposal of used rollers/trays/masking tape/gloves.

Step 1

Masking: Before painting, apply masking tape along the waterline. I find it best to use a good-quality plastic masking tape, as there will be no seepage of paint beneath the tape and it will be easy to remove the tape after you have finished painting. Cheaper masking tape can be very hard to peel off if left for more than a few hours and you can end up with an uneven edge. Take care to keep the masking tape straight, working it along the existing waterline without it kinking. Also mask off anything that does not need antifouling, including sacrificial anodes, transducers and the log impeller.

Step 2

Stirring the paint: Stir the paint well using a wide stick. This will take several minutes as the biocides are thick and heavy and need to be mixed well into the paint. When you are satisfied it is completely mixed, pour some into a paint tray and reseal the lid. The last thing you want to do is step back to admire your handiwork and kick a tin of antifouling over by mistake. It is a good idea to stir the paint each time you refill the tray as it can get very thick and sticky near the bottom of the tin otherwise.

Step 3

Painting: Be generous with the paint. Go back after you have finished the first coat and add extra layers along the leading and trailing edges of the keel and rudder. Use a roller as much as possible, but also have an old brush to reach the inaccessible places. If the paint dries out quickly, you can apply a second coat of antifouling on the same day, but I usually come back the next day to do the second coat.

Step 4

Underneath the cradle pads: If your boat is supported by cradle pads, then to do a proper job you need to paint beneath the pads. There are a couple of options for doing this. One is to ask the boatyard to move each of them just enough to enable you to come back and paint the patches. The other option is to wait for the boat to be lifted into the slings before launching and painting the patches on the day of the launch. The second option does not normally involve an additional cost, while the first option usually incurs a yard labour cost, which is fair enough.

Step 5

Rubbish disposal: Peel away the masking tape, dispose of all the used rollers, brushes, tape and debris, step back and admire your handiwork.

ANTIFOULING KEELS

Exposed keels (as opposed to encapsulated keels) require special attention as they are prone to corrosion. Most keels are made from either steel, iron, lead or a combination of a steel fin and a lead bulb. Note that lead does not rust, but it does need antifouling and requires an underwater primer to be applied.

Keels in good condition

- Before applying coatings, pressure washing is needed to remove as much loose material as possible.
- Abrade with 60- or 80-grit wet and dry sandpaper, used wet to prevent dust.
- Remove all residue and wipe clean with fresh water.
- Apply underwater primer as soon as possible, before the surface begins to oxidise. Usually at least three coats are recommended.
- Finally apply at least two coats of the same antifouling as used for the hull.

Keels in poor condition

- If there are signs of rust, pitting or small cracks along the keel surface, you will need to remove all of the surrounding paint.
- Use an angle grinder, wire brush or shot blasting to take the keel back to bare, shiny metal.
- Apply a rust preventer.
- If the metal is seriously pitted, the holes need to be filled. There are epoxy products

▲ Keels need special preparation. Any rust on iron keels has to be removed with an angle grinder. Then keel primer is applied and the surface faired before it is ready for the antifouling.

▲ This keel requires some serious attention. The keel bolts should be checked and may need replacing.

available to fill cracks and holes in iron keels.
- After filling with epoxy, fair the surface using 60- or 80-grit paper.
- Apply at least three coats of underwater primer or as recommended by the manufacturer.
- Finally, apply at least two coats of the same antifouling as used for the hull.

Note: If there is rust showing along the hull–keel joint, this could indicate the keel bolts are corroding. See **Keel maintenance and repair** overleaf.

KEEL MAINTENANCE AND REPAIR

There is a broad diversity of keel types found within the boating spectrum. By far the most common type used for sailing yachts is the bolted-on fin keel, usually made of cast iron, which is bolted through the underside of a GRP hull with substantial stainless steel bolts. Other types of keel include bilge keels, shoal keels, encapsulated keels, lifting keels and canting keels, as used on racing yachts. While iron is the most common type of ballast, lead is also widely used. Cement or concrete is sometimes used in combination with scrap iron as ballast for wooden and steel boats, but this can lead to steel rusting from the inside and is not considered good practice. Some modern racing yachts have water ballast which can be pumped into tanks to help counterbalance any heeling.

Whatever the shape and type, the job of a sailing boat's keel is to control sideways movement through the water and to provide a counterweight to the sideways force of the wind on the sails, which causes a boat to heel over. Keels are designed to act as underwater foils that generate lift as the boat moves through the water, counteracting the leeward force of the wind and enabling the boat to sail closer to the wind.

Clearly, motorboats do not require deep keels to counterbalance the heeling effect and sideways force of a boat under sail, but nonetheless they do have keels designed to keep them stable and provide structural integrity. Displacement hulls are often ballasted to increase stability. As a result, they have a low centre of gravity, making them less susceptible to the wind and waves than planing hulls, which are designed for speed and performance.

KEEL PROBLEMS

It is very rare for a keel to fall off a boat. When this happens the incident often receives a lot of press attention as the subject is understandably of concern to boatowners, builders and designers. Marine accident investigators are usually called in and reports are published explaining the probable causes of these accidents.

There are more common incidents involving keels that require inspections and repairs to be carried out.

KEEL BOLTS INSPECTION

Keel bolts should be inspected once a year for signs of corrosion. Most keel bolts of modern boats with cast iron keels are studs, threaded into a tapped hole in the keel. Keel bolts can be made from either stainless steel or galvanised steel.

Lead keels often have J-shaped bronze bolts cast into the lead. Bronze is only used with lead keels as bronze and cast iron create a galvanic reaction.

An inspection entails looking from the inside and outside of the boat:

Outside check
- If there is rust appearing along the hull–keel joint this is a clear warning sign that the studs may be corroding.
- Look for any signs of movement between the hull

▲ Iron keel pitting.

▲ Keel movement, possibly resulting from grounding.

▲ Rust streaks indicate bolts are corroding.

and keel, such as splits in the seal or cracks in the hull area around the joint.

Inside check

- Do a visual check of the fastenings in the bilges, making sure you take a look at all of them, even if they are hard to access.
- Dry and clean the bilges. The bilges should be kept dry at all times to help prevent corrosion of the fastenings, even if they are stainless steel.

- Some staining and minor rust is quite common, but heavier corrosion needs to be checked over carefully.
- Surveyors tap the studs with a hammer and know what sounds to listen for. A ringing sound is good; a dull sound is not good.
- Check for any stress cracks in the bilge area around the keel bolts, which indicate there has been movement. If you see damage like this it would be wise to have the keel removed for further inspection.

▲ A stress crack needs checking by a surveyor.

KEEL BOLT CORROSION

Keel bolts can sometimes be withdrawn for inspection to check their condition and for any signs of corrosion. This entails first removing the nuts one by one and inspecting the threads for signs of crevice corrosion.

Quite often, it is the middle part (the waist) of a bolt where the corrosion is taking place, which is where the hull joins the keel. This is caused by the failure of the seal at the hull–keel joint, which allows sea water to reach the bolts and corrode them. Under these circumstances, the seal will need to be replaced as well as any corroded keel bolts.

If you have any cause for concern it is wise to ask an expert to take a look and advise whether the keel needs to be removed for further investigation and repair.

1. Rust along hull-to-keel joint indicates keel bolt corrosion.
2. Sealant has been applied prior to reattachment of the keel.
3. A bilge keel has been detached for inspection following impact damage.

KEEL BOLT AND HULL–KEEL SEAL REPLACEMENT

A typical repair involving keel bolt replacement and new hull–keel joint proceeds as follows:

1. A frame is prepared to support the keel when it is separated from the hull.

2. The boat is supported in the boatyard hoist or crane.

3. The keel bolt nuts and washers are removed from inside.

4. The boat is hoisted a little off the cradle.

5. As separation begins steel blades are inserted into the hull–keel joint crack to cut through the seal. Steel wedges may be hammered into the joint to encourage separation. This can take several minutes as seals are sometimes reluctant to give way.

6. Once the hull and keel are separated, the boat is lifted clear from the keel. The keel now rests in the wooden frame.

7. The keel bolt studs are inspected. If any are badly corroded or distorted they are removed and replaced.

8. The old sealant is ground away from the flat surfaces of the hull join and keel top.

9. The fibreglass hull around the join area is checked for stress cracks. If these are found the hull will need to be strengthened with new layers of woven fibreglass mat and epoxy.

10. The hull and keel top are prepared thoroughly for priming so that the new sealant can be applied.

11. The boat is slowly lowered back down on to the keel, then the backing plates, washers and nuts are fastened. Excess squeezed-out sealant is wiped off.

12. The nuts will need to be torque-tightened according to the recommended keel bolt diameter torque settings as the seal beds down and checked again after the boat is relaunched for any signs of leakage.

GROUNDING DAMAGE

If you have ever witnessed a boat colliding with a rock or other submerged obstacle you will know that there is an almighty thump and the whole boat shakes and judders. While such hard groundings seldom result in catastrophic keel failure, something has to give and even the sturdiest keels can easily be damaged by such an impact.

Following a hard grounding it is always recommended to contact your insurance company as you may be covered for this. It will advise you how to proceed. The boat should be hauled out and a surveyor needs to inspect the keel and hull for damage.

Fin keelers

A hard grounding can cause the keel–hull joint of a fin-keeled yacht to split open as the keel is forced away from the keel stub by the impact. Aside from any damage to the joint and keel bolts (see **Keel bolt and hull–keel seal replacement** above)

the impact can cause cracks in the gelcoat which need to be repaired. More seriously, it can also force the aft end of the keel upwards, damaging the hull laminate in the process. This is repaired as follows:

- The areas of damage around the hull–keel join area are identified and marked.
- Splits in the laminate tend to be on the outside of the hull forward of the keel and inside the hull aft of the keel.
- The damaged areas are ground back and repaired with layers of glass fibre and epoxy resin, before being faired, primed and painted.

Encapsulated keels

Although encapsulated keels are generally thought to be more robust than exposed keels, damage can still occur after a hard grounding. A gash in the GRP keel coating needs to be treated as it can lead to bigger problems if water reaches the iron ballast, which will begin to rust and expand as a result, eventually splitting the encapsulated laminate. This should be dealt with as follows:

- For superficial damage to the keel coating, wash and clean the damaged area. Then roughen the edges of the gouge with coarse 40-grit sandpaper.
- Wipe clean with acetone and dry the area thoroughly.
- Apply a clear coat of epoxy resin, followed by a second coat of epoxy resin mixed with micro-balloons.
- Cover the patch with some

waxed paper taped to the keel in order to hold the epoxy in place until it hardens.

- Sand the patch when dry. Fill any voids with more epoxy if necessary and then sand smooth.
- Apply a two-part epoxy primer to the patch, building up several layers of primer to create a waterproof barrier coat. Lightly sand when fully cured.
- The repair is now ready for priming and painting.

Bilge keels

A problem with bilge keel boats kept on drying moorings is that the keel bolts and hull–keel joints sometimes fail due to the constant flexing load caused by the continuous grounding that occurs at every tide.

This problem can be solved by strengthening the hull on the inside with epoxy resin and glass cloth. This is in addition to replacing the worn keel bolts and resealing the keels (see **Keel bolt and hull–keel seal replacement** opposite).

LIFTING AND SWING KEEL INSPECTIONS

There are two main types of lifting keels fitted to sailing yachts: those that lift up vertically like dagger boards and those that pivot at an angle. Both forms have lifting tackle which needs to be inspected and maintained on a regular basis according to advice given in owners' manuals. Manufacturers usually advise owners which maintenance work they can do themselves and the work that should be carried out by suitably experienced boatyards.

Most swing keel lifting mechanisms have four basic parts: a winch, a cable, a pivot bearing attached to the keel and turning blocks. On larger boats, keels are often lifted by electric motors and hydraulic systems.

LIFTING KEEL MAINTENANCE

Most lifting keel maintenance needs to be done ashore with the keel lowered, in order to get access to the keel housing, but some systems can be checked

and maintained with the keel raised. Annual checks and maintenance should be done in accordance with owners' manuals and are likely to include:

- Winch mechanism inspected for corrosion and smoothness of operation, and lubricated.
- Centre-board pivots inspected for wear.
- If applicable, lifting tackle rope checked for chafe.
- If applicable, wire cabling checked for condition. If any wires are broken the cable should be replaced.
- Condition of the eye bolt inspected where the winch cable attaches to the keel.
- Turning blocks inspected for wear and lubricated with marine grease. Worn blocks to be replaced.

For a complete refurbishment of a swing keel, all the equipment will need to be disconnected and removed, the keel shot-blasted for rust removal and then repainted. Bearings, seals and cables will also need to be replaced.

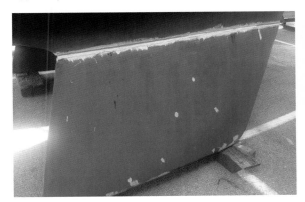

▲ Bilge keels have considerable lateral forces exerted on them when ashore or on drying moorings.

▲ A pivoting centre-board type lifting keel. The pivot bolt should be checked for wear annually.

RUDDERS AND STEERING SYSTEMS

A rudder is one of the most critical parts of a boat and should be near the top of your annual maintenance checklist. Rudder failure is a common occurrence on neglected or overworked boats and a very unpleasant and potentially dangerous thing to happen when you are out at sea.

It is important for a boatowner to fully understand how their boat's steering system works.

For example, do you know whether your rudder stock is hollow or solid? Is it made from stainless steel or aluminium, or is it composite? More importantly, do you understand how the system can fail? It is always best with boats to leave nothing to chance and to know how to spot early signs of trouble. This particularly applies to rudders.

Take a look around the average boatyard and you will see examples of all kinds of different rudders and steering

systems. Some rudders hang off the transom, some hang beneath the stern, others are built into the back of the keel, some look fine and elegant, others are crude and square – there really are all sorts.

One thing they all have in common is that they have three main parts that need to be checked: the rudder, or a steerable drive leg in the case of many powerboats; the system that joins the rudder to the steering; and the steering control itself.

▲ Metal spade rudder.

▲ Fibreglass spade rudder.

▲ Balanced spade rudder.

▲ Metal spade rudder.

▲ Skeg-mounted rudder.

▲ Skeg-mounted rudder.

TRANSOM-HUNG RUDDER

Traditional, aft-hung rudders with tiller steering are the simplest form of rudder. A common form is the three-point hung type with a laminated tiller attached through a hole in the top of the rudder. Fixed to the transom there are usually two or three metal eyes or gudgeons (made from bronze or stainless steel), through which metal pintles, with tangs attached to the rudder, slot into place. This forms a hinge. At the base of the rudder is a heel bearing which helps support the rudder. There are different ways for the rudder to be connected to the transom and to the keel, depending on keel type. Some tillers are attached to the head of the rudder stock by metal straps.

Transom-hung rudder checks

Check whether the pintles and gudgeons are worn and how much play there is in the rudder as a result, by moving it from side to side and up and down. The pintles and gudgeons should

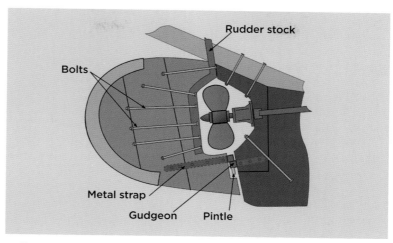
▲ The wooden rudder shown here is supported by a rudder stock. The pintle passes through the gudgeon to hold the rudder in place.

be replaced if there is excessive wear – 2–3mm is about the limit.
• Check for loose fastenings. If these are found inspect wooden rudders or transoms for signs of rot.
• Inspect stainless steel gudgeons and pintles for signs of corrosion. Be prepared to remove the rudder in order to make a full inspection.
• Check the pivot bolt for wear.

▲ Check pintles and gudgeons for wear.

▲ Pivot bolts should be checked for wear.

▲ Lower rudder bearings should be checked for wear.

▲ A badly corroded pintle needs replacement.

SKEG RUDDER

A skeg rudder is a variation of the transom-hung rudder used by boats without a full-length keel. The skeg hangs down below the hull in place of the keel, providing support and protection for the rudder. A full-skeg hangs down the full length of the rudder, while a half-skeg supports the upper part of the rudder only.

Skeg rudder checks

As with all types of rudder, if there is a distinct vibration in the tiller when sailing, this indicates bearing failure.

- Check all the pivot points for wear.
- Check the condition of the skeg, as skegs are subjected to very large stresses at sea. Check the seam is not cracked and the laminate waterlogged as a result.
- The bottom bearing of a skeg-hung rudder is usually very reliable, but if there is excessive play this will need to be replaced.

SPADE RUDDER

The spade rudder system is common on many modern designs of both sail and powerboats. This type is known as a balanced rudder, meaning that it pivots at a point well back from its forward edge (whereas transom-hung rudders are referred to as unbalanced rudders). This makes it easier to turn than a transom-hung rudder. A spade rudder is suspended beneath the hull, well astern of a fin keel.

▲ A half skeg rudder.

▲ Check the pivot points for wear.

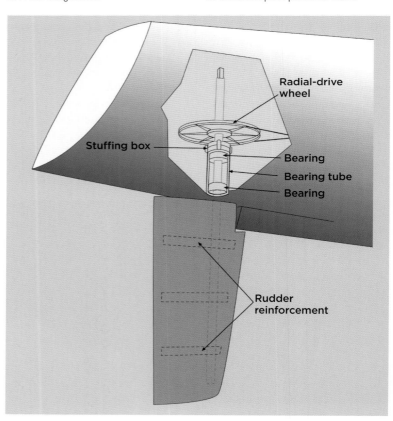

▲ A typical spade rudder.

GALVANIC CORROSION

Rudders, rudder fittings and sterndrives are at risk of galvanic corrosion. If your boat's rudder is made of metal it will most likely have a sacrificial anode bolted to it. This will need replacing when more than half of the anode has been lost to corrosion. Points worth remembering are:

- Anodes will not work if they are painted over.
- Make sure the metal is bare beneath the anode.
- For outdrives, check your engine manual to be sure how many anodes you need and where they should go.

Top left An anode in need of replacement.
Top right The results of not replacing an anode.
Bottom left A wasted ring anode urgently needs replacement.
Bottom right Failure to replace anodes has resulted in a badly corroded prop shaft.

Spade rudders have a rudder stock which reaches from the bottom of the rudder up into the hull. The stock can be hollow or solid and made from stainless steel, aluminium or composite materials. The rudder blade is built around the stock and reinforced with a frame which is welded to the stock. So when the rudder stock is turned, the frame and blade turn as one. The blade itself is usually made in two halves of fibreglass which are bonded together. The core is usually filled either with foam or plywood and occasionally is a solid laminate.

On most spade rudders, there are two bearings contained in a bearing tube. One of these bearings is at the point where the rudder stock enters the hull and another one higher up at the top of the tube which may also have a seal.

Spade rudders are subjected to considerable stresses and, some experts would say, are more vulnerable to failure than the old-fashioned transom-hung varieties. This is partly because they are hidden from sight and therefore difficult to inspect when afloat and partly because there is more that can go wrong if a spade rudder

isn't inspected regularly. The big issue is that it is very difficult to prevent water from getting into the core, causing corrosion and, eventually, rudder failure.

Spade rudder checks

- Check if water continues to drip from the rudder after the boat has been hauled out.
- Check for any rust-like stains on the rudder surface. These are an indicator of crevice corrosion.

BEARING FAILURE
- Check bearings for excessive play when ashore by moving

the bottom of the rudder blade from side to side. Up to 2mm play is acceptable.

- Check the bearing tube–hull joint for any signs of cracking.
- Check the flexible rubber bellows type of seal is in good order.
- Stiff steering can be caused by plastic bearing failure. Roller bearings can fail suddenly.

RUDDER STOCK FAILURE

- Check sea water has not penetrated the bearing tube as this will cause a stainless steel rudder stock to corrode and eventually fail.
- The rudder stock's lower bearing where it enters the bearing tube should be inspected for excessive play or signs of crevice corrosion and galvanic corrosion.
- Check the shaft seal for signs of leaking. If it is leaking it needs to be replaced.
- Check the upper part of the bearing tube is well supported and not showing any signs of movement.

FRAMEWORK FAILURE

- Check for water penetration into the rudder blade. This can cause corrosion of the metal frame, resulting in the rudder stock breaking away and failing to turn the blade.
- Check if there is any movement between the rudder and the rudder stock. If so, the rudder will need to be repaired or replaced.

DELAMINATION

- Check the rudder blade for bulges, an indicator that water has penetrated the rudder and is causing delamination.
- Check the edges of the blade for signs of cracking or splits which could allow water to penetrate the blade.

PREVENTATIVE MAINTENANCE

Preventative maintenance is especially important for rudders. However, the annual maintenance of a rudder and steering system should be approached with some caution as there are not really any hard and fast rules that apply to all. It is always best to follow manufacturers' recommendations. However, if you are unable to access this information or are unsure how best to proceed, check with your boatyard or surveyor to find out precisely what needs to be done before going into DIY mode.

Take rudder bearings, for example. Some should never be greased; others require special synthetic grease. Roller bearings and seals should be replaced on a regular basis, normally every five years, according to manufacturers' recommendations.

It is good practice to remove a rudder for a thorough inspection every four or five years and certainly before a long offshore voyage.

STEP-BY-STEP

REPLACING RUDDER BEARINGS

1. Find out in advance where you can get the replacement parts as this may take some time. If you need to arrange for parts to be machined it will be necessary to take measurements after the rudder has been removed.

2. Work out how much clearance from the hull bearing to the ground will be required for the rudder to be dropped clear of the hull.

3. Try to find out how heavy the rudder and shaft will be – rudders can be surprisingly heavy with most of the weight being in the rudder stock.

4. Discuss your plans with the boatyard and decide how much assistance you will require to remove the rudder.

5. Support the rudder blade from beneath before you start disconnecting it. To do this, rig a line from a cockpit winch down under the rudder blade on one side of the hull and back up to a winch on the other side. Most of the weight will be in the rudder stock so it is important to place and adjust the line accordingly. This is probably a two- or three-person job to avoid mishap as rudder blades can be very heavy.

6. If your boat has wheel steering, disconnect the steering mechanism and remove the quadrant.

7. With the rudder blade supported, unscrew the collet that holds the rudder in place.

8. Lower the rudder gently to the ground.

9. Remove the old bearings by sliding them off the shaft. These are often made from a very hard-wearing engineering plastic known as polyoxymethylene (POM), commonly referred to as Delrin. Note that plastic bearings on small yachts tend to be plain bush-type bearings. Yachts over 10m tend to have roller-type bearings. Take expert advice on which type you will need.

10. Take accurate measurements of the rudder stock and the shaft to be sure of the internal and external measurements required for the new bearings.

11. Slide the new lower bearing on to the rudder stock before refitting the rudder.

12. Ask the boatyard to help with lifting and refitting the rudder.

▲ A hole has been dug to enable this rudder to be dropped.

▶ The rudder back in place with new bearings.

▼ A two-part collet holding a rudder stock in place is removed.

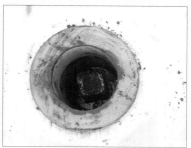

REPAIRING A RUDDER WITH A WATER-SATURATED CORE

While replacing rudder bearings is not overly challenging for the average DIY boatowner, more major repairs to rudders are not so straightforward. Here are the basic steps involved in repairing a rudder with a water-saturated core:

1. Drain out the water from the rudder by drilling a number of holes at the base of the blade.

2. Cut the seam of the rudder blade using a circular saw and separate the two halves of the rudder. If the rudder is foam filled, this can be removed. Now the damage can be fully assessed.

3. Check over the condition of the frame and stock. If the framework is badly corroded this will need to be replaced with a new one that will need to be welded to the stock.

4. Fill the void with expanding foam.

5. Rejoin the two fibreglass halves of the blade using thickened epoxy for maximum strength and laminate together.

▲ A foam-filled rudder suffering from water ingress has been cut open for repair.

▲ The foam has been removed and the foil placed in a mould for rebuilding.

▲ The void is being filled with fibreglass rather than foam to make the rudder less prone to water ingress.

▲ The rudder after repair.

WHEEL STEERING SYSTEMS CHECKS

Wheel steering systems include cable-operated types, push-rod and hydraulic systems. Here are some of the usual checks, but for all the specific requirements for your boat, refer to the manual.

- Check cables for broken strands, which will need to be replaced if found.
- Check and adjust cable tension if necessary, being careful not to overtighten.
- Check all pivots, connections, split pins and adjusters.
- Check the condition and tightness of bearings at the end of push-rods.
- Check the fluid level in the reservoir of hydraulic systems.
- Check for leaks.
- Check all pivots for wear and all steering locking devices.

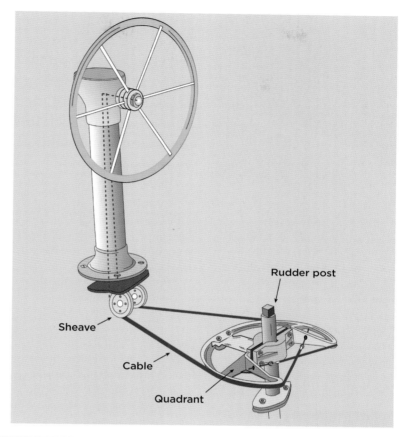

▲ A cable steering system.

◀ Wheel steering systems operated by cables should be checked for tension and tightness regularly. Chains and pinions should be greased but not the cables or pulleys. Nylon bushes need special lubricant. The whole system should be inspected annually.

The whole structure of a boat at sea is rocked and twisted as it pitches, yaws and rolls through the waves. This motion exerts considerable stresses on the hull, decks and superstructure as anyone will appreciate who has experienced the continuous slamming of a boat through rough weather at sea.

The deck and superstructure are often overlooked as structural components, but they need to be checked over on a regular basis. When inspecting their boat's deck it helps owners if they are aware of how these parts of their boat have been designed and constructed. What goes on beneath the smooth flowing lines of their pride and joy? Does the deck have a foam core, or

is it balsa or plywood? How is it supported, where has it been strengthened, how is it joined to the hull?

The deck and superstructure of a medium-sized GRP yacht commonly consists of a deck, coachroof and cockpit in one moulding. The deck, coachroof walk area and cockpit seats are usually stiffened by glassed-in members, and areas of load are backed with plywood plates. Down below, structural bulkheads are built in to provide strength and reduce flexing. The whole deck moulding is attached to the hull via a hull–deck joint (see more on page 119).

Not all boats are built to the same design standards. For example, an inshore motorcruiser is not designed to cope with ten-metre waves, while an ocean-going tug most definitely will be. This may seem obvious, but it is important to be aware of a boat's limitations and not to subject it to conditions it was not designed for.

◄ Check around the mast foot for any signs of cracking.

If you are not sure how your boat is constructed, it will help you if you can find out, so that nothing is left to guesswork. The first thing to do is try to get hold of plans, then get in touch with other owners of your class of boat, join class associations and forums, ask your surveyor and talk to your boatyard manager.

INSPECTION

A deck and superstructure inspection can be done at any time, but adding it to your to-do list of jobs to be done immediately as the boat comes ashore is a good plan. You don't want to delay carrying out the inspection and then discover there are things that need fixing the week before you have planned to relaunch the boat.

The deck of a boat is constantly exposed to the elements and should be inspected on a regular basis. Particular attention needs to be given to the overall condition of deck fittings such as the stanchions, cleats and chain plates.

▲ Check for signs of stress cracks around chain plates, the base of stanchions and leaking deck fittings.

▲ Check the bow fittings are all secure.

Here are the checks:

- Walk around the deck and test for any signs of flexing, which can indicate degradation of the core caused by rot. If the deck remains firm this is a good sign.
- Look for stress cracks around the deck fittings.
- Check for any loose fittings, which could be the cause of deck leaks.
- Check through-bolts for tightness. Note that fastenings are not always easy to inspect as they can be hidden behind cabin panelling or may be glassed in.
- Inspect all the windows, checking them for secureness, signs of leaks, stress cracks and the condition of the seals.
- Check the secureness of guardrails, stanchions and handrails. Also look out for stress cracks where they meet the deck.

- Check that the lifelines are in good condition and well secured.
- Look around the mast foot for any signs of cracking or damage.

- Check all hatches are watertight. Also check the condition of their seals, hinges and fastenings.
- Inspect for any holes left by old deck fittings or fastenings that have been removed.

Surveyor's tips: deck and superstructure

- If you do find an area of 'spongy' deck or superstructure on your vessel, it is best to address the problem sooner rather than later. If this area is relatively small and not near any major structural areas, your surveyor may suggest that simply rebedding nearby deck fittings is all that is required. In more serious cases, the area of degraded deck core may need to be removed and replaced with a marine plywood patch. If left, leaking deck fittings will cause an area of degraded deck core to spread, creating a more expensive problem to fix in the long run.
- Merely putting silicon sealant around a leaking deck fitting or window will only temporarily solve the problem. Any leaking fittings should be removed and rebedded using a marine-grade bedding compound.

TEAK DECKS

A teak deck has enormous appeal, much in the same way as a beautifully maintained lawn has. It looks good, it is nice to walk on and grips well, it is nice to lie on – who wants plastic? The only problem is that a teak deck needs regular care and attention to stay in good condition.

Modern teak decks are very different to teak decks of old, which would have consisted of teak planks laid over timber frames beneath. Today, with teak in short supply, most production boats with teak decks have thin planking only a few millimetres in depth. This is laid over a solid deck beneath, so these teak decks act more like a thick skin over the deck itself.

Timber decks today can be applied to a sub-deck of GRP, wood, aluminium or steel. Steel and aluminium decks usually need to be levelled with a polyurethane-based system before the decking is laid over the top.

When inspecting a teak deck, look out for loose caulking, splits in the timber and movement of the wooden plugs over screw heads. If there are some minor signs of these, they should be able to be repaired relatively simply. However, be aware that teak decks do not last for ever. If the problem is more extensive, then the whole deck may be worn out and need replacing.

CLEANING

Regular washing of a teak deck – preferably using salt water as it keeps rot at bay – is essential to keep it in good condition. It is important to prevent dirt from working its way into the surface as this will increase wear as well as being unsightly. The decks should be washed using a soft brush across the grain. The reason for this is that the wood fibres between the grains are soft, so hard brushing scrubs them away, wearing the deck out in the process.

Remove stains using teak cleaner that contains oxalic acid. Brush the teak cleaner on to wet teak and leave it for a while before rubbing it with an abrasive pad and then rinse thoroughly with plenty of water.

Teak care summary

Wash gently, on a regular basis. Clean the deck with a soft sponge and light detergent, if necessary scrubbing against the grain with a soft brush.

- Check the condition of the caulking on a regular basis and repair before it deteriorates.

▲ A router being used to remove a damaged deck plank.

Caution (TiP)

Oxalic acid is a bleaching agent that removes tarnish as well as rust stains. Like most powerful acids, it is toxic and needs to be used with caution. Wear gloves when using it and do not breathe the vapours.

LOOSE CAULKING

If a section of a teak deck's caulking is flaking or loose it needs to be cleaned out and replaced. This is not just for cosmetic purposes, as water could work its way into the deck and cause serious problems.

- Cut the seam caulk diagonally a few centimetres either side of the damaged section, using a craft knife. Then carefully cut along the edges of the caulk seam, using a metal straight edge as a guide.
- Dig out the old caulking, using a reefing tool if you have one

or alternatively with a sharp wood chisel the same width as the groove. Clean up the groove with acetone, removing all traces of the old caulking using a scraper, craft knife and sandpaper. Don't be tempted to use a router as this could go horribly wrong and make a mess of your deck.

- Mask the groove with tape and then apply new caulking into the groove. A polysulphide sealant is best.
- Finish off with a palette knife. Then remove the masking tape before the sealant cures.

- Resist the temptation to scrub using a hard brush with all your might; this will only wear the deck out.
- Sanding the deck is not advisable as it will shorten the life of the deck.

REPLACING WOODEN PLUGS

When teak decking gets very thin due to excessive wear, the plugs over the fastenings can lift, split or generally pop out and fail. This needs to be dealt with, as now the fastenings are open to the elements:

- Remove the screw and check whether moisture has made its way into the deck beneath. A cotton wool bud or piece of wire wrapped in cotton wool can help.
- Replace the screw, rebedding it in polysulphide sealant.
- Clean the hole with acetone

and, once it is dry, put a new teak plug into the hole, coating it with epoxy glue, wiping away any excess. Make sure the wood grain of the plug is following the line of the planking grain.

- Once the epoxy is dry, use a sharp chisel to cut along the grain of the plug at deck level. Finish by sanding with 120-grit paper.

REPLACING A TEAK DECK PLANK

If you are contemplating whether to replace some damaged teak planking, it is advisable to make a thorough check of the deck to try and fathom out why the planking has gone rotten or split. Consider whereabouts on the deck the damaged planking is. Rot can occur by water from leaks in other parts of the deck working

its way under the teak planking to the lowest point of the deck. If seams have split because the caulking has failed, these will have to be repaired before patching in new planks. Likewise, the wooden plugs covering the fastenings may be the cause. Leaks could have occurred because deck fitting seals or cable glands have failed. Be sure you have identified where the possible leaks have come from and repair these first.

The worst-case scenario is that there could be a more serious underlying problem and that water has penetrated the deck core, in which case this needs to be repaired before new teak planking can be laid – clearly a major job. If in doubt, have a surveyor or shipwright take a look before you start peeling parts of the teak decking up.

STEP-BY-STEP

The following assumes that new planking is replacing old planking covering a GRP deck. The basic principles also apply to other substrates.

1. Remove the plugs and unfasten the screws.

2. Use a sharp knife to cut through the caulking all around the damaged plank.

3. Make a note of where the screw holes are by marking the adjacent planks with chalk.

4. Removing the old plank may be a question of destroying it completely if it can't be persuaded to separate from the bedding compound, a possible scenario if polysulphide was used, but more than likely if polyurethane was used. Use a flat-bladed knife to prise up the plank, taking care not to damage the surrounding planks or the deck beneath.

5. Once the old plank is removed, scrape away all the old bedding compound. Check the condition of the core beneath and decide if you need to lift more planks before laying down replacements.

6. Clean out the old screw holes prior to filling each hole with epoxy filler. This can entail enlarging the holes by using a bigger drill bit, before injecting the epoxy into the holes.

7. Prepare the new plank to the same dimensions as the old one. Dry fit the new plank in place.

Drill new holes through the plank and deck for the screw fastenings. Also counterbore holes for the new plugs.

8. Clean the deck and underside of the plank, lightly abrading the contact area with a sanding pad. Wipe clean with acetone prior to applying primer to the underside of the teak.

9. Apply polysulphide adhesive to the deck using a comb trowel. Sikaflex 298 is suitable, which is a one-component adhesive designed for the purpose. It is essential that no air pockets are left between the planking and the substrate so the planking needs to be held in place by weights.

10. Screw down the plank and leave it to cure.

11. Install the plugs with epoxy and trim them when dry.

12. Caulk the seams using a caulking compound such as

Sikaflex 290 DC PRO. Note the planks need to be primed and thoroughly cleaned before applying the caulking with a handgun applicator. Sika primer acts as a link between substrates and adhesives and is formulated for the treatment of bond faces prior to application of the caulking compound. Apply a thin coat of the primer using a brush, cloth or foam applicator, ideally at temperatures between 15°C to 25°C. Manufacturers advise that high-quality industrial dispensing applicator guns are used for applying caulking in order to achieve full control and the best finish. While Sikaflex 290 DC PRO can be handled between 5°C and 35°C, they advise the optimum temperature is again in the 15°C to 25°C range. Finish the caulking off with a flexible metal spatula.

13. Sand in two steps, first with 80-grit and finishing off with 120-grit paper.

WINCHES

SERVICING

It is not essential to service the winches when a boat is ashore, but if time allows I prefer to do this maintenance job when the boat is on dry land, mainly because the retaining clips, pawls and pawl springs can easily go flying overboard as a winch is dismantled, especially if the boat is rocking about. Manufacturers recommend that winches are serviced at least twice during the sailing season so getting this done before the boat goes back in the water is a good plan.

Particular attention needs to be given to the condition of the pawls and pawl springs, which may need replacing.

Most manufacturers provide downloadable service manuals and give detailed instructions for your specific winch models. Here is a reminder of how to go about things:

Things you will need

Small flat-bladed screwdriver, old toothbrush, cotton rag, paper towel, paraffin or white spirit, light machine oil (3-in-One oil is good), winch grease and two old plastic containers for cleaning the disassembled parts. Spare parts: springs and pawls.

Disassembly

When taking a winch apart it helps to take photos to remind you how to put it back together again later. These are in addition to the manufacturer's service manual illustrations.

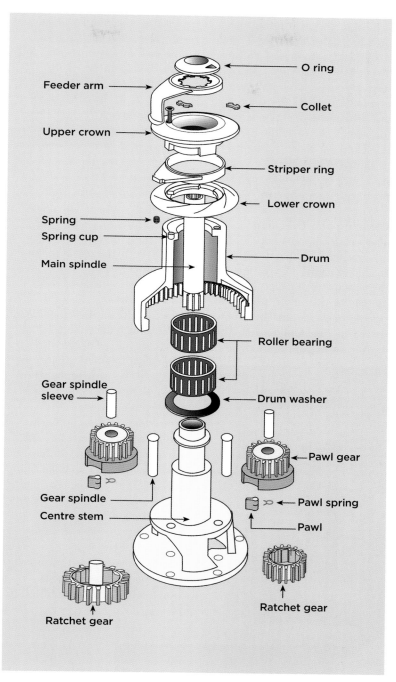

▲ A self-tailing winch. It really helps to have manufacturers' cutaway diagrams of specific winches to show how they work. This helps to avoid confusion when it comes to reassembly or when ordering new parts.

Like almost everything else on a boat, winches differ from manufacturer to manufacturer. To start the disassembly, some have a big slotted screw at the bottom of the handle socket and others have a circlip at the top, which can be fiddly to pry open and put back. Yet others, as shown in the photo opposite, have slots on the top that you can push with a screwdriver.

Cleaning and checking

The winch components should be removed one by one and soaked in paraffin using one of the containers as a bath. Remove all the old oil and dirt from each part in turn – an old toothbrush makes an ideal tool for this. Then dry the parts and put them in the

other plastic container prior to oiling and reassembly.

As you remove each part, check the condition, paying particular attention to the pawls and springs. If the pawls show signs of wear or chipping, they need replacing. If the springs show signs of corrosion or loss of tension, they should be replaced. These parts are cheap and it is wise to carry spares on the boat. Other parts will be more expensive but still need to be checked: the gears for wear or broken teeth, the inside of the drum for corrosion.

Lubrication

Lubricate the pawls with 3-in-One oil. Lubricate the ratchet tracks, gear teeth and bearings with a light smear of winch grease. Do not apply excessive amounts of grease as this can collect in the pawl pockets, preventing the pawls from working properly. The grease will attract dirt and salt, which could lead to the pawls binding and no longer working. If any of the bearings in your winches are plastic, do not grease them.

Reassembly

Before you begin the reassembly, make sure the base plate is completely clean. Any dirt left in the winch can cause wear, so it

is worth taking the time to do a thorough cleaning job.

I have to confess I am not brilliant at reassembling winches. There always seems to be something I leave out or put back upside down and invariably I have to start again. The main thing here is not to try to force the whole thing back together. If you meet resistance you are probably doing something wrong and need to start again.

When you finish the reassembly, the best moment of this sometimes fiddly and messy task is to test the winch is working nicely. Then reassure yourself it will be a joy to use when you get back on the water.

◀ Choosing the right winch for your requirements is not always easy. Manufacturers' winch selection guides are a good place to start as they help with size selection, purpose, dimensions and power ratios.

STEP-BY-STEP

1. Unscrew and remove the top cap, lift off the feeder arm and remove the two retaining collets.

2. Lift off the drum.

3. Remove and clean the drum bearings and washer.

4. Remove and clean the gear spindle and gear.

5. To remove the main spindle, rotate it in a clockwise direction as you lift it. Also remove the ratchet gear.

6. Lightly grease the ratchet gear, place it in position with the ratchet facing up.

7. Reassemble in reverse order. Remember to lightly grease all gears, ratchet tracks, spindles and bearings.

8. Remove the three fixing screws holding the crown assembly to the drum.

9. Carefully lift off the crowns and lift out the springs.

10. Remove, clean and inspect pawls and pawl springs. Look for excess wear; replace as necessary. Lubricate pawls with a light machine oil. Reassemble.

11. To fit the drum, you will need to use a small-bladed screwdriver to close the pawls.

LEAKING DECKS

Leaking decks are perceived as a nuisance by some boatowners, who are often prepared to put up with them and turn a blind eye: 'That's boats for you!' The reason for this might simply be because many boats are only used when the weather is fine. If rain isn't falling and water is not washing over the decks then a leaking deck can easily be forgotten about when the sun is shining, even if there are telltale signs of water ingress below in the cabin and bilges.

The problem here is that if the leaks are ignored a much more serious situation may well be developing, especially in the case of boats with balsa or plywood deck cores. Rot is likely to be occurring. Rot can't be ignored on a boat, even on a fibreglass boat, as wood is used to strengthen the structure both of the hull and deck. So deck leaks do need to be investigated and dealt with.

SOURCES OF LEAKS

It can be quite a challenge to find the source of a leak. It helps if two people are involved in the search, with someone up on deck with a bucket of water or a hose and another down below looking out for the drips. Common sources of leaks include:

Deck glands

The fittings where wires and cables pass through the deck can fail because the rubber gaskets wear out. Or sometimes the glands are not the right size for

▲ Every deck fitting is a potential cause for a leak.

the wires passing through them. These can be fixed easily by replacing the rubber gaskets or by using a good-quality silicone sealant such as Sikaflex 291i, which is ideal for bedding deck hardware.

Deck fittings

The average boat has a considerable number of deck fittings serving a variety of purposes. Each one of these could be the potential source of a leak. Removing them all and rebedding them would be a major task, ideally done when the boat undergoes a major refit.

It is best to start with the most likely culprits, those that are subject to heavy loads. These include mooring cleats, stanchion bases, genoa tracks, winch bases, toerails as well as pushpit and pulpit bases. The fact is that a lot of deck fittings are subjected

to heavy loads and all have to endure a marine environment. See **Rebedding deck fittings** on page 120.

Windows

Leaking windows are easy enough to detect, but if in doubt the bucket of water test or hosing the window from outside will confirm if there is a problem. Window seals fail when the gasket or sealant hardens with age and no longer provides a flexible seal. The temptation is to try a quick fix by simply running some new sealant around the edge of the window – but this is not the answer.

Repairing a leaking window can be a time-consuming job if it is done properly. The window needs to be removed completely in order to replace the seals. See **Replacing window seals** on page 122.

Chain plates

It is wise to do an annual check of the chain plates. Chain plates fail for the same reasons standing rigging fails: corrosion and metal fatigue. On many boats access to the bolts that secure the plates to the bulkheads or knees is difficult as they are buried out of sight behind bulkheads, or glassed in completely.

If a bulkhead shows signs of damp, a leaking chain plate could be the cause. A full inspection needs to be done, not only of the chain plate fixing itself, but also checking for rot in the deck core and where the plate is attached. If you suspect this may be the case, access is essential as the fitting will need to be cleaned up and resealed with a flexible non-setting sealant and possibly new bolts will be needed, depending on their condition.

Stemhead chain plates, which secure the forestay, can also be difficult to access. Some are located in anchor lockers where they come into contact with salt water, which is not good.

Hull-deck joint

Most GRP boats are constructed with separate hulls and decks. These can be joined together in a number of ways: Some have an inboard flange on the top edge of the hull on to which the deck is bolted, others have an outboard facing flange on the hull and deck and a third type has a joint where the deck fits over the hull, like the lid of a shoebox. All joint

types are coated with sealant, bolted together and rubber or wooden strips are added to finish them off.

These joints can fail after impact damage or when a boat has been subjected to the considerable stresses incurred when pounding through rough seas, causing the hull and deck to twist, distort and ultimately separate. See **Repairing a leaking hull–deck joint** on page 124.

FILLING OLD SCREW HOLES

When deck fittings are removed or upgraded the old screw holes need to be filled to ensure no water can find its way into the foam or wooden core beneath. The best way to do this is to clean the old hole up with

▲ Deck leaks can cause wooden cores to rot. If so, this needs repairing before the fitting is replaced.

acetone, or if necessary first enlarge it with a slightly bigger diameter drill bit and then clean and dry it. Next fill the hole with epoxy resin mixed with glass bubbles which results in a strong, lightweight filler that can be sanded and then painted.

▲ Removing a deck fitting.

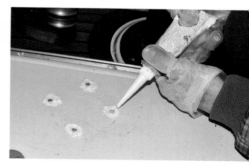
▲ Putting sealant around the screw holes.

▲ Tighten the fastenings until sealant appears, allow to cure then fully tighten.

REBEDDING DECK FITTINGS

Stanchions, pulpits, pushpits, cleats – the list goes on. Over time and with continued exposure to the marine environment, all deck seals will eventually start to break down, which can allow water to seep into the hull and begin to cause problems. On older boats there comes a time when it is wise to rebed the fittings in order to stop any leaks from developing and to protect the core.

There is no easy fix here; simply smearing extra sealant around the fitting is not the solution. The worst part of the task, at least in my experience, is trying to remove the old screws and bolts without damaging the fitting or the deck. You usually have to say goodbye to the screws and bolts, but you should not need to replace the fittings themselves as they usually clean up pretty well.

Another challenge is getting access to the nuts on the underside, which can entail the removal of cabin ceiling liners. Worse still is when you discover they are glassed in, which is especially maddening when you find yourself wedged into a forepeak and have to grind away at a lump of glass fibre in order to get to the underside of a stanchion base fastening.

How to undo seized fixings and fastenings

Before you damage the screw head or bolt slot of a fixing that refuses to budge, tell yourself that patience will be rewarded. Be wary of power drivers – in my experience these can easily strip

screw heads of seized or corroded fastenings. Here are some tips:

Penetrating fluid: Start by applying good-quality penetrating fluid and leave it for at least 15 minutes and longer if necessary. Do not expect this to work instantly. Covering the fastening with clingfilm will prevent evaporation of the fluid.

White vinegar: This is good for freeing things up, especially

if a fitting has been exposed to salt water. Vinegar is especially effective at freeing up seized aluminium fittings where corrosion may have set in. Allow white vinegar plenty of time to work.

Tapping the screw head with a hammer: The vibration this causes can free up a corroded fastening. The best way to do this is to place a tightly fitting screwdriver (or box spanner over a bolt), hold it tight, turning it in the right direction and then tap the back of the screwdriver.

Impact driver: These are specifically designed to undo screws that are stuck fast. They take a bit of practice to use, but they are effective. It is important to use the right-sized bits for it to work properly. Then it is a matter of holding the handle of the driver firmly with a little turning pressure applied and tapping the end with a hammer. Little by little the screw should begin to move.

Locking pliers: Pliers, vice grips, mole grips and long-nose locking pliers can sometimes be more effective than a screwdriver, provided you can get a good grip on the screw head.

Friction enhancer: This is a type of fluid mixed with metallic particles that help tools get a better grip on a seized fastening. Alternatives include using steel wool or rubber bands placed over the screw head to help the screwdriver grip more effectively. Try this in combination with pliers to get more torque.

Heating and cooling: For obvious reasons go carefully here. There are products that can freeze a bolt, causing it to contract, which is probably a better option than setting fire to your boat. If it is safe to do so, heating a nut is best rather than the bolt itself, using a propane torch.

Drilling: The last resort is to drill out the old fixing. This entails filing the fastener flat if possible and then drilling a pilot hole before resorting to a larger drill bit. It is best to use a left-hand twist drill bit as this will turn in the direction that fastenings are removed. If this does not work completely there are specialist extractor tools available which may be worth looking into.

Removing fittings sealed with polyurethane

There can be one last hurdle. If the fitting was originally bedded with polyurethane the fitting may well be stuck fast, even if you have managed to extricate the fastenings. There is a risk that your soul could be almost destroyed at this point, but remind yourself that perseverance wins through in the end.

There may be a way to cut through the polyurethane bond, if the sealant is thick enough and you can reach around the fitting. A cheese wire type wire saw can work, allowing you to saw through the seal. Maybe.

Another option is to try separating the fixing by driving a chisel under one edge and then leaving it for a few hours. This can stretch the old sealant little by little and is known to work.

There are chemical products that can work, including DeBond Marine Formula. This is expensive, but by now you won't mind. Heat can work, but you don't want to risk melting the deck or setting fire to it.

RESEALING

The next stage is to apply new sealant and rebed the fitting. It is probably best to avoid using polyurethane sealant as this will create a permanent bond that will be almost impossible to remove in the future. For more information about which type of sealant to choose, see **Sealants, adhesives and sealant adhesives** on page 50.

- With the fastenings and fittings removed, remove any old sealant or bedding material, clean up the area with acetone and then dry it thoroughly.
- Mask the area around the fitting to prevent any excess sealant from making a mess of the deck. Mask right up to the edge of the fitting, tracing around it if necessary before applying the sealant.
- Apply the sealant evenly to both surfaces of the fitting. I use an old artist's palette knife to do this, which is very effective. The main thing to watch out for here is to keep the sealant even and smooth and avoid getting into a mess.
- Place the fitting carefully into position. Add a little sealant to the underside of the mounting bolts or screws.
- Assemble the fastenings until they are finger tight, enough for the sealant to begin bulging slightly around the fitting.
- Wait until the sealant is cured before tightening the fastenings to ensure a good fit.
- Trim any excess sealant that has bled out around the fitting, using a thin, sharp blade.

REPLACING WINDOW SEALS

Window leaks usually develop because the window seals fail. The main causes for this is are the deterioration of the seal due to ultraviolet radiation, weathering and flexing of the deck and superstructure. Quick fixes such as spreading silicone around the window edges may sound tempting, but they will only work for a short while – and look messy. To do a proper job requires resealing the glass (or Perspex) and rebedding the window fitting entirely.

Portlights vary in design, but the following principles for an aluminium-framed portlight apply to most types.

STEP-BY-STEP

Things you will need
Silicone adhesive sealant, rubber gasket, acetone, masking tape, screwdrivers, flat blade and locking pliers.

Dismantling the portlight
1. Peel away the inner rubber seal, if there is one. The window pane is usually held in place by inner and outer frames, which are either bolted or screwed together, normally from the inside. Some have a gasket between the frame and the glass, which will need to be replaced if it shows any sign of deterioration.

2. Take care when removing the fastenings as these will need to be reused – ordering replacements can prove tricky and time-consuming. It is best to use a regular screwdriver as power tools can easily strip the heads. If some of the fastenings are hard to remove, leave them and remove those that will undo first. See **How to undo seized fixings and fastenings** on page 120.

3. With the fastenings removed, lift off the inside frame. This will most likely need a good clean.

4. Remove the outside frame. Start by pushing gently on the pane from the inside and see if the frame moves, mindful that it will also be sealed from the outside. Then on the outside, use a flat blade between the frame and the hull to prise the window free from the seal.

5. With the inner and outer frames and pane removed, thoroughly clean around the opening, removing all the old sealant – acetone normally works well. Use a scraper if needed, taking care not to scratch the hull or superstructure.

6. Check the condition of the edges around the opening.

If there are any signs of rot in the exposed core, this needs to be scraped out to a depth beyond the bolt holes. Make sure this is cleaned out as well as possible and left to dry. The resulting cavity can then be filled with epoxy and left to harden.

7. Undo the frame and remove the glass. The frame is normally made in two halves held together by a fixing plate. This needs to be unscrewed. The frame can then be gently prised apart and the window pane removed, peeling away the old rubber gasket. Keep the old rubber gasket as a template for ordering a new one.

8. Thoroughly clean the frame and window pane, ensuring any residue left by the old seal is removed. Check if the old gasket was bedded in by silicone, as this is often the case with aluminium windows.

Reassembly

1. Replace the rubber gasket window seal. Your boat manufacturer might be able to supply suitable spare gasket material. It is often best to contact a window seal specialist, providing them with the measurements you require and, if necessary, sending them a short section of the old gasket to be sure.

2. Fit the new rubber gasket into the frame, pushing it well into the corners to check the length required. Cut the rubber approximately 25mm overlength to make a really tight butt joint. Ensure the butt joint is at the top.

3. Remove the gasket and apply a bead of silicone into the window pane seal and fit the window to the gasket.

4. Apply silicone sealant into the channel of the frame and fit the window pane and gasket to the frame, pushing it gently into place, making sure it beds in completely.

5. Reassemble the frame around the pane. If some of the sealant oozes out, clean this off before it cures.

6. Dry fit the reassembled portlight from the outside. Then apply masking tape all around the edge of the portlight to the hull.

7. Remove the portlight once again, wiping around the edge of the opening with acetone.

8. Apply silicone adhesive or suitable caulking all around the opening as recommended by the manufacturer.

9. Fit the portlight in position and hold it in place with tape. Better still, have someone outside hold it in place for you.

10. From the inside, refasten the inner frame to the portlight, tightening the screws little by little to ensure they will all fit properly. Take care the portlight does not shift around as you tighten all the screws. Allow the silicone to cure before fully tightening the screws.

11. Clean up the outside, running a scalpel or razor blade around the edge of the frame and then remove all the tape.

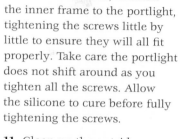
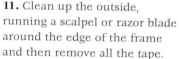
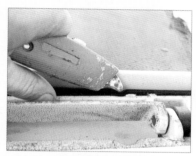

REPAIRING A LEAKING HULL-DECK JOINT

If you suspect a hull-deck joint has failed, then being absolutely sure where the actual leak is occurring is of prime importance. Areas to check are near the deck fittings, where the decks may be put under considerable stress by the rigging and the continued flexing of the hull. Another area to check is where mooring cleats have been subjected to excessive strain or when a boat has been left tied alongside with insufficient fenders in place.

Hull-deck joints are designed not to come apart, so they are permanently bonded, often covered up and some are even glassed in. This can make repairing them very challenging.

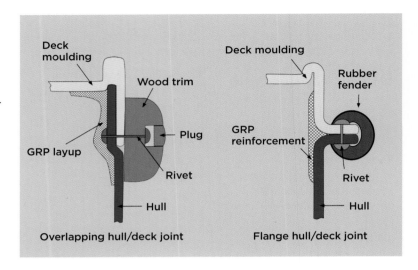

Overlapping hull/deck joint

Flange hull/deck joint

1. Getting access

Hull-deck joints are usually fastened with bolts from above and nuts below. Others are fastened by screws and others by rivets. Getting access to the underside of the fastenings usually entails stripping away the headlinings or panels. So the first thing to do is check what type of fastenings you have on your boat and then work out how you are going to get access to them and remove them.

2. Loosen the rigging

Before you begin to unfasten things, it is a good idea to slacken off the rigging to ease the tension acting along the length of the joint.

3. Removing the rail

Back on the outside, it is common for the joint to be protected by a rubber fender or toerail, which may be constructed either from aluminium or wood. The rail invariably needs to be removed first. Metal rails might be bolted, screwed or riveted. Wooden rails will be bolted or screwed.

4. Inspection

With the rail removed, closely examine the joint and get a better idea of where the problem lies. It might be that there are only a few places where leaks are occurring, meaning that a localised repair is all that is required. A thorough inspection at this stage will help you decide.

5. Unfasten the joint

Remove the fasteners holding the joint in place around where the problem lies. The reason for this is that you need to open up the joint in order to apply

new sealant for the repair. Alternatively you may choose to rebond the entire length.

6. Remove the old bedding compound

Before new sealant can be added, all the old bedding compound must be removed, using a reefing iron or similar to scrape out the old material. Use wedges to separate out the joint flanges enough to get access for the repair.

7. Fill the joint with new sealant

With the old joint cleaned out as well as possible, fill the joint with polyurethane sealant, ensuring there is sufficient to reach well into the joint beyond the fastening holes. Once the sealant has been applied, remove any wedges and, where possible, clamp the joint to ensure there will be a good seal along its length.

8. Refasten the flange

Refasten the flange with through-bolt fittings if possible, but if not, use self-tapping stainless steel screws. Apply extra sealant beneath the heads of the bolts or screws, but leave the nuts beneath clear of sealant to make it easier for the joint to be undone in the future. Clean up any excess sealant before it cures.

9. Refasten the rail

Refasten the rail, bedding it with polyurethane sealant and bolts or screws. Reattach the fender strip if there is one.

▶ *Top left* Removing the old fastenings.
Top right Cleaning out the joint.
Bottom left Applying sealant.
Bottom right Clamping the joint.

STRESS CRACKS

It is quite common to find cracks in the gelcoat when inspecting the deck and superstructure of a GRP boat. A trained eye will be able to inspect these and know whether they are purely cosmetic or of structural concern.

It is important to differentiate between a crack and a scratch. Scratches in a gelcoat may be unsightly, but these are surface blemishes only. Cracks, on the other hand, go right through the gelcoat and are an indicator that there has been some level of structural failure beneath. How do you tell the difference if the answer is not obvious? See the table, right.

Difference between cracks and scratches

Cracks	Scratches
Always narrow	Variable width
Go through the gelcoat	Shallow, do not penetrate the gelcoat
Bottom of crack can't be seen	Bottom of the scratch can be seen
Sharp edges	Ragged edges
Can run in parallel lines	Hardly ever run in parallel lines
Can form starburst patterns	Never form starburst patterns
Can branch and spread out	Do not branch or spread out
Do not crisscross	Can crisscross
Seldom single	Can be single

▲ Linear cracking caused by bending or flexing.

▲ Linear cracking around a cockpit locker.

▲ Mast deck mount crack.

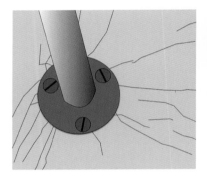

▲ Star cracking at stanchion base.

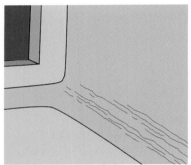

▲ Linear cracking along cockpit moulding.

Causes

The main causes of gelcoat crazing are stress and movement. Gelcoat is hard and brittle while by comparison the glass fibre laminate beneath is softer and more flexible. So if the laminate bends or moves, the gelcoat won't bend with it and cracks as it is brittle.

There are two main types of stress crack: linear cracks and star cracks. Linear cracks tend to run in parallel lines and star cracks spread out in a starburst-type pattern. The patterns of cracks are a clue to what caused them:

- **Star cracks:** Star cracks are caused by external impact, with the central area of the crack being the point of impact and concentric circles spreading outwards, like a spider's web. They are also caused by flexing around a point, for example around a stanchion base that has been leant on or pulled heavily by crew members getting aboard.

- **Linear cracks:** Linear cracks indicate damage caused by bending or flexing. These occur, for example, along deck edges, where the deck meets the cabin sides, where the moulding curves upwards away from the cockpit area to the deck or around the edges of cockpit lockers.

Repairs

The underlying cause of stress cracks needs to be identified before a repair is carried out, because if there is a structural problem beneath the deck this will need to be repaired first. This may be a question of fitting backing plates or stiffening an area with additional glass fibre laminates. Check the integrity of the laminate beneath the affected area and see if it is watertight.

Taking advice on how best to proceed at this stage would be wise, as it will depend on your specific circumstances.

Thankfully, most deck stress cracks can be repaired fairly easily, providing the underlying laminate is intact. Here are the steps involved:

Step 1

Remove any deck hardware necessary to gain access to the whole length of the crack (or cracks).

Step 2

Grind out the cracks using a small, high-speed rotary tool. An alternative is to use the corner of a good-quality scraper to open the cracks up, chamfering both edges in the process.

Step 3

Clean the cracks and repair the area with acetone.

Step 4

Mask the repair area off prior to filling. This will prevent the surrounding gelcoat and fittings from being damaged when sanding the repair.

Step 5

Decide whether you need to tint the filler to match your gelcoat, using gelcoat pigments. This will require some practice to get a good result (see **How to colour match gelcoat** on page 63).

Step 6

Fill the exposed cracks with gelcoat filler using a plastic spreader, making sure the cracks are completely filled.

Step 7

Leave the filler to harden off. When fully cured, sand the filler with 240-grit wet and dry paper, used wet.

Step 8

Check the filler repair is flush and refill if necessary. Then rub back and smooth off with a finer 600-grit wet and dry paper.

Step 9

When the gelcoat surface is flush, remove the masking tape and apply rubbing compound to give a gloss finish to the repair, which can then be polished with a wax polish.

◀ Many parts of the deck are subjected to heavy loads, including the bow area. Any voids in the lay-up can cause the gelcoat to crack.

VOIDS

When fibreglass decks are being laid up, pockets of air can get trapped in sharp bends and corners of the moulding, also known as radiuses. This happens because the lay-up mat or cloth does not completely fill these corners. The gelcoat beneath will have done so, being a lot more fluid during the construction stage and the result is a weak spot with a void beneath. When pressure is applied from above, the gelcoat will crack like an eggshell, exposing the void beneath.

Repairing a small void is a similar process to repairing a stress crack, but a larger void will require filling the cavity

with polyester resin, followed by gelcoat filler. Here are the steps involved:

1. Chip out the void, removing all the cracked gelcoat. This can be done with a rotary tool, angled scraper or similar. Chamfer the edges of the gelcoat around the void.

2. Clean the area and exposed void with acetone.

3. If the void is large, fill it with polyester resin mixed with chopped strand mat (CSM). This will bond well to the laminate beneath. Leave enough depth for the gelcoat filler to be applied at the surface.

4. When the polyester resin has hardened, fill with the gelcoat filler.

5. When the gelcoat filler has hardened, sand the filler with 240-grit wet and dry paper, used wet. Check the filler repair is flush and refill if necessary. Rub back and smooth off with finer 600-grit wet and dry paper.

6. When the gelcoat surface is flush, apply rubbing compound to give a gloss finish to the repair, which can then be polished with a wax polish.

The rig of a sailing boat is put under huge stresses and strains so it is important for inspections of a yacht's spars and rigging to be carried out at regular intervals.

All the elements of a sailing rig – the mast, spreaders, boom, kicker, stays and the fittings that hold everything together – are subjected to considerable forces when at sea.

Less obvious perhaps is that the process of cyclic loading, the cause of metal fatigue, continues unabated even when a boat is rocking gently on a sheltered mooring. The rig components continue to push and pull against each other, day in and day out. Added to all the stresses and strains imposed on the rig components are their susceptibility to different kinds of corrosion, caused in the case of aluminium masts both by exposure to the marine environment and by galvanic corrosion. Galvanic corrosion occurs when stainless steel or bronze fittings are fitted to aluminium masts and not adequately insulated from each other, which causes the aluminium to corrode. While wooden masts do not suffer from galvanic corrosion, they are susceptible to rot and delamination.

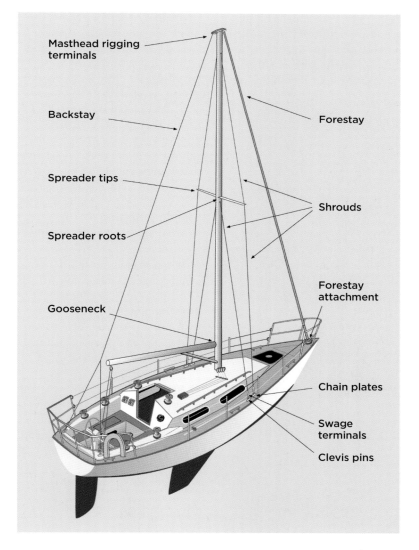

- Masthead rigging terminals
- Backstay
- Forestay
- Spreader tips
- Shrouds
- Spreader roots
- Gooseneck
- Forestay attachment
- Chain plates
- Swage terminals
- Clevis pins

RIG CARE

As with many other kinds of boat care, regular checks, preventative maintenance and the correct set-up of mast and rigging are key to ensuring longevity and preventing failure. With sailing boat rigs in particular, the integrity of all their parts is vital. The mast and rigging are a lightweight structure designed to be rigid and strong, a bit like a house of cards – if one of the components fails the whole house comes tumbling down. Even if one part becomes loose this can increase loads on other parts, causing them to fail.

While doing regular checks of your rig throughout the sailing season is good practice, so too is a more detailed inspection when the boat comes ashore and the mast can be taken down. Even if the rig remains unstepped ashore, it still needs to be checked by a trained eye.

UNDERSTANDING YOUR RIG

There are many kinds of mast and rig configurations for sailing boats and it is important for boatowners to fully understand the rig set-up of their particular boat. This understanding will help them know what to look out for when doing their regular checks. Here are a few questions that owners should be able to answer:

Standing rigging

*   What are the main causes of rig failure?
*   When was the mast last unstepped? Once every two or three years is generally recommended.
*   When was the standing rigging last inspected? Annual inspections are usually recommended.
*   When was the standing rigging last replaced? Once every ten years or so is usually recommended for wire rigging and about fifteen years for rod rigging.
*   Where are the main stress points on your rig?
*   How do you check the rig alignment?

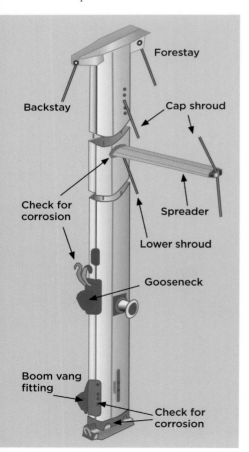

▲ Galvanic corrosion will occur if aluminium is in contact with stainless steel, as seen here.

Running rigging

*   When was the running rigging last inspected?
*   When should it be replaced?
*   What maintenance needs to be done?

CAUSES OF RIG FAILURE

While many sailors live in fear of rogue waves and capsizing, most dismastings happen either because of equipment failure or operator error. Leaving aside operator error, the main reasons include the failure of chain plates, spreaders, turnbuckles and tangs caused by either metal fatigue, corrosion or a combination of the two.

Chain plate failure is one of the most common causes of dismasting. Chain plates are not easy to inspect as they are hidden from view beneath the deck. Corrosion happens out of sight where the metal cannot be

Forestay

Backstay

Cap shroud

Check for corrosion

Spreader

Lower shroud

Gooseneck

Boom vang fitting

Check for corrosion

inspected without the plates first being removed.

Other causes are the failure of terminal fittings, clevis pins, cotter pins and all the parts that hold a rig together.

Surprisingly perhaps, the mast and stays are rarely the components that break first and cause a dismasting.

STRESSES AND LOADS

The components of a rig are designed to withstand certain stress levels and loads caused by a boat under sail in varying conditions. The correct adjustment of the rig is important to maintain the rig's strength and longevity for a number of reasons – not just the boat's performance and ability to point to windward:

- If the rigging is slack problems can develop as it moves about, causing fatigue.
- Rig components can become weakened by vibrations (caused, for example, by sails flogging in strong winds) or by shock loading (caused, for example, by accidental gybes).
- The misalignment of part of a rig can cause other parts to be overloaded, resulting in metal fatigue and eventual failure.
- Stress, coupled with corrosion, will accelerate the potential for rig failure.

CREVICE CORROSION

Some surface rust on stainless steel rigging is normal and usually polishes off very easily. While stainless steel does not rust in the way that regular steel does, it does suffer from crevice corrosion.

▲ Regular checks will help identify potential rig failure.

Crevice corrosion occurs because the stainless steel has been deprived of oxygen. As a result its protective oxide film breaks down, allowing chlorides to infiltrate and corrode the metal. This happens around joints and under fastener heads and where pieces of metal are in close contact. Chain plates often suffer from this type of corrosion where they pass through the deck and sea water has saturated the deck core.

Crevice corrosion also takes place where cyclic loading has caused stainless steel to develop hairline cracks on the metal's surface. Sea water then gets into the cracks and the corrosion slowly takes hold.

GALVANIC CORROSION

Aluminium masts with stainless steel fittings are at risk from galvanic corrosion. Galvanic corrosion is the transfer of electrons from one metal (the anode) to another (the cathode).

In this case, the anode is the aluminium and the cathode is the stainless steel. Positively charged electrons flow from the anode to the negatively charged cathode. Galvanic corrosion also requires an electrolyte, a liquid that enables the electron flow to take place. In this case, salt water is the electrolyte and a very efficient one.

All stainless steel fittings should be insulated from aluminium masts by washers or sealant.

▲ Corrosion on a mast base caused by water running down the halyards inside the mast.

▲ Galvanic corrosion clearly seen eating into the aluminium.

OWNER RIG CHECK

Some owners inspect their rigs before every cruise, others two or three times a year – to a certain extent it depends on how much sailing the boat has done. Rig tensions should also be checked and adjusted as necessary. The mast manufacturer will recommend what they think is best, as will your local rigger.

RIG GEOMETRY

It is best to check over the whole rig with the mast stepped. Look around the rig from all angles to check the geometry is correct. This means standing back and checking the mast is straight, with no bends visible. The shrouds and stays should also be well balanced and feel roughly at the same tension. Check they are correctly aligned from the top swage to the chain plate at deck level to ensure that the loads on the rig are even.

Once you are satisfied with the overall geometry, you need to take a closer look at all the rig components. The easiest way to do this is with the mast down as you can detach the stays and shrouds for a thorough inspection. A magnifying glass is useful for this, to check for hairline cracks and pitting.

▲ I normally take the mast down every other year for a thorough check.

CHAIN PLATES

• Check for excessive wear on spacers or bushes, signs of elongation in pin holes, alignment with bottlescrews, stay angles and evidence of fracture at deck level.

▲ Adjusting rig tension obviously has to be done with the rig up.

▲ Look out for seized, overloaded or distorted blocks. They all need checking.

▲ Chain plates need very careful checking.

▲ For total peace of mind call in a professional rigger to ensure everything is OK.

- Check the condition of the chain plate fastenings to the hull below decks. Check for signs of leaking and crevice corrosion. The tiny cracks tend to occur horizontally due to a combination of stress and corrosion.
- Be aware that chain plates can fail because the structure that supports them rots due to water ingress in the deck core.

DECK CHECK

- Check split pins, adequacy of threaded fittings, chafe or breakage of stranded wires, rig cracking, rust streaking, condition of mast collar sheaves.
- Check the mast foot of aluminium deck-stepped masts for signs of corrosion, cracks or movement. Also check halyard alignment and halyard chafe guards.

- Check the mast foot of aluminium keel-stepped masts for signs of corrosion caused by sea water in the bilges.
- Check for water and rot in wooden mast foots.
- Check the condition of running rigging lead blocks and their attachments.
- Check all rope clamps are operating correctly and their mounting points are secure.

MAST STAY WIRES AND MAST FITTINGS

- Check all the shrouds and stays for fraying, making sure there are no broken strands of wire, visible signs of cracking along swage sections or signs of rust streaking.
- Check T-bar plates have retaining plugs or locking tabs. Look for corrosion around mast tangs.

- Check fastenings are secure, that threaded fittings are sound and rigging screws are locked with split pins or seizing wire.
- Check wire terminals, toggles, extension links, rigging screws, shackles, clevis pins and split pins for wear, distortion or cracks.

MAST AND BOOM – ANODISED

- Check all fittings and holes for cracks, fastening wear, deformation and corrosion.
- Check all welded fixtures for cracks around the welds.
- Check keel-stepped masts for cracks and dents at deck level.
- Check genoa halyard leads (if fitted) for wear and replace if necessary.
- Check all moving parts are moving freely – sheaves, locking arms, etc.

▲ The gooseneck pin should be checked for wear.

- Check for signs of corrosion, that split pins are protected to safeguard sails and all fastenings are securely riveted.

- Check the gooseneck pin has washers to protect it from vertical movement.

MAST AND BOOM – PAINTED

- Carry out the same checks as for an anodised mast and boom on the previous page.
- Check for any damage to painted sections.

MAST AND BOOM – WOODEN

- Check varnish or paint finishes for signs of peeling, cracking and blistering.
- Check for areas of chafe.
- Check for signs of water ingress and rot damage around fasteners. Fasteners that are put under a lot of stress can crush the wood beneath, allowing water to penetrate and rot to start.

SPREADERS

- Check for broken wire strands in the area where the spreader end is connected to the shroud.
- Check the spreader roots for any signs of cracks, movement or mast corrosion.
- Check for signs of cracking, that fastenings are secure and that there are no signs of rust streaking, chafe or corrosion. Look out for covered spreader tips as they can trap water, which leads to corrosion. Avoid putting too much tape around spreader tips as this tends to trap moisture.
- Check the condition of rubber pads if your spreaders have them.
- Check the spreaders are angled correctly, slightly

▲ A professional rig report with recorded observations should be done every five years or so.

upwards, never downwards. The reason for this is that when the shroud is under a heavy load it will pull the spreaders downwards and could pull the spreader base away from the mast completely, leading to rig failure.

- Also check that the spreaders bisect their shrouds.

MASTHEAD

- Check the halyard sheaves rotate freely and are not worn, and check the condition of the bushes and split pins.
- Check that the halyard shackles are in good condition.
- Check the electrical wires are clamped correctly and are chafe free and that the lights are operating.
- Check the VHF aerial wire is securely fastened and in good condition.
- Check the windex and wind gear are operating correctly.
- Check the forestay and backstay mounting holes for signs of wear or elongation.

FORESTAY

(See also: **Mast stay wires and mast fittings** on page 133).

- Check the roller-furling headstay.
- Check halyard leads are at the correct angle to the swivel car.
- Inspect halyards for wear on sheaves, fairleads and check swivel cars.
- Check for corrosion around mast tangs.
- Check the condition of threaded fittings.
- Check there are no broken strands of wire in the forestay.

BACKSTAY

(See also: **Mast stay wires and mast fittings** on page 133).

- Check the condition of the backstay adjustment system.

SPINNAKER POLE RING

- Check the attachment points are secure.
- Check for signs of corrosion around mast tangs.

INSULATORS

- Check for sunlight degradation of plastic insulators.

PROFESSIONAL RIG INSPECTION

Periodically, every five years or so, depending on usage and your mast manufacturer's recommendations, a full professional rig inspection needs to be carried out, which will involve disassembly of the rig. This will comprise a visual inspection, sometimes aided by ultrasound tools, dye penetration testing, or X-rays, which reveal surface flaws not visible to the naked eye. The full inspection will look for items such as cracks in rigging components, misalignment of stays and corrosion. A written report will record observations and any work carried out to help with future inspections.

MAINTENANCE
General

- Stainless steel rigging should not be left in contact with an aluminium mast when it is unstepped in order to avoid galvanic corrosion.
- Routine cleaning of stainless steel components should be done throughout the year.

Standing rigging

- As well as rinsing with fresh water to remove salt, with the boat in the boatyard it is a good idea to clean everything with a cloth and polish out any surface rust spots.
- Any traces of rust should be removed and the area inspected

▲ This 20-year-old mast has recently been repainted.

for hairline cracks or signs of damage to the metal. Use stainless steel cleaners only as some cleaners contain chlorine, which destroys stainless steel. Don't use wire wool as this can leave tiny particles in the rigging which will rust.

- If corrosion has gone deep and cannot be removed by polishing, the part should be replaced.
- Clean the rigging screw threads using a degreasing solvent – an old toothbrush is ideal for this. Dry the threads and then lubricate with rigging screw oil.
- If a single strand of wire has failed, the shroud or stay should be replaced with a new one. It is good practice to replace wires in pairs: for example, if one cap shroud has failed, the opposite one must be replaced as well.

- Don't wrap rigging terminals in tape as this deprives stainless steel of oxygen and causes corrosion.

Mast and boom – anodised

- Rinse the mast and boom with fresh water, then wash with liquid detergent. Rinse off thoroughly with fresh water to remove all traces of salt water and detergent, not forgetting the inside of the mast.
- Flush the sail track and slides to remove salt crystals and lubricate them with track lubricant – some people use Vaseline.
- Remove and grease the screws of the boom outboard end-fitting.
- Coat all aluminium surfaces and cast metal parts with paraffin oil or wax to seal and preserve the surfaces.

Mast and boom – painted

- Carry out the same maintenance as for an anodised mast and boom above.
- Use coatings that are suitable for use on aluminium and follow the manufacturer's instructions.
- If you drill holes into a painted mast, there is a high probability that corrosion will spread under the paint, which will cause blistering. To prevent this happening, ensure that fittings are properly bedded down on to the mast with mastic-type sealant. If there are any exposed edges, these must be protected with a suitable primer and topcoat.

Log it

Keep a maintenance log of your boat's rig. This should include details of inspections, replacement parts, wire sizes and expenditure so that at a glance you can be aware of what is likely to need doing and when and what the costs should be.

Masthead

- Clean and inspect the masthead sheaves. Check they run freely and that the bearings are in good order. Then lubricate them with a light machine oil.
- If they are badly worn replace them. Also check the retaining pins are secure.

Roller-furling

- Wash and rinse the furling system with fresh water and a mild detergent to remove dirt and salt.
- Polish the luff extrusions with silicon-free polish or wax. This prevents dirt from staining the sail.
- Clean and polish any stainless steel components.
- Halyard leads should be inspected for wear and any sharp edges should be filed smooth. Halyard leads need to be replaced when wear reaches 50 per cent.
- Lubricate roller-furling gear according to the manufacturer's recommendations. The bearing assemblies need to be

lubricated with grease. Getting access to these is normally possible via greasing holes.

- Grease the halyard swivel, which may have an upper and lower bearing.

WOODEN MASTS AND BOOMS

It is no secret that varnished wooden spars require a lot of maintenance. Even the best quality varnishes are unlikely to last two seasons given their exposure to the sun and UV, especially in hotter climates. For this reason, some wooden spars are painted on the upward-facing surfaces, particularly spreaders. In some cases, the whole mast is painted. While a painted mast may not be as attractive to look at, it can last up to five years before needing to be repainted.

As soon as varnish begins to crack and peel, moisture can penetrate the wood beneath, leaving a telltale dark stain, which, unless dealt with, can quickly cause rot.

REPAIRS

Most wooden masts and booms are hollow. Typically, they are constructed in a series of sections

Looking after wooden masts (TiP)

Little and often maintenance is the best way to look after wooden masts.

- Repair any rot damage as soon as it appears.
- Rub back old varnish and apply new coatings where necessary.

connected together by scarf joints to form the finished box-shaped spar. A scarf joint comprises two tapered pieces of wood that are glued together.

Being hollow, wooden spars are susceptible to rot from both outside and inside. The outside is visible, of course, and can be easily checked, but the inside is hidden from view and if the wood begins to rot from the inside, this can be very bad news. Consequently all hollow wooden spars need to be treated internally to protect them from rot. This means gaining access periodically and treating the insides with rot-proofing fluid.

Damaged spar

An area of damaged or rotten spar can be repaired, but it is usually a specialist job unless the repair is very minor. You need excellent woodworking skills and the know-how to make tight-fitting scarf joints, access to the best quality timber, a large workshop with good supports for the mast while it is being repaired and plenty of clamps to grip the repaired area as it glues.

▲ A major wooden mast repair in progress. Scarph joints are used to join the new wood with the old.

RUNNING RIGGING

As soon as the boat is ashore in the boatyard, one of the first things I do is remove most of the running rigging and take it home for cleaning, then dry and store it for the winter. While rinsing blocks and lines in fresh water regularly during the sailing season is a good idea, if they are left unattended dirt and salt easily gets ingrained into rope fibres and blocks, shortening their lifespan and making them unpleasant to use.

AFTER LIFT OUT

- Before removing the running rigging, take photos of everything in situ, especially which block goes where.
- Label all the major components to remind you where they go when you rig the boat again at the beginning of the season. Replace the halyards with mousing lines and store in preparation for cleaning. (I put all the ropes in an old sail bag and the blocks in a plastic box and take them home.)

HOW TO WASH ROPES

- Check all the halyard ends are properly sealed or whipped before cleaning them.
- New rope should not be washed, a light scrubbing with a brush is ample.
- Soak older ropes in warm water and a mild detergent for at least an hour. A bath or large, deep sink is best.
- Heavily soiled ropes can be cleaned in a washing machine,

▲ Take the running rigging home over the winter. Don't forget the blocks!

but care needs to be taken when doing this: rope ends need to be whipped and stitched or fused to stop them from fraying. Ropes should be coiled tightly and any spliced shackles should be covered with old socks to protect the machine and ropes.
- Put the ropes in mesh laundry bags or pillowcases, tying knots in the ends.
- Use a mild detergent or fabric softener and a gentle cycle.

- Leave rope to dry slowly and never use excessive heat as the core and sheath will shrink differently, causing the rope to be distorted and weakened.

MAINTENANCE OF BLOCKS

Blocks need the minimum of maintenance. Simply rinse in hot soapy water to remove salt and greasy deposits. If they remain stiff after cleaning, some light lubrication with WD-40 may help but shouldn't be needed.

Washing instructions

- Do not use strong laundry detergents as marine ropes have coatings that protect them from UV radiation and abrasion. Do not use bleach as this significantly reduces a rope's breaking strength.

- Tests have shown that machine washing a rope is to be avoided as splices come undone and the core of double-braided lines gets pulled out by the wash cycle action.

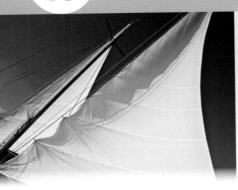

10 SAILS

At the end of the sailing season, sails should be washed and inspected carefully for damage, including small tears, stitching failure, UV damage, stains and mildew.

Many boatowners send their sails off to their sailmakers to be laundered, checked, repaired and stored for the winter. Whether it is the sailmakers who do this work or the owners themselves, they should be stored in safe conditions for the winter, out of harm's way. It is a false economy to leave sails on the boat or store them in a damp garden shed as this will more than likely shorten their life considerably.

One of the most critical things is to wash or hose down the sails to remove dirt and salt. The other is to store the sails where they are safe from moisture, extreme temperatures and pests, all of which can inflict damage to sails over prolonged periods. Before going into details of basic sail care advice and maintenance, here is a quick aide-memoire on types of sailcloth and sail construction.

Budget factor **TiP**

Remember to factor sail valeting and repairs into your budget.

MATERIALS AND CONSTRUCTION

TYPES OF SAILCLOTH

When thinking about the care, maintenance and repair of sails it helps to have some understanding of the properties of the ever-growing range of modern sailcloth and the fibres they are made from, as opposed to the traditional canvas sails of the past. Some sail fibres are tougher than others, some are very light, others are more stretchy, some are best for racing sails, others for cruising sails, some are ideal for spinnakers and some are designed to stand up to the harshest marine environment. Added to which, sailcloth varies in price quite considerably.

Being aware of what materials your sails are made from is a good idea, as some materials require more sensitive treatment than others. For example, flex resistance is critical to the longevity of a sail. If a sail can flex without being damaged it is going to last longer as the fibres that make up a sailcloth are flexed every time a sail is folded, creased or flogs in the wind.

Some sailcloth is impregnated with UV inhibitors to protect it from the sun's harmful rays, providing a sailcloth which is both tough and durable.

The main types of sailcloth are:

Polyester

The most commonly used sail fibre is strong and long-lasting, has good UV resistance, good flex ability and is comparatively inexpensive. Woven polyester is often called Dacron, the brand name given by DuPont to their Dacron yarn introduced in 1951, and known as Terylene in the UK.

Polyester fabric is used as a stand-alone woven sailcloth and as a component part of laminate sailcloths which are impregnated with resin to reduce the stretch and make them airtight. This gives better sail performance than basic Dacron but makes the sails less durable. PEN polyester is one such variation.

Nylon

Lightweight and strong, nylon is ideal for spinnakers and gennakers. It absorbs shocks well and is stretchy, which is less of a problem for downwind sails as it

▲ In my experience, sailmakers are always happy to explain the pros and cons of different types of sailcloth. It does help to do some homework before getting into discussion when ordering new sails.

is not so critical for them to hold their shape as it is for upwind sails. Note that nylon is easily damaged by exposure to chlorine, so never use bleach when cleaning nylon sails.

Aramid

Fibres include Kevlar, Twaron and Technora. These are all lightweight performance fibres used for racing sails. They are also used in some laminated cruising sails. Aramid fibres are sometimes mixed with carbon fibres, resulting in very low-stretch, high-strength sails.

Vectran

This liquid crystal polymer fibre has excellent flex life and low stretch on the plus side but offers poor UV resistance and is expensive.

Ultra PE

These fibres are processed polyethylene and include Dyneema and Spectra. They have good UV resistance, very high strength and very low stretch. Ultra PE is expensive but has a long life and is often used for upmarket cruising yacht sails.

Carbon fibre

This has very low stretch and very good UV resistance. Carbon fibres are used widely for top-end high-performance racing sails. Their weakness is that the fibres easily break if they are flexed sharply, for instance if the sail is creased when a sail is folded, making them vulnerable if they are not properly handled.

SAIL CONSTRUCTION

Sails are designed to have depth in their shape to make them work as efficiently as possible. One way a sailmaker adds shape to a sail is to add some curvature to the edges, particularly to the luff and foot but also to the leech. So when a sail with curved edges is hoisted up a straight mast the result is that the sail has depth in it, which will help its performance.

Another way the sailmaker creates depth is to add curvature to the seams of panelled sails. This has a distinct advantage over edge curvature because depth can be added exactly where it is needed to give the best performance. A combination of these two factors is desirable and knowing this can help when ordering new sails.

ULTRAVIOLET EXPOSURE

The two worst enemies of sails are salt and sunlight. All sails suffer from exposure to UV rays, although certain sailcloths are more susceptible than others. The UV rays degrade sailcloth and stitching by changing the chemical properties of the material, breaking down the chemical bonds of the fibres and rotting the stitching through the process known as ionisation. This causes the sailcloth to become weak and easily torn; eventually it breaks down completely. During the sailing season, the best protection from the sun is to remove the sails immediately after use, but this is not always practical on larger boats where several crew may be required to do this.

The importance of having UV protective strips for furling

▲ One of the worst enemies of sails is ultraviolet. It weakens the cloth and causes the stitching to rot.

headsails and boom covers for mainsails is therefore vital. If part of a mainsail is left exposed by an ill-fitting cover it will degrade quickly. Likewise, an incorrectly furled headsail can leave sections of the sail unprotected if the sail has been furled the wrong way round, which is a mistake easily made. The UV cover has to be on the outside.

It is always worth double-checking your sails are UV protected as much as possible through the sailing season to prevent them from becoming damaged, ensuring mainsail covers and UV strips are used and maintained properly. The stitching of covers and UV strips is susceptible to damage and is likely to need replacing more frequently than the sails' stitching.

WARNING SIGNS
The first signs of UV degradation of a sail is stitching failure. To check, look first for any stitching that has become unstitched, which will more than likely be caused by UV damage.

Sail care tips (TiP)

- **Flogging:** Do not allow sails to flog as this will reduce a sail's lifespan very quickly by the constant and rapid side-to-side motion. When motor-sailing avoid steering into the wind and instead allow the sails to fill, even if this means tacking. Better still, if heading into harbour, drop the sails completely and continue under engine.
- **Chafing:** Use tape or sail patches to protect the sails from sharp edges and fittings that might rub on the sails.
- **Flaking:** When flaking or folding a sail do not always follow the same crease as this will cause damage to the sail. Note that rolling rather than flaking a sail will prolong its life.

You can also test the strength of the stitching by plucking it gently with a sail needle or pointed tool. The thread should be able to be plucked without breaking, but if it is in poor condition it will be easily broken. If this happens ask your sailmaker to take a look. They may advise restitching the sail to strengthen it.

Another obvious sign of UV damage is discolouration of UV strips and any coloured materials on the sails, especially reds, oranges and yellows, which fade more quickly in the sun than blues and greens. White Dacron

sails fade to a grey colour as they become UV damaged, a sure sign of a weakened sail nearing the end of its life.

INSPECTION

- Check the sails for tears, cracks or signs of chafing, especially where they may come into contact with the spreaders, fastenings, exposed split pins, cotter pins or sharp edges around the mast. Look for wear along the foot of headsails, especially where they overlap the shrouds.
- Check that sail slides are in good condition and securely attached to the sail.
- Check the condition of the headboard, batten pockets, Cunningham and outhaul rings – look for chafed or broken stitching.
- Check seam stitching is in good condition and not degraded by UV damage. Mark any defects with vinyl tape.
- Check the battens are in good condition and remove these before winter storage.
- Check headsail UV strips are in good condition.
- Check the sail covers are in good condition.

CLEANING

Rinse your sails thoroughly with fresh water to remove all traces of salt and dirt and clean with a mild soap solution. Salt crystals are damaging to sails as they cause chafe, so the simple act of rinsing them will help to prolong

Zippers (TiP)

Rinse sail bag zippers and lubricate with silicone spray.

the sails' life. As well as damaging the sailcloth, salt also corrodes the fittings sewn to the sails.

Avoid heavy scrubbing of the sails or the use of harsh chemicals as this will damage the sailcloth coating.

Make sure the sails dry thoroughly before storing them for the winter – it is best to air dry them on a calm, sunny day outside, keeping them supported clear of the ground. If they are stored damp they will attract mould.

Note that sailmakers advise owners never to wash sails in a washing machine. There are a number of reasons for this, including that a sail's finish will be irreparably damaged by putting it through a washing machine, fibres will be broken down and the sail weakened, UV inhibitors will be destroyed, exposing the sail to UV damage and the sail's shape will be distorted, resulting in poor performance.

STAIN REMOVAL

It is always best to remove stains as soon as they occur. However, it is almost inevitable that a sail will have a few unsightly stains at the end of a sailing season. If using cleaning fluids, always double-check first with your sailmaker which products are harmful to your sailcloth and which are OK to use as chemical solvents and detergents can destroy the material integrity of a sail.

Here are a few tips on how to deal with stains:

- **Rust:** Wet the affected area and soak with lemon juice for about an hour and then rinse. Oxalic acid is another option, but it needs careful handling – mix 15g of crystals in 300ml of warm water.
- **Blood:** Bloodstains can be removed with soap and water. If this doesn't work try diluted oxalic acid (see for rust above) and rinse well.
- **Mildew:** Soak the stained area in a mild bleach solution, scrubbing lightly with a soft brush or cloth. Leave it for a while and then rinse with plenty of fresh water. Do **not** use bleach on nylon, aramid or laminated sails. Lemon juice will also remove mildew.
- **Oil and grease:** Rub the stain with a soft brush soaked in acetone. Then rinse and apply a mild soap, taking care to scrub the sail gently as excessive scrubbing will damage it. Also try hand-cleaning jellies used by car mechanics, such as Swarfega. Rub into the stain and scrub with warm water and soap. Rinse well with clean water.

STORAGE

Avoid folding sails on the same fold lines to prevent small creases from becoming permanent. Sails are best left loosely rolled with nothing heavy on top of them.

If you are storing your sails at home, they should be kept in well-ventilated clean conditions. Moisture increases the risk of mildew developing.

Watch out for pests including rodents and insects.

REPAIRS

Whether you make your own sail repairs will depend on your sailmaking skills. Areas of a sail that are not under too much load can be repaired at home by someone who knows what they are doing. Examples of such jobs are batten pockets, hanks and slides. Repairs to critical areas such as the clew, tack and head rings are usually left to the professionals who use specialist equipment.

RESTITCHING A SEAM

While major sail repairs are usually carried out by sailmakers, it is possible for restitching to be carried out by hand, preferably after a little bit of practice on an old or scrapped sail. This entails following the old needle holes using sailmaker's needles and strong polyester thread and a sail repair kit, which will include a sailmaker's palm, sail repair tape, needles and thread. Here's what to do:

Step 1

Use double-sided tape to hold the sailcloth in place while doing the repair.

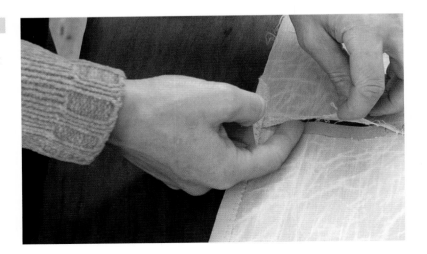

Step 2

Anchor the thread with a few stitches through two existing holes.

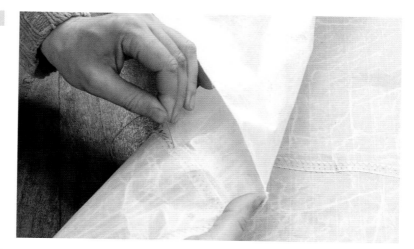

Step 3

Work along the seams with the needle and thread, following the existing holes in a zigzag direction.

Step 4

Stitch back in the opposite direction to complete the other side of the zigzag.

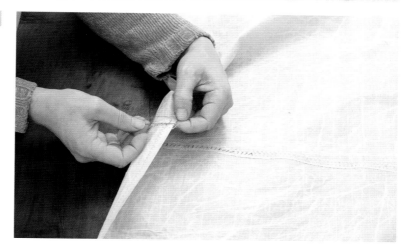

Boat engines come in all shapes and sizes and include inboards, outboards, petrol, diesel, electric and hybrid systems. Some engines are far more complex than others and should only be looked after by qualified engineers, while others can be maintained fairly easily by a savvy boatowner.

Irrespective of what kind of engine a boat is equipped with and who does the work, the care and maintenance of it is imperative. The most common cause of marine engine failure is widely known to be lack of maintenance.

Let's be honest, few boatowners want to spend the winter bent over double in cold, cramped engine bays. On the other hand, we don't want to spend half the summer working on our engines either, when we could be having fun out on the water. Most of us simply want to do the essential things as quickly and efficiently as possible without costing us excessive amounts of time, energy and money. This usually means spending a few hours changing the oil, replacing filters, draining and flushing the cooling system with fresh water, topping up with antifreeze, checking the impeller – which should be well within the DIY capabilities of most boatowners. Or, alternatively, paying a professional to do this work.

At the same time, as boatowners we also know that it is important to understand our

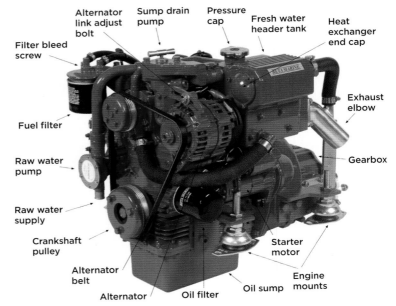

boat engines as well as possible so that in the event of an engine failure at sea we will have some idea of how to fix the problem ourselves. Most of us also know that the best way of avoiding engine failure is to carry out regular maintenance, some of which is simple, some of which is quite technical and some which might require professional assistance, all depending on our levels of expertise.

A few years ago this led me to remove my boat's Beta 14 diesel

engine one winter and take it home for a complete overhaul and repaint. I knew this was going to be a bit of a gamble as the last engine I had stripped down was a 175cc motorbike engine when I was 17 years old. In the end things worked out OK and doing this gave me the chance to become more fully acquainted with the boat engine well away from the very cramped engine bay in which it is housed – and it saved me quite a bit of money into the bargain.

KNOW YOUR ENGINE

Here are some thoughts about getting to know your engine. There are plenty of good illustrated reference books available on diesel engine maintenance and repair for boatowners (see **Further Reading** on page 218) as well as online forums and YouTube videos. While these reference sources may have lots of useful information about diesel engines in general, they are unlikely to include specific information about your own make and model of engine. So although these are worth buying or taking a look at, the most important reference by far is a copy of the engine maintenance manual for your specific engine.

ENGINE MANUAL

Your boat engine manual will most likely be a little dull to read, but it really is the best place to start and will provide you with the essential information to get started and gain confidence with working on your engine. The engine manual should cover the following essentials:

- technical elements of the engine
- maintenance and repair worksheets
- recommended lubrication for engine and gearbox
- common causes of breakdown and troubleshooting
- winterising.

In addition to these essentials, the engine manual will include other specific information like torque settings, how to bleed the fuel system, wiring diagrams and spare parts listings.

Engine manufacturers' manuals tend to be full of commonly used technical terms that may not be familiar to all boatowners, so be prepared to spend a little time deciphering precisely what all these mean. They include terms like bore, stroke, compression ratio and specific fuel consumption, which are not too challenging, but I can't resist including a couple of examples of what I mean from my engine's operating manual:

Operation at parameters outside the test parameters may affect the outputs/powers which in any case are subject to the ISO tolerance bands.

The exhaust back pressure, measured with the exhaust system connected and the engine running at full speed, must not exceed 80mmHg (3.1 inches Hg/42 inches WG).

TECHNICAL TERMS

- **bore:** cylinder diameter.
- **bottom dead centre (BDC):** a piston's lowest position at the bottom of the downward stroke.
- **compression ratio:** the ratio of maximum cylinder volume at bottom dead centre to minimum cylinder volume at top dead centre.
- **displacement volume:** the total volume of all the cylinders in an engine (litres or cubic centimetres).
- **four-stroke engine:** completes a power cycle every four strokes.
- **power:** engine power or horsepower is the maximum power that an engine can produce, expressed in kilowatts or horsepower. In physics, power is defined simply as the rate of doing work.
- **specific fuel consumption:** the amount of fuel consumed for each unit of power output, for example the quantity of fuel in grams needed by the engine to produce 1W/h (Watt per hour).
- **stroke:** *either* a phase of an engine's cycle during which the piston travels from top to bottom or vice versa; *or* the type of power cycle used by a piston engine; *or* the stroke length, the distance travelled in the cylinder by the piston in each cycle.
- **top dead centre (TDC):** a piston's uppermost position *or* the end of the upward stroke.
- **torque:** a force that causes something to rotate, measured in Newton-metres or lb/ft.
- **total volume:** the volume swept by a piston multiplied by the number of cylinders.
- **two-stroke engine:** completes a power cycle every two strokes.
- **volume swept by the piston:** the volume displaced by the piston between the top dead centre and bottom dead centre in cubic centimetres.

ENGINE TOOLS

Keep a small dedicated toolkit for working on your engine to ensure you have the correct-sized spanners and screwdrivers for maintenance purposes – this will save you a lot of time and avoid the frustration of spending ages hunting around for the correct tools to use.

Always choose good quality tools as although they will be more expensive, they will last longer. Cheap tools have a habit of not fitting properly and quickly rust. Give some careful thought when buying tools – for example, there is no need to buy a 200-piece socket set when you will only need ten at most for your engine.

Some engine manuals give a basic list of tools and sizes. If not, here are some of the tools you will need (note: engines manufactured in Europe use metric-sized spanners, while engines manufactured in the USA use spanners sized in inches):

- **Spanners:** Open-ended and ring spanners are both useful. Having both is advisable.
- **Socket spanners:** These can be very useful when accessing fastenings in confined spaces.
- **Screwdrivers:** Flat blades and Philips head come in several sizes with short and long handles. Small socket type heads are very useful.
- **Adjustable spanners and mole grips:** These are useful to have on board anyway but can come in handy when working on the engine.

- **Pliers:** square-ended and long-nose pliers.
- **Allen keys:** essential to have on board, as are the socket types.
- **Hacksaw:** a small hacksaw with spare blades.
- **Hammer:** occasionally invaluable.
- **Inspection mirror:** A telescopic inspection mirror is very useful for locating fittings that are out of sight or awkward to reach.
- **Multimeter:** Every boat should have one.
- **Feeler gauges:** A set will be required for checking alignments and precise settings.
- **Filter wrench:** for removing used filters.
- **Torque wrench:** You will need this to tighten bolts according to the manufacturer's specifications.

Engine maintenance tips

Keep two copies of the engine manual for your boat, one on the boat and the other at home.

- Keep the engine and the engine bay as clean as possible. This will make it easier to spot any leaks in hoses and seals.
- For those with little or no engine maintenance experience, the RYA diesel engine one-day course is well worth doing. The course includes basic maintenance and engine care, explaining the basics of the four-stroke cycle, cooling and air systems, engine electrics, winterisation and servicing. See www.rya.org.uk for information.

HOW DIESEL ENGINES WORK

The basic principle of a diesel engine is less complex than that of a petrol engine. A piston traps a quantity of air in an enclosed cylinder, then rises up the cylinder and compresses the air. As the air is compressed into a small space it heats up to a very high temperature, about 600°C. Diesel fuel is injected under high pressure into the small space. The fuel ignites when it comes into contact with the very hot compressed air. Bang!

The resulting expansion of gases pushes the piston back down to the bottom of the cylinder, creating a powerful force, which is used to drive a crankshaft. As this happens, the piston is pushed back up the cylinder and the exhaust gases escape through an exhaust valve and then the process or cycle begins again. This is known as the four-stroke cycle

– literally four strokes of the piston – consisting of induction, compression, power and exhaust.

No spark plug or ignition system is needed, making the basic diesel engine a comparatively straightforward system that results in fewer faults and has lower maintenance costs than the petrol engine.

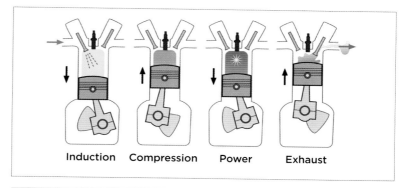

Induction   Compression   Power   Exhaust

VALVES

In order to get the air into the cylinder and the exhaust gases out of it, a combination of valves open and close through the cycle at precisely the right moment to either allow air in or exhaust out. When they are closed the valves need to be as tightly shut as possible to prevent the air, mixture and gases from escaping at the wrong moment. Strong springs called valve springs are used to hold the valves closed; the valves are opened by other lever type components called rockers. All the opening and closing of the valves is controlled by a camshaft which is connected to the crankshaft. The correct timing of the valves opening and closing is crucial, as is the gap or clearance of the valves.

Things get a little more complicated depending on the design of specific engines, number of cylinders and variations of ways the camshaft is driven – some use chains, some use gears and some use belts. It is probably best to hang on to the principle here rather than get too bogged down in the detail.

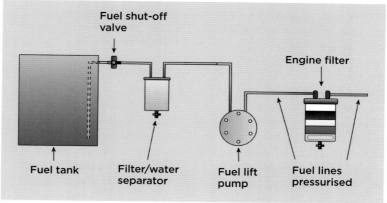

Fuel shut-off valve

Engine filter

Fuel tank   Filter/water separator   Fuel lift pump   Fuel lines pressurised

TRANSMISSION SYSTEMS

Most inboard engines of sailing vessels use one of two ways to connect the engine to a propeller, either a conventional propeller shaft with a stern gland or a saildrive transmission system. Many mid-range powerboat designs have sterndrive systems.

Conventional propeller shaft system

A coupling attached to the rear of the engine gearbox connects horizontally to a propeller shaft. The shaft goes in a straight line at a shallow downwards angle to the stern through a stern gland and exits the hull to the propeller. The stern gland prevents the ingress of water while allowing the propeller shaft to turn the propeller (see more on page 166).

Saildrive transmission system

A saildrive has a transmission system leading from an inboard engine which has a horizontal output shaft. This connects with the saildrive transmission which has a system of gears that drives an intermediate shaft vertically downwards through the hull to more gears that drive a horizontally mounted propeller. This system is sometimes referred to as an S-drive or Z-drive transmission due to the way the shaft is configured (see more on page 172).

Sterndrive system

Sterndrives are also known as outdrives and inboard/ outboards. As the names imply, these systems have an inboard engine which connects through the transom to a drive system that drops down via a shaft and gearbox to connect with the propeller. Unlike a saildrive, sterndrives can steer a boat by pivoting, similar to how an outboard engine works, with no separate rudder required for steering (see more on page 172).

EVOLVING TECHNOLOGY AND REGULATIONS

Boat engine technology and regulations have evolved considerably in recent years. It is a complex subject, made even more complex by the different marine exhaust emissions standards in force around the world, resulting in widely different rules that now apply for both commercial and leisure vessels in different territories.

As an example, at the time of writing, a mechanically controlled diesel engine may comply with the EU Recreational Craft Directive (RCD) but would not meet the US EPA domestic marine standard as it does not have electronic control and a common rail fuel system. While the DIY maintenance of mechanically controlled diesel engines is within the grasp of many boatowners, common rail technology is much more complex and requires professionals to carry out the maintenance and troubleshooting of these engines.

Common rail technology

Common rail technology is a digitally controlled very high pressure fuel injection and sensor system. This results in greater engine efficiency and reduced emissions than with mechanical systems, which is, of course, of environmental benefit and therefore a good thing. However, in the event of a breakdown out at sea, this is not such good news, unless you happen to have a professional engineer aboard with electronic diagnostic testing equipment to troubleshoot any problems that might arise.

These advanced engines are not DIY-friendly, unless you are a qualified engineer, but this is the way the world is going. If marine diesel engine technology is to survive well into in the future, it will have to meet the increasingly challenging emissions regulations needed to protect the environment. It will also need to compete with the rapid advancement of alternative technologies, in particular electric drive systems that do not produce exhaust gases or carbon emissions during use.

ELECTRIC MOTORS AND HYBRID SYSTEMS

As with the automotive industry, in recent years there have been considerable advances in the development of electrically powered propulsion in the leisure marine sector, resulting in electric drives that have increased power and much greater ranges than those in the past. This includes developments with inboard and outboard electric motors, hybrid systems, lithium-ion battery technology as well as solar-, wind- and hydro-powered generators.

Electric engines have been around for a surprisingly long time. For example, Frauscher Boats launched its first electrically powered motorboats back in 1955, but perhaps even more remarkable is that electric propulsion for boats dates way back to 1839 when the German inventor Moritz von Jacobi developed a 7.3m electric boat that carried 14 passengers at 4.8km/h. This predates the arrival of the first diesel engine by almost 60 years.

Until recently, three critical issues held back the widespread development of electric motors: battery constraints, cost and lack of environmental awareness by regulators. While cost still remains an issue, battery technology has come on considerably with the development of lithium-ion batteries, which are much lighter and hold their charge longer than traditional batteries and can deep-cycle repeatedly without damage. Even so, there is still the drawback that recharging a lithium battery takes considerably longer than topping up a fuel tank.

Most crucially, environmental concerns and pressures have risen sharply and tougher laws have been introduced to control water pollution.

As an example of where things stand with contemporary electric marine propulsion available in the leisure boating market today, one of the best known manufacturers is the German company Torqeedo, founded in 2005 (see www.torqeedo.com). Torqeedo produces outboard and inboard electric motors ranging from 0.5 to 100kW. Its lightweight Travel Series outboards, designed for tenders and daysailers up to 1.5 tons, deliver the equivalent of 3hp of power, while the Cruise Series motors can achieve planing speeds up to 12 knots on the right type of hull. Its top-of-the-range Deep Blue 40 SD saildrive can propel 13m sailing yachts at speeds of up to 10 knots, delivering the equivalent of 40hp of power. Another successful electric motor manufacturer is ePropulsion (www.epropulsion.com), which competes head on with Torqeedo in the small outboard market.

Despite these advances the marine internal combustion engine is not doomed, in fact far from it, as governments are not seeing electrification as the sole solution for marine craft in the same way as they may for road vehicles. In 2018 the International Maritime Organisation (IMO) announced its strategy on the reduction of greenhouse gases (GHG) from ships. This strategy commits the global maritime sector to reduce GHG emissions by at least 50 per cent by 2050. The objective is to develop engines that run on alternative fuels, including hydrogen, methanol, ammonia and bio-diesel, as well as fully electric vessels that will use electric motors and batteries. Another objective is to continue to encourage the development of hybrid electric vessels, where the use of electric motors and batteries complement other energy sources such as diesel.

The fact is that as things stand today, the range of an electric propulsion system is nothing like the range of a traditional diesel system, so as yet few coastal and bluewater cruising sailors are opting for pure electric solutions. Instead, hybrid systems are seen by many as more attractive.

HYBRID SYSTEMS

There are two main types of marine hybrid systems that combine internal combustion and electric power: the parallel hybrid and the serial hybrid.

Parallel hybrid

The parallel hybrid has two propulsion systems that operate in parallel on the same shaft. One is a conventional combustion engine, gearbox, propeller shaft and propeller drive train, which all work together in the normal way. This is used for propulsion when the vessel's maximum hull speed is required. The other is an electric motor/generator used in low- to mid-power cruising speeds up to two thirds of maximum hull speed. During the low- to mid-power cruising mode, the electric motor/generator propels the vessel using the stored energy in the battery bank. Once depleted, the combustion engine restarts and the electric motor/generator switches into generator mode to recharge the battery bank.

This combination of internal combustion with electric power is designed for maximum efficiency at high and low speeds, reducing the high drain on batteries that occur during high-speed cruising.

When a vessel with a hybrid system is under sail, the propeller can freewheel and drive the electric motor/generator, providing one of various alternative ways to recharge the battery bank in addition to the main engine. Solar panels, wind generators and shore power can also be used.

Serial hybrid

The serial hybrid also has an internal combustion engine but, unlike the parallel hybrid system, the combustion engine of a serial hybrid is solely a generator – there is no mechanical link between the engine and the driveshaft. The system has a substantial battery bank charged by the generator, which can be backed up with solar, wind, hydro and shore power.

Two examples of hybrid system manufacturers include the British company Hybrid Marine and the Finnish company Oceanvolt:

- Hybrid Marine produces parallel hybrid systems in association with Beta Marine and Yanmar (see www.hybrid-marine.co.uk).
- Oceanvolt produces electric motor and serial hybrid systems in partnership with monohull and multihull designers and builders around the world (see www.oceanvolt.com).

OUTBOARD MOTORS

The story of the outboard engine goes back a long way – in fact all the way to 1881 when the first external boat motor was invented by the Frenchman Gustave Trouvé. This was a battery-powered electric motor that Trouvé fitted to a 5m boat which was capable of speeds up to 2.5m/s (9km/h).

Most of today's leading outboard manufacturers built their reputations by designing two-stroke engines fitted with carburettors. These engines were lightweight, low cost and comparatively simple designs that became incredibly popular with small boatowners in the second half of the 20th century. This was despite the fact that they were noisy, smelly and had very poor fuel consumption due in part to leaving trails of unburned fuel oil on the water. Towards the end of the century emissions standards were introduced in Europe and the USA to control pollution levels, leading to the development

▲ Outboard engines should be winterised. Check the manual for guidance.

of four-stroke outboards, which were quieter, less polluting, more economical and more complex than the very popular two-stroke.

While a small number of advanced two-stroke engines are still produced, most outboards today are four-stroke engines ranging in power from 2hp to more than 400hp.

WINTERISATION
Winterisation will vary a little from one outboard to another. As with inboard diesels, it is always advisable to check your engine manual for details. The basic principles remain the same across all types: desalting and lubrication of the engine to protect against corrosion.

If an outboard is used in salt water, it should be flushed out with fresh water after every trip to remove any salt deposits from the cooling system to prevent salt clogging or corroding the internal parts of the engine. When it comes to winterisation a thorough flush through of the cooling system with fresh water is a good place to start:

Step 1
Flush the motor with fresh water for ten minutes or so. With some outboards this means attaching flush muffs over the water intakes and connecting them to a garden hose. Others have connections for hoses to attach directly into the outboard.

Step 2
Check that the telltale flow is strong and regular, indicating

there are no blockages. A weak telltale jet will alert you that there is a problem to investigate.

Step 3
Add an enzyme fuel treatment petrol additive to the fuel. This helps to prevent fuel oxidisation and to stabilise the fuel. It eliminates carbon build-up in the fuel system and on exhaust components.

Step 4
Spray fogging oil through the carburettors to leave a protective coating on the internal surfaces of the engine.

Step 5
Change the engine oil according to manufacturer's recommendations.

Step 6
Remove the spark plugs and spray in fogging oil before replacing the plugs.

Step 7
Spray the whole power head with a water repellant oil such as WD-40.

Step 8
Clean and regrease control linkages and grease points.

Step 9
Change the gearbox oil as recommended by the manufacturer.

Step 10
Store your engine vertically in a dry, well-ventilated place.

DIESEL ENGINE WINTERISATION

Why is engine winterisation so important? The answer is because an inactive boat engine needs to be protected from corrosion caused by the rising humidity levels through the cold months and the salty coastal air. This applies to both boats left afloat and hauled out over the winter.

Assuming the boat is coming ashore, it is best to winterise the engine in two stages: firstly when the boat is still in the water so you can run the engine and secondly as soon as possible after the boat is secure in the boatyard. You need to allow a few hours to do the work. If other commitments prevent you from doing this within a

▲ Diesel engines can be easily damaged if they are not properly winterised.

couple of weeks of lift out, then it would be a good idea to make arrangements for a service engineer to do this for you as winterising should be carried out before corrosion can set in.

Winterisation will vary a little from engine to engine, so do check the manual. The following is a basic guide that applies to most engines:

Stage 1: boat in the water	✔
Run the engine until it is warm. Check all the fuel lines and engine cooling hoses for leaks.	
Stop the engine, drain the oil and change the oil filter. It is much easier to pump warm oil out of an engine than trying to do it when the engine is cold.	
Refill the engine with new oil as recommended by the manufacturer.	
Run the engine to check the oil filter is properly sealed. Switch off and double-check that the oil level is correct.	
Fill up the fuel tank to eliminate water condensation in the tank – this is also easier to do before lift out as you can come alongside a fuel berth. Water entering the fuel injection system can cause considerable damage. Added to this, water in the fuel stimulates the growth of bacteria, which clogs up the filters.	
Smear some Vaseline around the fuel filler cap threads to make it 100 per cent watertight and easier to open in the spring – there is nothing more maddening than a seized fuel filler cap that will not budge.	

Stage 2: in the boatyard	✔
Once ashore, protect engine cylinders by removing the injectors and spraying anti-corrosion oil into the cylinders while turning the engine by hand, Plain engine oil can be used, but special anti-corrosion oil is best. Use a ring spanner on the crank pulley to help turn the engine.	
Engines with closed-circuit fresh-water cooling systems should contain a 50:50 solution of antifreeze, or as recommended by the engine manufacturer. Drain the circuit and replace as necessary.	

Stage 2: in the boatyard cont.	✔
Drain and flush the sea- or raw-water circuit with fresh water before filling it with an antifreeze mixture to protect it over the winter months. Do this as follows: (i) Close the inlet sea cock to the engine (engine stopped). (ii) Disconnect the sea water inlet pipe and dip it into a bucket containing 50:50 antifreeze solution. (iii) Start the engine (out of gear) and run for ten seconds or so until the antifreeze is used up and can be seen coming out of the exhaust outlet. (iv) Shut the engine off and reconnect the inlet pipe to the sea cock.	(i) (ii) (iii) (iv)
Remove the water pump impeller. The reason for doing this is that if the vanes remain in one position for months on end they can become permanently deformed and more prone to failure.	
Most engines with raw-water cooling have sacrificial zinc anodes to protect the engine from corrosion. The easiest time to replace this is during winterisation. Check your manual to find out where the zinc anode is. On my engine it is attached to a bolt that screws into one of the end caps of the heat exchanger. Slacken the alternator and water pump drive belts to extend their life.	
Protect the instrument panel and give the key switch a spray with WD-40 or equivalent.	
Protect the engine electrical circuit by disconnecting the connections and spraying them with WD-40 or a water-repellant spray.	
Clean and inspect the engine from all angles, making sure there are no water, fuel or oil leaks and that all the jubilee clips are in good condition and tight.	
Clean the bilges to help reduce humidity and to make it easier to check for leaks that might develop.	
Lubricate the throttle and gear levers and linkages.	
Plug the exhaust outlet and air intake with rags to prevent any moisture from reaching the engine.	
Disconnect the engine battery and clean the terminals. Take the batteries home so they can be trickle-charged and stored where they cannot freeze. Some owners store batteries on board if they have shore power for trickle-charging and can keep the boat interior above freezing through the winter.	

OTHER ENGINE MAINTENANCE ASHORE

Once all the winterisation tasks are complete you will have done the lion's share of a full diesel engine service. Assuming everything has been done correctly this will have saved yourself a lot of labour charges – very satisfying.

What more needs to be done to the engine while the boat is ashore in the boatyard? If they are installed and serviced correctly most marine engines are very reliable, but they are not infallible and problems are more likely to occur if an engine is not taken care of and inspected from time to time, in addition to carrying out the all-important engine servicing. Reading through the troubleshooting and fault-finding section of your engine manual on a dark winter's evening will certainly provide some insight into what can go wrong with your engine, the possible causes and the possible solutions – in theory, of course.

FUEL SYSTEM

Regular checks of the fuel system are necessary throughout the year, especially the primary filter of a diesel engine fuel system. With the boat in the boatyard, it is a good opportunity to replace the fuel filters and then bleed the system to remove any air that might have entered the system as a result of replacing the filters. You will need to buy replacement filters as recommended by your engine manufacturer in advance.

CHANGING THE FILTER

PRIMARY FILTER

This catches any water and dirt that might be in the fuel. Typically, this has a sealed glass bowl underneath where dirt and water get trapped. To replace the primary filter:

1. Make sure the tank fuel stopcock is closed.

2. Diesel is harmful to the skin, so wear protective gloves in case of fuel spillage (which is more than likely to occur). Also have some rags or paper towels at hand.

3. Use a suitable container such as a glass jar or plastic container to catch all the fuel which will drain from the filter and bowl.

4. Undo the drain screw at the base of the glass bowl to drain off the fuel into the jar.

5. Now undo the central retaining bolt that holds the glass bowl and filter in place, carefully separating these from the retaining bracket above. There are normally rubber O-ring type seals between the bracket, filter and bowl. New seals are normally supplied with filters – it is best to check when ordering.

6. Clean all the parts, paying particular attention to all the contact surfaces.

7. Reassemble with the new parts, including the new seals, taking care not to overtighten the bolt securing the bowl, filter and

bracket together – only moderate pressure is required. Smear some diesel on the seals to help them bed in properly.

8. Open the fuel stopcock and check for leaks.

SECONDARY FILTER

Also known as a fine filter, the secondary filter is needed to separate the extra-fine particles in diesel fuel that could damage the injectors. It does not need replacing as often as a primary filter; normally manufacturers recommend doing this after 200 hours' use. There are two main types of secondary filters: spin-on style, where the filter is contained in a metal canister, and cartridge-type filters, where only the filter medium is replaced.

The replacement procedure for a spin-on filter is as follows:

1. Make sure the tank fuel stopcock is closed.

2. Unscrew the filter a half turn using a filter wrench, pipe wrench or strap.

3. Now hold a plastic bag around the filter and continue to undo it by hand, being aware that it will be full of fuel. Then dispose of it in the boatyard's recycling containers.

4. Replace the rubber seal, smearing a little diesel fuel on the new seal to help it bed in.

5. Carefully pour some diesel fuel into the new filter. This will help make bleeding the fuel system quicker. To prevent spillage, do not attempt to do this with a primary filter as in my experience assembling the new filter, seals and glass bowl is tricky enough without the new filter having fuel in it.

6. Screw on the new filter and hand-tighten it only.

7. Bleed the fuel system and check for leaks.

STEP-BY-STEP

BLEEDING THE FUEL SYSTEM

When you replace the fuel filters, air gets trapped in the fuel system. This also happens if you run out of fuel. When you try to start the engine the trapped air prevents the fuel from flowing properly, hence the engine will run badly and may not start at all. This happens because if air bubbles get into the injector pipes the injector valve does not operate. Some engines do not require bleeding as they are self-bleeding, but many do. These are the steps to bleed a fuel system:

1. Turn the fuel tank stopcock on.

2. You need a container and rags to catch drips from the fuel system as you bleed it and a small screwdriver and/or spanner as required. If in doubt, consult the manual. Wearing protective gloves is also a good idea.

3. Identify where the hand priming lever is on the fuel lift pump and where the bleed screws are on the filter bodies and injection pump. These can be a little tricky to find for the first time in a cramped engine bay.

4. If the primary filter is at a lower level than the fuel in the tank undo the bleed screw.

You don't need to unscrew it completely.

5. Fuel with bubbles will begin to appear, so hold a container beneath the filter to catch the drips. When the fuel runs clear, close the bleed screw.

6. Wipe the primary filter dry.

7. Unscrew the bleed screw on top of the secondary filter.

8. Operate the hand priming lever on the fuel lift pump. If the lever won't move, this will most likely be because the engine will have stopped where the pump is at the end of its travel. Try turning the engine over a little, either with the starter or by hand, then try the pump again.

9. Keep working the priming lever until clear fuel comes out with no bubbles and then tighten the bleed screw.

10. Wipe the secondary filter dry.

11. At this point the system should be bled and the engine should start, but if not the injection pump and high pressure line may need bleeding.

12. Bleed the injection pump next, having located the upper bleed screw.

13. The last parts to bleed, but only if necessary, are the injector pipes. By this point, an extra pair of hands will be of help to operate the starter.

14. To do this, slacken the pipe connectors that join the pipes to the injectors one by one, cranking the engine in short bursts and checking for fuel escaping from the unions. Take care as fuel escaping from the injection pipes will be under very high pressure.

15. Finally retighten all the fittings through the system, shut off the fuel tank stopcock, wipe everything dry and dispose of any spilt fuel.

A final note on this: some boatowners prefer to wait and bleed the fuel system when the boat is back in the water. This enables the engine to be run for a while and checked over with the cooling system operational.

OIL SYSTEM

The key oil system-related things to do when the boat is ashore for the winter are:

- Change the oil and replace the oil filter (see **Winterisation** on page 152 for details).
- Check for oil leaks.

Why is it necessary to change the oil when the engine is not going to be used over the winter? Leaving old oil in the engine over the winter is not a good idea as it will be contaminated with the harmful by-products of combustion, making the oil very acidic. This corrodes the engine and shortens its life. Replacing the old oil with clean new oil will protect the engine.

It is important to buy the grade of oil recommended by your engine manufacturer, so once again consult the manual for the correct specification. This may prove to be more expensive than the average car engine oil, but when it comes to boat engines it is best to follow the manufacturer's advice. This can be a particular problem for older engines where the specified oil is not widely available.

The recommended grade of oil for your engine will be given as an SAE (American Society of Automotive Engineers) grade. The SAE grade system refers to the viscosity or thickness of the oil where the higher the number, the greater the viscosity; for example, an SAE40 is thicker than an SAE30. A low viscosity oil such as 10W ('W' stands for winter) will flow better in low temperatures as it is thinner, meaning the engine will be easier to start and better protected in colder temperatures.

Today we have multigrade oils which are designed to work efficiently in winter and summer. For example, an SAE15W/40 means that the oil is a multigrade oil with a viscosity of 15W when cold and a viscosity of SAE40 when hot. Multigrade oils have chemical additives mixed with the oil to change its characteristics at different temperatures.

It helps to check and learn the specific requirements for your engine and to keep a record of when you change the oil and filter. It also helps to keep a log of the engine hours and the manufacturer's recommendations for oil changes – usually every 200 or 250 hours or so.

Why is oil so important? Most of us know that checking the oil regularly is a good idea and that oil reduces friction and wear of an engine's moving parts, but engine oil does more than this. As it circulates, it helps cool the engine, reduces corrosion and cleans the engine by removing carbon deposits and tiny metal particles. Failure to change the oil results in increased engine wear as all the carbon and metal particles build up, making the oil dirtier and dirtier.

Oil leaks

If your engine has been leaking oil it would be wise to check out what is causing the leak – either a failed gasket, a failed seal or worn piston rings. Some leaks are easier to deal with than others, so you will need to decide whether this calls for a professional repair or if it is something that you can do yourself. This very much depends on your engineering skills and experience.

The first thing to do is to wipe the engine and bilges clean and try to pinpoint where the leak is coming from. This is easier said than done in a cramped engine

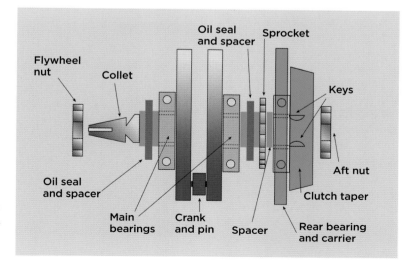

bay, but rather easier when all round access to the engine is possible. Then check:

- **Head gasket:** This is the biggest gasket and subject to very high pressure and temperatures. To replace this entails removing the cylinder head, which can be done in situ.
- **Sump gasket:** Not as critical as the head gasket, this will require the engine to be removed for the repair.
- **Camshaft seals:** The camshaft cover and pulley will need to be removed, but the engine should not need lifting.
- **Crankshaft seals:** The front crankshaft seal can be repaired fairly easily, while the rear seal is more challenging as you have to remove the flywheel and gaining access is normally an issue.
- **Valve seals:** Replacing valve seals normally requires removing the camshaft.
- **Worn piston rings:** Oil leaking into the combustion chamber is caused by worn piston rings. The telltale sign of this is blue smoke coming out of the exhaust. This a major job which could entail a complete engine rebuild.

DRY FRICTION

After a long period of disuse (over the winter, for example), all the oil makes its way down into the sump. When the engine is started, the moving parts including the cams and bearings may have become completely dry and will be subject to dry friction, causing harmful metal abrasion.

To overcome this problem at the beginning of the season, you can spray a small amount of oil into the air inlet and then turn the engine over without starting it. This will provide a coating of oil in the cylinders and reduce the friction.

AIR FILTER

It is best to clean or replace the engine air filter annually. This is an easy task involving either unclipping or unscrewing the air filter cover and replacing the paper filter element. Cleaning the filter with a brush is an option if the filter is still in good condition. Some air filters have wire gauze elements instead of paper. These should be rinsed in paraffin or washing-up liquid in hot water and replaced when dry.

EXHAUST SYSTEM

Most marine exhausts are water-cooled, with water from the engine's raw-water cooling system used to cool the exhaust gas. The water and exhaust gas

mix together in the injection bend, where it turns into steam before cooling and condensing back into water which then makes its way out of the hull via the exhaust system.

Inspection

With the boat ashore, it is wise to inspect the exhaust system for corrosion damage, especially around the injection bend:

- **Injection bend:** This is where the raw-water cooling system meets up with the exhaust gases in order to cool the gases enough to prevent the flexible rubber sections of the exhaust from melting. Check the condition carefully, looking for any signs of corrosion.
- **Exhaust piping:** Look for external signs of deterioration in the flexible rubber piping, connections and clips, checking the condition of the double clips all along the system. Any signs of white crystals indicate there have been sea-water leaks.

▲ Clear evidence of an exhaust leak.

Smoking exhaust

If you have noticed the engine exhaust smoking a lot during the sailing season this can indicate a number of potential problems with the engine that may need to be rectified. It is normal for an engine exhaust to smoke until it is warmed up so you only need be concerned if the exhaust is smoking after the engine has fully warmed up.

The colour of the smoke can be a guide to what might be wrong. White, blue or black smoke from a diesel exhaust indicates there is a problem.

- White smoke has two general causes: overcooling, where proper combustion is not taking place, or worn piston rings.
- Blue smoke comes from burning oil. It can be caused by worn valves or piston rings.
- Black smoke typically indicates partially burned fuel, worn injectors or clogged air filters.

The chart below looks at possible causes and solutions. To help solve the mystery you may need advice from your boatyard mechanic.

▲ A perished engine hose in need of replacement.

Possible cause	Solution
White exhaust smoke	
Blocked injectors	Service the injectors
Water or air in the fuel	Defective seals, possible leaking head gasket
Breather pipe is obstructed	Remove and clean out
Reduced cooling water flows	Check the raw-water system
Blue exhaust smoke	
Engine oil level too high	Check the oil dipstick. If too high, pump out some of the oil
Worn valve guides and seals	Replace oil seals
Piston ring and bore worn, giving a low compression	Get compression checked by a boatyard pro
Leaking turbocharger seal	If fitted, get the turbocharger checked by a boatyard pro
Black exhaust smoke	
Blocked air filter element	Inspect and replace
Inadequate ventilation in engine compartment	Check the ventilation isn't blocked
Blocked or damaged exhaust hose	Check the exhaust hose isn't blocked or restricted in any way; internal inspection may be required as inner layers of exhaust flexible hose can collapse
Malfunctioning fuel injection	If the airflow is unobstructed and the engine not overloaded, poor injection could be the problem
Overpitched propeller – engine will not reach its full rpm	Check the engine will reach full rpm in neutral; if it does not get the propeller checked/repitched if necessary
Accumulated debris on hull	Inspect and clean if required

COOLING SYSTEM

Some engine breakdowns are unavoidable, but those caused by lack of maintenance or regular checks can be avoided. Failure to maintain an engine's cooling system is a well-known example of this, so it is well worth spending time checking over the cooling system thoroughly when the boat is ashore, as well as throughout the season. In particular, it will help to be aware of the damage that salt water passing through a cooling system can do to an engine and therefore why the need to keep an eye on things is so important – more on this below.

Many boat engines are cooled by a combination of fresh water and sea water, also known as raw water, using a system known as indirect cooling. Raw water refers to the water that the boat is floating in, hence on an inland waterway this may be fresh water and at sea it will be salt water.

An indirect cooling system works as follows. Raw water enters the boat via a sea cock and passes through the raw-water filter to remove weeds and debris. It then passes through hoses and a pump to a heat exchanger and back out of the boat via the exhaust system.

The fresh water is contained in an enclosed system similar to a car's cooling system, using a combination of fresh water and antifreeze supplied by a header tank which can be topped up when required. The main difference between the car and the marine engine is that the marine engine uses a heat exchanger instead of a radiator. The fresh

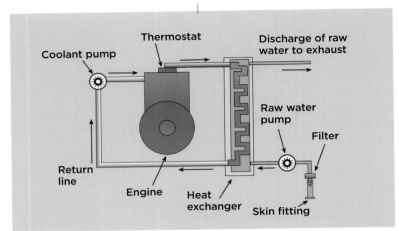

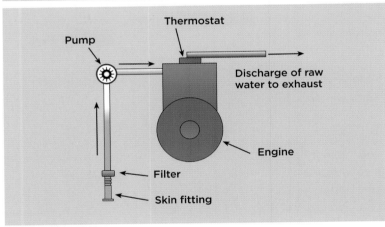

water circulates around the engine and passes through the heat exchanger, which usually forms part of the header tank on smaller engines but may be separate on larger engines. Once in the heat exchanger, the fresh water is cooled by the raw water which is pumped through small-diameter cooling tubes – note that the raw water and fresh water do not mix together. The sea water is then pumped into the exhaust system where it mixes with the exhaust gases and ends up being pumped out of the exhaust into the sea.

Direct cooling

The more basic system of engine cooling is direct cooling, where raw water is pumped through the engine block and back out to sea, with no secondary fresh-water system used at all. This might sound more straightforward, but the problem of corrosion can become a big issue.

It can get confusing when several different names are given to parts of a boat and the cooling system is no exception. To summarise, sea-water cooling is also raw-water cooling.

As a bonus it is also called a direct cooling system if no fresh water is involved. Fresh-water cooling is also known as indirect cooling if raw water is involved. Confused? Hopefully the illustrations will help explain this better.

Inspection

Here are some things to check for:

• **Sea cock hose:** Check the condition of the hose that connects the sea cock to the raw-water filter. Any signs of swelling in the hose is a sign that it is deteriorating. Check there are double hose clips in place and that they are free from corrosion.

• **Raw-water filter:** Although this should be checked throughout the season, give this an extra special clean and double-check the condition of the wire strainers, the hose connectors either side of the filter and look for any signs of leaks in the system.

• **Raw-water pump:** Check for any signs of leakage around the pump. Open it up and inspect the condition of the impeller. Some people remove the impeller

▲ Check the condition of the raw water filter.

▲ Heat exchanger tube stack before removal.

completely for the winter to help preserve its shape and condition. Replacing the impeller on an annual basis is normally recommended (see **Replacing the water impeller** overleaf).

• **Sea water hoses:** Check all sea-water hoses for condition and signs of corrosion at the connections. If in doubt, replace these every two years as a sensible precaution.

• **Gaskets:** Check the cylinder head, thermostat housing and manifolds for any signs that salt water has been weeping through the gasket surfaces.

• **Fresh water circulating pump:** The pump itself does not need servicing, but check the condition of the drive belts and beware of shaft bearing and seal failures.

• **Heat exchanger:** The heat exchanger tube stack needs to be removed and cleaned annually. The reason for this is that fine seaweed and other debris can get past the raw-water filter and then get trapped in the tube stack. Pieces of a disintegrated rubber impeller can also get trapped in

▲ Check the raw-water pump impeller.

▲ Removal can be tricky. Tap gently.

▲ Clean it in hot water, remove all debris from the tubes.

the tube stack, so this is the place to look and remove them if the impeller has failed. Refer to your engine manual for advice on how to do this.

• **Injection bend:** see page 158.

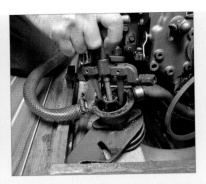

REPLACING THE WATER IMPELLER

Every boatowner knows to check that water is flowing from the exhaust pipe after starting the engine as this indicates the raw-water cooling system is working properly. If water isn't flowing it may simply mean that the raw-water sea cock has not been turned on, but it could also mean that the raw-water pump has failed.

The most common reason for the failure is that the rubber impeller has disintegrated. To be on the safe side, most manufacturers advise the impeller is replaced annually. Certainly it needs to be inspected when the boat is ashore, even if it has been replaced during the season, and many boatowners remove it during the winter as this helps to prolong its life.

You will need a replacement impeller and gasket. When ordering remember to have your engine number at hand to ensure you get the correct parts. This is how to replace it:

1. Remove the circular face plate by undoing the screws holding it in place.

2. Note how the impeller fits into the pump – taking a photo will help.

3. Withdraw the rubber impeller from its drive shaft using a pair of pliers, gently coaxing the impeller bit by bit from the

pump. Take care not to scratch the inside surfaces of the pump.

4. Smear the new impeller with washing-up liquid and push it on to the shaft, making sure that the rubber vanes are facing the same way as the old ones did – checking the photo you took will help if you've forgotten.

5. Fit the new gasket. If necessary, use some washing-up liquid or a little Vaseline to hold it in place.

6. Then place the cover plate back on and screw it tight.

ENGINE ELECTRICAL SYSTEM

Boatowners who grew up sailing boats without engines often treat the idea of boat engine maintenance with a fair amount of trepidation, whether inboard or outboard varieties. This trepidation has a tendency to go up a notch when the subject of maintaining an engine's electrical system is contemplated.

As with all things boating, it helps to gain some understanding of the basics of all the systems found on a boat – including the electrical system of the engine – in order to avoid running into a problem at sea that could either have been avoided by regular maintenance or even be dealt with by a competent skipper without having to call the rescue services. This is particularly useful when tracing and rectifying a fault that may be as simple as a loose wiring connection that costs nothing to fix except some time and a little patience.

The typical basic electrical system associated with a marine engine includes a dedicated engine starting battery, a starter motor, a charger in the form of an alternator, a solenoid and some engine sensors and instruments. For the engine to remain operational and healthy these few components and the wiring that connects everything together need to be kept in good working order. This system is self-contained with its own battery and wiring that is separate from the rest of the boat's electrics.

BATTERY CARE

Battery installation and maintenance is covered in Chapter 12.

ALTERNATOR BELT

Most small- to medium-sized inboard engines are fitted with a single belt to drive the battery-charging alternator and fresh-water circulating pump. If the belt is slipping or fails, there will be reduced electrical output from the alternator and the batteries will discharge. Belt tension needs to be checked regularly through the year when the boat is being used and adjusted where necessary. It is also a good idea to check the belt when the boat is ashore and decide whether it needs replacing or not.

Adjusting belt tension

There are usually two bolts that first need to be slackened: a link adjust bolt and a support bolt on which the alternator pivots.

- With both bolts slackened, swing the alternator outwards to tension the belt by pivoting it on the support bolt. Tighten the link adjust bolt.
- Check the tension of the belt by pressing downwards on it with your thumb. The belt should not depress more than 12mm (0.5in).
- Retighten the bolts.
- Take care not to overtighten the belt because this will put too much load on the alternator and water pump bearings and cause them to fail.

Black dust

Black dust on and around the alternator is very unsightly, but more importantly it indicates the sides of the belt are wearing significantly. This can be caused by corrosion of the pulleys,

▲ Black dust indicates this belt is wearing fast. Poor alignment or corroded pulleys could be the reason.

or could mean the pulleys are out of alignment or the engine compartment temperature is too high.

Rusty pulleys can become very abrasive and quickly chew their way through an alternator belt. To remedy this, remove the belt and sand smooth the pulleys with emery paper. If they are very badly corroded, consider replacing the pulleys completely.

Check the pulleys are all aligned correctly; if they are out of alignment the belt will wear through very quickly.

If the engine compartment temperature is very high, improving the compartment ventilation should help.

Your engine manufacturer may also advise replacing the belt with one with a higher temperature tolerance.

ALTERNATOR CARE

Alternator care and maintenance is covered in Chapter 12.

WIRING CHECKS

Your engine manual should include a wiring schematic of your engine wiring. This will help to identify the wiring and which wire belongs to which component. A telescopic inspection mirror can help with these checks:

- Bearing in mind the cramped conditions of many engine bays, check the wiring as best as you can, for signs of chafe or melting of the wire insulation.
- Check for corrosion on the connections.
- With so much vibration

caused by the engine, it is wise to check the integrity of connections to the instruments, ensuring the engine wiring loom and any stray cables are properly clipped in place.

- Check that the engine instruments and warning lights are all working. It will help to refer to the engine manual fault-finding section as helpful information is usually provided.
- Replace any wiring or connections with marine-grade materials – only the best available are recommended as you don't want to cut corners with boat wiring.

For more information about wiring in general, see Chapter 12.

ENGINE CONTROL SYSTEM

It is easy to take engine controls for granted, possibly because we are so used to car engine controls which need virtually zero maintenance. However, with boats it does pay to inspect the controls and their cables annually and to do a bit of greasing.

They may be awkward to get to, but getting access to service the control mechanisms that connect the helm positions to the engine will help to ensure that they continue to work smoothly through the boating season. This may entail dismantling a steering pedestal or crawling into a cockpit locker or (as in my boat's case) working your way headfirst into a pilot berth with no headroom.

The object is then to:
- Clean the old grease from the mechanism with a paraffin-soaked rag.
- Check that the nuts, bolts, pins and links holding the throttle and gear selectors are all in place and everything is well fixed.
- Check the cabling is not frayed and in good condition.
- Lubricate with waterproof grease.
- Work the control levers a few times to check they are all operating smoothly.
- Remember to check the cabling all the way through to the engine and gearbox, greasing the connections along the way.

EXCESSIVE ENGINE VIBRATION

If you have become concerned about excessive engine vibration during the boating season, then, with the boat ashore, there are some checks you can carry out. Before doing so, bear in mind that even a well-tuned and properly installed engine will vibrate quite a bit and in a small boat this is one of those facts we have to live with.

Here are some possible causes and solutions to excessive vibration. Be aware that some of the remedies involve a considerable amount of work and can only be done with the boat out of the water, so do these checks as soon as possible after the boat comes ashore to allow time for the work to be done in the boatyard.

Possible cause of vibration	Solution
Loose securing nut on engine mount	Check alignment and retighten nut
Engine mounts have not been adjusted correctly	Check each mount is adjusted to take an even amount of weight
Engine mount rubbers have perished	Replace the engine mounts (see **Engine mounts** on page 181). Note that diesel fuel or oil spillage over engine mounts can destroy rubber
Poor engine alignment to shaft	Have the alignment checked, even if your engine has a flexible coupling
Loose zinc anode on the shaft	Tighten or replace
Worn cutless bearing or shaft	Replace (see **Cutless bearing** on page 170)
Weak engine bearers	Have these checked by the yard

▲ Check the gearbox oil for level and colour.

GEARBOX

A boat engine's gearbox connects the engine to the propeller shaft. It has a forward and reverse gear and neutral, so it is not overly complex compared with a car's gearbox. In fact, it has very little in common with a car's gearbox.

One of a boat gearbox's functions is to provide a reduction gear that reduces the high input speed of the engine's crankshaft revolutions to a lower output speed for the propeller shaft. Reducing the propeller's rotation ratio maintains good propeller efficiency, as a propeller is more effective when it is larger in diameter and rotates more slowly than a small, fast-spinning one. For example, a reduction ratio of 2:1 means the crankshaft is rotating two times faster than the propeller. The important thing to bear in mind here is that reducing the shaft speed in this way increases the torque or turning effort.

There are several types of boat engine gearboxes, including epicyclic, twin-shaft, bevel gear and layshaft. You can find details of how all these gearboxes work in other publications – hopefully understanding the basic gearbox functionality is all that is required here.

What is important for now is that different types of gearboxes need different types of oil and they do not mix, so it is critical to know what type of gearbox your engine has, its capacity and how often the oil needs to be changed. Your engine manual will be the best place to find this information. Although gearboxes need very little maintenance, nonetheless there are a couple of things to be done.

Checking gearbox oil

Getting access to the gearbox dipstick can be quite a struggle in a cramped engine bay and you will find that it needs a strong

▲ When changing gearbox oil, check the manual for the right oil to use.

pull to remove it for checking. Changing the oil itself entails locating the gearbox drain plug. When filling with new oil, take care not to overfill the gearbox as this can cause serious damage – detailed instructions will be given in the engine manual.

Gear selector mechanism

Check the selector mechanism is adjusted correctly, according to the engine manual. This will prevent the clutches slipping when under load.

▲ A three-bladed propeller fitted to a 12m cruising yacht.

▲ A rope cutter fitted to a propeller shaft will help protect the stern gear from damage.

STERN GEAR

The term 'stern gear' encompasses propellers, propeller shafts, shaft couplings, rudder tubes, rudder assemblies, propeller shaft brackets, propeller shaft seals, stern tube assemblies, bearings and more.

The stern gear of a boat needs to be checked carefully when the boat is in the boatyard as this is something that can only be done when it is out of the water. The same applies for any maintenance and repairs that may need doing, so it is best to check it all over as soon after lift out as possible.

There are a number of ways that inboard boat engines can be connected to their propellers. The conventional system has a straight line of components leading back from the engine, including a gearbox, engine coupling, propeller shaft, stern tube (or shaft log), then through the hull to the propeller. Other arrangements include saildrives, sterndrives, hydraulic transmission and water jet propulsion.

Stern tube

The stern tube can be made of metal and built into the deadwood at the stern of a hull or embedded in a resin glass moulding through which the propeller shaft passes. The forward end of the stern tube has a watertight stern gland and a bearing for the shaft may also be incorporated.

STERN GLANDS

The stern gland, or stuffing box, is the clever part of the stern gear that prevents water from entering the hull while at the same time allowing the propeller shaft to rotate at high speed – it is an ingenious type of seal, in other words. The gland is packed with three or four rings of compressible material around the shaft (traditionally greased flax). This enables the shaft to turn without abrading the metal and prevents water from getting into the hull. More modern materials used include graphite, acrylonitrile and Kevlar. The packing material is compressed by a large nut which encompasses the shaft. This can be tightened as the packing material slowly wears away. In time the packing gets worn away to the point that it needs to be replaced with new packing material.

▲ A traditional stern gland arrangement. Lubrication is via the white tube.

▲ This stern gland's rubber is split and needs replacing.

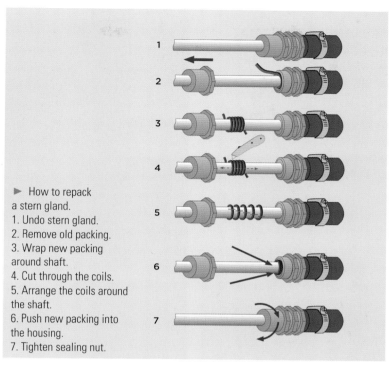

▶ How to repack a stern gland.
1. Undo stern gland.
2. Remove old packing.
3. Wrap new packing around shaft.
4. Cut through the coils.
5. Arrange the coils around the shaft.
6. Push new packing into the housing.
7. Tighten sealing nut.

It should be noted that while this is a clever and well-proven system, the traditional stern gland arrangement is not 100 per cent watertight and is designed to allow a tiny bit of water to drip into the bilges – in the region of one drop every minute or so when the engine is running. The gland needs to be adjusted just tight enough to prevent the shaft from overheating, enabling it to turn. If the packing is overtightened, the friction on the shaft is increased and it will heat up as a result, which is not at all desirable. Worse still, the shaft will struggle to turn and may fail completely, which is not pleasant to contemplate.

There are many variations of stern glands and it is worth studying your boat's particular arrangement, taking expert advice if in any doubt about how it works. Most stern glands incorporate a greaser that allows grease to be injected into the gland through a tube. The grease is applied every few hours of engine running time by turning a small handle on the stern tube greaser reservoir. Here are some stern gland maintenance tasks and tips:

- If your boat has a traditional type of stern gland, it needs to be checked and tightened if necessary when the boat is ashore.
- Remember not to overtighten the packing.
- Care should be taken not to overlubricate as this can cause packing to run hot.
- Check and refill the stern greaser with waterproof grease.
- It is recommended to change the packing material in most stern glands every two or three years.

- Many arrangements include a section of heavy-duty rubber hose in the stern gland which is held in place by stainless steel jubilee clips. If your boat's system has this, check the condition of the hose as this can perish. If it is in bad condition, it will need to be replaced. This is probably best done by a professional as it is a tricky job which involves disconnecting the prop shaft, which puts everything out of alignment.

Aside from the traditional stuffing box type stern gland there are two other groups of seals which are more recent developments and are collectively referred to as dripless shaft seals (DSS).

DRIPLESS SHAFT SEALS

As their name implies, dripless shaft seals are designed to completely stop water from entering the hull via the stern tube. There are two main types of DSS, known as face seals and lip seals, which many boat manufacturers now fit to production boats. They can also be fitted as replacements to boats with traditional stuffing boxes.

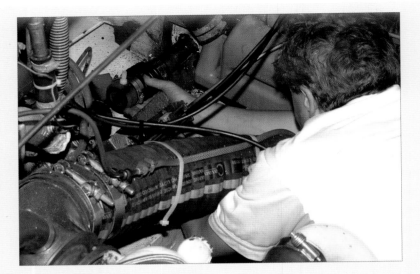

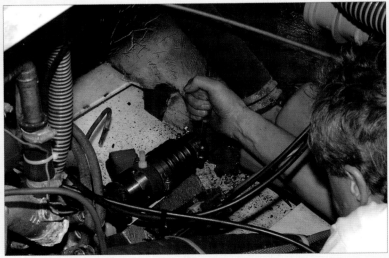

Face seals

A face seal has a flexible bellows attached to the stern tube that presses a carbon or graphite flange against a stainless steel rotor, or sealing ring, which is attached to the spinning propeller shaft, making a seal between the spinning rotor and the flange. Once installed correctly, they should not need adjustment or maintenance, aside from a check every now and again of the hoses, clamps and sealing faces.

These are popular as they are considered maintenance-free and keep the water out even if the shaft is slightly out of alignment. However, while they are known to last for more than five years with no problems, if either the setscrews that hold the rotor in place or the bellows fail, water can quickly flow into the bilge and serious problems will arise. This might occur because of fatigue of the bellows material or improper installation. If your boat is fitted with a face seal, you need to be aware that it is definitely not maintenance-free. Here are some maintenance checks:

- The bellows should be inspected every six months and checked for signs of cracks, splits, tears or brittleness.
- If leaks are noticed where the bellows attach to the shaft log or flange, check the hose clamps for looseness or damage.
- Be aware that if the seal or bellows are attached incorrectly the seal faces will be subjected to uneven pressure which will cause uneven wear.
- A common cause of minor leaking is where foreign material gets between the rotor and flange – a grain of sand can cause the seal to be broken. The remedy for this is to clean the two surfaces, which is easier said than done with the boat in the water but more easily done in the boatyard.
- The bellows can lose tension over time due to slippage, which can result in leaks as the pressure on the face seal reduces. A remedy that can prevent this is to clamp a propeller shaft anode right alongside the face seal.
- Face seals are lubricated by water and if air is trapped in the bellows, for example after the boat has been out of the water, then the seal will no longer be lubricated. Some systems have a water injection tube to deal with this, but others need to be manually squeezed or 'burped' once back in the water so that the air can escape. If in doubt your yard should be able to assist with this.

Some manufacturers advise the bellows should be replaced every six years or less, even if they appear to be in good condition. As always, it is advisable to check through your manufacturer's instructions and include the seal inspection as part of your winter maintenance schedule.

Lip seals

Lip seals also use a flexible rubber-type sleeve to keep the water out, but, unlike face seals which use a stainless steel rotor, the seal is made from nitrile rubber and bears directly against the propeller shaft. The shaft rotates inside the seal and no water escapes into the boat. Most lip seals are lubricated by water that comes from the engine's raw-water system, while some are oil-lubricated. There is no dripping of water and the seal does not need to be tightened. Things to be aware of about lip seals include:

- Lip seals need a smooth, pristine shaft surface. If the shaft is not in an unblemished and polished condition it will leak.
- They rely on a water supply for lubrication, which should be checked periodically.
- Oil-lubricated lip seals are supplied by a small header tank of oil, which needs to be kept topped up. If this runs dry the seal will heat up and fail.
- Correct installation is vital so it would be advisable to have this done professionally to avoid any leakage.

The only maintenance required is as follows:

- Lip seals should be greased with manufacturer's recommended waterproof grease every 200 hours of operation or once a year.
- Replacement of the seals is usually advised every five years or after 500 hours of operation.

- As with face seals, lip seals need to have any trapped air removed from them after launching. This is done by squeezing the sleeve and pushing it back towards the stern.

CUTLESS BEARING

Just before a propeller shaft meets the propeller it passes through a bearing known as the cutless bearing, which supports the shaft and helps it rotate smoothly.

Cutless bearings are tube-shaped and typically made from bronze, marine-grade brass or stainless steel and are lined with nitrile rubber. The rubber is grooved where it meets the propeller shaft to enable water to pass through the grooves in order to lubricate the bearing. The bearing is usually located in a strut or bracket suspended from the hull or in traditional deep-keeled vessels may be enclosed in the deadwood part of the stern through which the propeller shaft passes.

Cutless bearings can last for many years, but if the propeller shaft is out of alignment they will wear through more quickly. If you have noticed a clunking sound when motoring, it could be a worn cutless bearing that is causing the problem. With the boat out of the water it is a good opportunity to check:

- Try moving the propeller shaft or propeller itself from side to side and up and down.
- There should be a very small amount of movement, about 2mm, to allow the propeller shaft to be able to rotate inside the bearing.
- If the shaft moves more than 3mm this indicates either that the cutless bearing is worn, or possibly that the propeller shaft and cutless bearing are both worn, which is a more complex problem. Either way, further inspection is required.
- The condition of the cutless bearing can provide a clue to the exact problem. If the bearing is worn unevenly, on one side only for example, this indicates the shaft is likely to be out of alignment. You can only check this by removing the shaft.
- A worn cutless bearing can be relatively easy to replace, but if in doubt it will be a good idea to ask your boatyard's advice to help ascertain exactly what the problem is.

While on some boats the procedure for replacing a cutless bearing is relatively straightforward, on others it involves specialist tools and several pairs of hands to do what amounts to a lot of hard work – followed by a trip to the chiropractor. Being aware of what is involved will be of benefit before deciding on your best course of action.

STEP-BY-STEP

REPLACING THE CUTLESS BEARING

The typical procedure for the replacement of a cutless bearing is as follows, noting that the first big challenge is to get the old cutless bearing out:

1. Remove the propeller.

2. Remove the propeller shaft (necessary in most cases).

3. Remove the stern gland (sometimes necessary).

4. If the cutless bearing is embedded in a strut or bracket, it should be held in place by some locking screws either side of the strut. These need to be located and removed.

5. Old cutless bearings can be very hard to remove as when installed they have to be a very tight fit. There are several ways to remove them: a bearing puller tool can be used, in some cases without having to remove the propeller shaft, so a good option if you can get hold of one. Another method is to use a section of tubing with an inside diameter equal to the shaft, which is then hammered to force the old bearing out. Caution is required to avoid damaging the bracket. Alternatively, cut lengthways into the old bearing using a hacksaw, taking great care not to cut through the bearing into the bracket itself. The old bearing can then be prised inwards but

Cutless or cutlass? TiP

The name cutless is derived from the 'cut-less' design of these bearings which enables small particles to pass through grooves in the bearing without cutting or wearing the rubber surface. Not to be confused with a 'cutlass' sword which has zero association with the design.

will usually still need knocking through with considerable force and skill to prevent damaging the bracket.

6. Once the old bearing is finally removed the bracket or shaft opening needs to be cleaned up and checked for condition – any damage or corrosion will need to be dealt with. Also clean and polish the shaft using fine-grade wet and dry paper.

7. Meanwhile, the replacement bearing will need to be ordered with highly precise measurements and specification given for length, outer diameter and inner diameter. Given an option, it will always be worth going for high quality here as you want the next bearing to last as long as possible.

8. The last part of the process is to refit the new bearing. This should be a very tight fit but not so tight that it might be damaged

▲ *Top* To check the cutless bearing for wear, move the shaft up and down and from side to side. If there is more than 2mm of play, it will need replacing.
Bottom A vernier gauge is very useful if you need to measure the diameter of a propeller shaft when replacing a cutless bearing.

by being forced into place with a mallet. Professionals sometimes leave the new bearing in a fridge for a few days to contract the metal a fraction to help it slide into place.

9. With the bearing in place, the locking screws are inserted and the propeller shaft and propeller reattached. Remember that aligning the propeller shaft itself is a skilled procedure.

SALIDRIVE MAINTENANCE

There are less maintenance tasks to carry out on a saildrive transmission than on a traditional inboard shaft drive system with its associated stern gear. For example, you don't have to worry about engine alignment, cutless bearings and stern glands. I owned a boat for seven years that had a saildrive transmission system and this caused no problems during my ownership. However, there are a few critical things that require maintenance. These are as recommended in detail by the engine manufacturers and should be adhered to.

Corrosion

- Drive leg housings are made from aluminium and they must therefore be well protected from corrosion, requiring a special copper-

free antifouling paint, plus undercoats. The housings also need dedicated sacrificial zinc anodes to prevent them from galvanic corrosion.
- Carefully inspect the drive leg for any damage to the paintwork. Any exposed aluminium will quickly corrode in salt water. Look for any white corrosion beginning to form on places where paint may have been chipped off. If any such damage is found, it will need to be ground back before the unit becomes seriously damaged.
- Anodes are designed to protect saildrives from electric currents generated while in sea water.
- The electrical system of the engine will need to be an isolated system, not one that is grounded to the battery negative.
- When a non-aluminium propeller is fitted, additional anodes are required.

Oil change

- Regular checks of saildrive transmission oil are important. Any signs of milky-coloured oil indicate water has found its way into the system. This could occur because of a shaft seal failure or defective drain plug seal.
- Manufacturers usually recommend that the transmission oil is changed annually, which can only be done ashore by draining the oil from the base of the leg. On some systems the oil can be

removed using a hand pump operated from the engine bay. In order for the oil to drain completely, remove the filler cap on top to allow air in.
- Always use the manufacturer's recommended oil and be careful not to overfill the system.
- Be aware that some manufacturers recommend a torque setting for the oil drain plug and advise that the seal is replaced regularly, because if there is the smallest crack in the rubber seal it will leak.

Rubber seal

- The saildrive leg passes through a thick rubber seal that attaches to the base of the hull. These seals usually last for seven years or so and replacing them is a fairly major job as it entails lifting the engine. Clearly this has to be done ashore. The part itself is pricey, but significant additional cost needs to be factored in for the engine lift and labour involved.

OUTDRIVES/STERNDRIVES

Sterndrives are a popular form of propulsion in the powerboat market. While popular, they do require a fair amount of maintenance. Aside from the inboard engines that drive them, their care and maintenance can keep a DIY boater very busy.

The main factors to be aware of are salt-water corrosion, lubrication and regular inspection of the bellows, the condition of which is vital to prevent water from entering into the hull.

▲ A Volvo Penta saildrive. The three holes on the leg are used for raw water intake.

Stern gear • 173

▲ A sterndrive ready for painting.

Surveyor's sterndrive tips (TiP)

As a rough guide, the bellows on your sterndrives should be replaced every two years. Some manufacturers will state that their bellows will last for longer than this. However, I feel that it is best to err on the side of caution and replace them every two years. At a minimum, properly inspect the bellows yearly for any signs of damage or cracking.

Bellows inspection

There are three types of bellows – for the exhaust, drive shaft and gear cables – and they all need careful inspection with the boat out of the water:

- Some bellows can be partially covered up by protective caps or steering helmets and these will need to be removed to make a proper inspection.
- Check for signs of cracking in the rubber. If the rubber is becoming brittle it is time to replace the bellows.
- Look out for any marine growth and remove any barnacles, which are very sharp and can easily damage the rubber.
- Check the condition of the stainless steel clamps.
- Check inside the hull for any signs of water ingress.
- Check for any damage that may have been caused by fishing line wrapped around the propeller. This will entail removing the propeller. (See **Propellers on saildrives and sterndrives** on page 179).
- Replace bellows if there are any signs of damage.

Corrosion inspection

Sterndrives, like saildrives, have aluminium housings and these remain in the water when the boat is afloat. This means that if they are used in salt water they must be protected from galvanic corrosion by sacrificial zinc anodes and well-maintained paint layers:

- Check the owner's manual for the location of all anodes.

▲ Sterndrives need regular maintenance to protect them from galvanic corrosion.

- Check the condition of the sacrificial anodes and replace them when they are 50 per cent wasted. If unsure how much 50 per cent is, buy spares so you can double-check.
- Remember never to paint anodes with antifouling as their surfaces must be in direct contact with water to be effective.
- Carefully check the condition of the painted surfaces of the sterndrive before applying any antifouling. If any repainting is necessary, this must be done first (see **Painting a sterndrive** below).
- Make sure the whole sterndrive is free of any standard antifouling bottom paint that may be used for the rest of the hull below the waterline.
- Apply copper-free antifouling paint suitable for aluminium outdrives as recommended by your sterndrive manufacturer. These paints should contain copper thiocyanate rather than copper oxide.

Painting a sterndrive

The key to all boat painting and varnishing work is to prepare the surfaces thoroughly. Anything less than this will result in wasted effort and frustration when the job has to be done again. Sterndrive surfaces are fiddly and uneven, so sanding back is best done by hand – a good supply of 80-, 120- and 240-grit aluminium oxide wet and dry paper and a wire brush will be needed. These are the steps involved:

Surveyor's anode tips

- It is always a good idea to check the electrical continuity between the anode you have fitted and the items that you are trying to protect. This can be done with relative ease, by setting a multimeter to its 'continuity' setting and touching one lead firmly to the anode and the other lead firmly against the stern gear you are trying to protect. You may have to scratch away at the anode and stern gear to make sure that both leads are touching good metal.

- If you are switching a vessel from fresh water to salt water (or vice versa), it is worth checking if the anodes you currently have fitted are correct for the type of water your vessel will be moving to. Magnesium anodes tend to perform better in fresh water, whereas zinc anodes tend to perform better in salt water. You might have to ask local suppliers for the best option if your boat is moored in brackish water.

Step 1

When the boat is hauled out, ask the yard to give the sterndrive a thorough pressure wash. Before doing any sanding, make sure that all barnacles are removed. Use a plastic scraper for this if needed.

Step 2

If the paintwork is in good condition and there is no sign of underlying corrosion, wet sand using 120-grit paper to provide a key for new topcoat.

Step 3

If there is any loose or flaking paint or any sign of bubbling, this must be removed. Use 80-grit wet and dry paper for this, removing all signs of aluminium oxide in the process. A wire brush may be needed on badly pitted surfaces.

Step 4

Rinse thoroughly with fresh water – a high-pressure hose is best. Wipe dry with an old towel.

Step 5

Apply an etch primer. This paint is designed to bond itself to the substrate and contains acid so the use of rubber gloves and protective gear is essential.

Step 6

Apply two coats of antifouling primer. Allow to cure and dry between coats according to the paint manufacturer's instructions.

Step 7

Lightly sand back any paint drips or imperfections using 240- or 400-grit paper.

Step 8

Apply two coats of antifouling paint.

Lubrication and other checks

- Check the condition of the cabling.
- Check the hydraulic hoses for steering and trim, making sure they are not cracked and their connections are all in good condition.
- Check hydraulic system fluid levels and if necessary trace and repair any leaks.
- Check gearbox oil condition. If this is milky in colour, then this indicates a seal has failed, allowing water ingress. The shaft seals will need to be replaced.
- Check and grease all grease points off the drive as recommended in the sterndrive instruction manual.

Sterndrive propellers

- See **Propellers on saildrives and sterndrives** on page 179.

PROPELLERS

Have a look around any boatyard and you will notice quite a variety of propellers – some have two blades, some have three and others have four or more. While most propellers are completely rigid, some have blades that fold. Propellers can

▲ Three-bladed propellers are normally used for powerboats and sometimes on large cruising sailboats.

be right-handed, where they turn clockwise as they move forward, or left-handed where they turn anticlockwise. All these variations come about because different types of propeller are suited to different types of boats, engines and transmissions.

How a propeller works

The scientific theory behind how a propeller works is quite complex and if you are contemplating buying a replacement propeller for your boat, it would be advisable to read up about propeller theory and hydrodynamics in some detail – what follows here are just a few basics.

◄ To measure the diameter of a propeller, measure the distance from A to B and double the result. The pitch of a propeller is the distance the prop would move forward in one complete rotation.

Diameter

Pitch

A ship's propeller is often referred to as a 'screw', but since water is a liquid rather than a solid this analogy is a little misleading as a propeller can also be described as a type of foil or pump, which are nothing like a screw.

A propeller works by converting torque (a force that causes something to rotate) into thrust. A turning propeller moves water downwards and behind the blades, in other words an action that produces a thrust of water from the blades. Each blade has a distinctive curved shape which as it turns helps to move the water down and behind it, acting like a foil in the process and then pumping the water out behind. It acts like a foil because the angle of the blade creates lift as it moves through the water, in a similar way to how a wing creates lift through the air, with a positive pressure, or pushing, on the underside and a negative pressure, or pulling effect, on the top side. This accounts for why a propeller blade is also twisted – its shape helps it create lift.

Going back to the screw analogy, if a propeller was screwing its way through a piece of wood, the distance it would move in one revolution is equivalent to the propeller's pitch, for example 20cm. The diameter or width of the propeller might be 40cm. Diameter and pitch are the two key dimensions given to describe a propeller and are usually marked on the hub of a propeller, for example in this case 40 × 20.

Two other factors to be aware of are 'advance' and 'slip'.

Advance refers to the actual distance a propeller moves through one rotation and slip refers to the difference between the pitch and the advance.

Number of blades and folding props

Why the different number of blades? What about props that fold? The quick answers are as follows:

- Two-blade propellers are the best option for sailing boats under 10m in length, giving adequate performance under power and causing less drag through the water when under sail.
- Three-blade propellers give greater thrust than two blades but increase drag. Three-blade props are more commonly used for powerboats, but some larger sailing boats use them. Three blades usually give a slightly better top-speed performance than four blades.
- Four-blade propellers tend to be quieter and vibration-free.

They produce more lift at the stern, which can help with acceleration.
- Folding or feathering props are designed for sailing boats and minimise drag when the boat is under sail. These are very effective but a lot more expensive than standard propellers.
- Boat type, engine power, displacement and desired boat speed are all factored in when choosing the exact type and specification of propeller.

Propeller care and maintenance

Given that the shape of a propeller is so critical to a boat's performance, fuel consumption and ride, it makes sense to keep your propeller in good working order. Propellers are complicated and repairs should be done by specialists, but owners can carry out checks and some routine maintenance themselves when the boat is in the boatyard.

▲ Replacing a shaft anode.

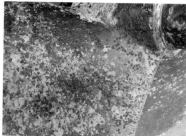

Regular maintenance is the key to preventing propeller corrosion. Change anodes when they are less than 50 per cent wasted. Prop anodes will corrode more rapidly when the boat is in use. Regular cleaning is also advisable.

Here are some checks and maintenance jobs:

- Clean the propeller thoroughly, removing all marine growth. Using a plastic scraper to remove barnacles is preferable to a metal one to avoid scratching the blade surface. I find mixing up a paste using white vinegar, flour and salt works well. Apply the paste to the surface and leave it for about 15 minutes. Then rinse with warm water and polish, being prepared to use plenty of elbow grease. Use superfine wire wool to help things along if absolutely necessary, but whatever you do, don't use a grinder.
- Grease the propeller as recommended by the manufacturer's instructions. Note that folding and feathering propellers need to be greased and the manufacturers provide advice and a kit for doing this.

- Check the surface of the blades for any dents, scratches or nicks, paying particular attention to the blade tips.
- Check for any hairline cracks in stainless steel blades, especially around the edges. These can be repaired for much less than the cost of a new propeller, but if ignored the propeller will soon deteriorate to the point that it will have to be replaced.
- Minor nicks and scratches can be filed smooth, but take care not to grind too much as you could easily alter the blade

geometry. Filing the nicks smooth will be worthwhile as the smallest of imperfections will affect performance.
- Check the propeller and prop shaft stern bearing for signs of fishing line caught around it, which can easily damage shaft seals. This may require removing the propeller to carry out the check.
- Check the condition of the propeller sacrificial anode if fitted and replace according to manufacturer's recommendations – it is normal practice to replace an

anode when half of it has been wasted away. Anodes do an essential job protecting bronze or aluminium propellers from galvanic interaction with stainless steel propeller shafts. A missing or badly wasted anode will result in very rapid corrosion of the propeller as soon as it is back in the water. Make sure you clean the contact point between the anode and the propeller shaft before replacing it.

- Check for areas of pitting in the blades of faster boats that can be caused by cavitation. Cavitation is a highly complex phenomenon that causes bubbles to form on the back of a propeller blade due to the negative pressure created when a propeller spins at high speeds. Over time these

▲ Standard antifouling is not recommended for most propellers. If in doubt check with the manufacturer.

bubbles hammer away at the blade and can cause pitting damage, which leads to vibration. Ask an expert's opinion on the best course of action to repair the blade and whether they think cavitation is the cause.

- If a blade has been bent out of shape or chunks of metal are missing this will not only affect performance but also cause vibration, risking damage to struts, bearings, seals and drive shafts. The solution is to remove the propeller and ask your yard to recommend a specialist who can repair it for you. They will have the right equipment to get the propeller back into the correct shape – if it is repairable. Trying to hammer it back into shape yourself is clearly not an option.

Vibration
There are quite a few possible causes of vibration in addition to propeller blades being out of shape and cavitation, as outlined in the checks above. Vibration from the engine and drive system is not good news (see **Excessive engine vibration** on page 164) and several other checks can be done at the same time as checking the propeller if vibration has been an issue:

- Check the integrity of the bracket or strut supporting the propeller shaft and propeller. If this is at all loose it should be looked into.
- The propeller shaft may be worn or slightly bent, so check this over carefully for

any signs of wobble when turning it.
- The engine and shaft may be misaligned – it will probably be best to have this checked over by an engineer, unless you have the skills to do this yourself.

Removing a propeller
Some propellers can be removed fairly easily, which can help with maintenance, while others will be more stubborn and require some specialist tools and an extra pair of hands to assist. The basic steps are as follows:

FIXED-BLADE PROPELLER ON A SHAFT DRIVE
1. Remove the split pin from the prop nut.

2. To stop the propeller from rotating as you undo the prop nut, use a large wooden block to hold the propeller in position.

3. Loosen the prop nut with a large wrench with plenty of leverage.

4. The next step sounds easy enough – now slide off the propeller. If it refuses to budge some extra persuasion using a well-aimed mallet can work, but proceed carefully. A better solution is to borrow a propeller puller tool which can be controlled and is less likely to damage anything.

5. With the propeller off, remove the key from its slot in the shaft. This may need some gentle hammering and chiselling to prise it free.

FOLDING/FEATHERING PROPELLERS ON A SHAFT DRIVE
These are more complex than fixed-blade propellers. For example, Darglow's Max-Prop 3 Blade Classic should be removed as follows:

1. It is very important to put the propeller blades in the feathered position (sailing position). Mark the position of the outer hub in relation to the inner hub with a marker pen or similar.

2. Remove the anode.

3. Remove the securing split pins on the end cap and the outer hub. Remove the six screws which hold the end cap in place.

4. Remove the end cap with the blades and the spacer still in place. Keep the end cap, spacer and blades away from any dust/dirt, etc.

5. Ensure that the marker line you made has not moved during this process.

6. The central bevel gear of the prop will now be exposed at the end of the shaft.

7. Carefully look out for a blind drill hole within the surface of the outer hub directly below the bevel gear. The hole will be adjacent to one of the splines of the bevel gear. Note down the letter shown at the top of the spline. This is the 'Y' mark.

8. Now undo the bolts and remove the two halves of the outer hub.

9. Around the base of the central bevel gear, you will find a spot mark. Note down the letter shown on the inner hub that is adjacent to the spline with the spot mark. This is the 'X' mark.

10. Next remove the central gear. There will also be a small cut out on the base of the cone gear on this marked tooth.

11. The propeller nut can then be unscrewed after the two holding pins (new props)/locking pin (older props) have been removed.

12. The inner hub can now be removed from the shaft using a propeller puller.

Propellers on saildrives and sterndrives

Saildrive and sterndrive propellers are mounted on splined shafts. The method for removal will vary according to the type of blade fitted and locking systems used, but essentially follow the same procedures as the shaft drive systems outlined under **Propeller care and maintenance** on page 176. It will be best to refer to the manufacturer's manual for detailed instructions on how to get access to locking devices and securing nuts.

As for the maintenance of saildrive and sterndrive propellers, likewise, follow the recommendations above, first checking them for damage and then greasing the shaft according to manufacturer's instructions.

With the propeller off, check for fishing line that may

▲ A Darglow FeatherStream folding propeller with a new anode attached. Darglow advise that only specialist antifouling products that are safe to use with bronze propellers should be applied.

be caught around the prop, inspecting the seal in front of the prop for signs of damage.

OVERHAULING AN ENGINE

It is easy to be lulled into a false sense of security with a boat engine. You might assume that if you dutifully change the oil, replace the filters, impellers, anodes and the alternator belt according to the engine manufacturer's recommendations, the well-maintained engine will last for thousands of hours and go on for ever.

My boatyard manager, Tim, says on this subject:

▲ A badly corroded engine mount.

Marine engineers will often tell you that diesel boat engines hardly ever wear out through mechanical failure, but they are prone to long-term salt-water corrosion and cooling problems. It is these factors that are most often the cause of their eventual demise. The salt-water environment attacks engines without mercy, especially those that are raw-water-cooled. One of the most critical parts of the engine that receives constant punishment is the heat exchanger. It is part of boating folklore that heat exchangers are often neglected, which leads to engines overheating and blown head gaskets, cracked heads and complete engine failure.

With corrosion and cooling problems in mind, it can help to prolong the life of an ageing engine if it is lifted out and overhauled ashore in the comfort of a home workshop. This doesn't necessarily mean doing a complete rebuild, so those of us with limited marine engineering skills can consider doing most of the work ourselves and asking marine engineers to do the more highly skilled work that requires specialist knowledge.

PRIOR TO ENGINE LIFT OUT

Most boatyards have plenty of experience with lifting engines and the process is not as daunting as you might imagine. However, there are a number of things that need to be done prior to the engine lift out:

- **Fuel supply:** Shut off the fuel supply to the engine and drain the fuel lines and fuel filters into suitable containers. Then disconnect the fuel lines.
- **Wiring:** Unplug the engine wiring harness. It is common

to have a plug with two halves into which numerous pins or connectors are pushed together. Prising these apart without damaging them can be difficult, especially if there is any corrosion. Also disconnect the positive and negative wiring cables from the battery.

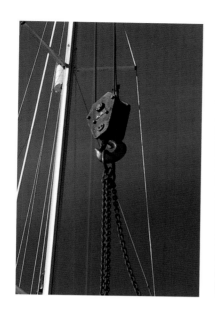

Lifting the engine: tips TiP

Most boatyards have had plenty of experience with lifting engines. They will advise what needs to be done and whether or not you are likely to have problems lifting your engine through the main hatch.

- Don't book the boatyard crane until you are sure the engine is ready for lifting. Unbolting corroded nuts and bolts can delay proceedings.

- Apply penetrating oil to all the nuts and bolts a couple of days beforehand to make the task easier.

- Give serious consideration to replacing the engine wiring if lifting an engine out for an overhaul. I didn't and regretted not doing so.

- **Cooling system:** Drain the cooling system and disconnect the raw-water inlet and calorifier system pipes if fitted.
- **Exhaust:** Unbolt the exhaust pipe and remove the hose connecting the heat exchanger with the injection bend where fitted.
- **Gearbox couplings:** Unbolt the gearbox coupling to the propeller shaft. There are usually half a dozen or so bolts in place. Try to prevent them from dropping out of reach into the bilge (if this happens a magnet on a stick is a good way to retrieve them).
- **Engine mounts:** Unbolt the engine mounts. Doing this sounds simple enough, but access to the mounts and shifting the bolts can be quite a challenge in a cramped engine bay. If penetrating oil and elbow grease doesn't work,

drilling through the nuts is sometimes the only option.
- **Alternator:** It is wise to remove the alternator if it is protruding in order to enable the engine block to fit through the hatch.

LIFTING THE ENGINE
Lifting an engine can be very straightforward or quite challenging, depending on the size of the engine and the boat it is being removed from. Having ascertained how and whether the engine is going to fit through the hatch, it is worth finding out how heavy it is before you attempt the lift. Could two people lift it or will it take four? Will you need a chain hoist to lift it out of the hatch? Could you use the boom and mainsheet block and tackle instead? The Beta 14 engine in the photos overleaf weighs 90kg and can be moved relatively

easily by two people, but a larger engine such as the Beta 30 weighs 140kg and is therefore a lot more awkward. Time for some calculations.

ENGINE MOUNTS
With the engine lifted out, replacing the engine mounts is a straightforward enough task that most boatowners can manage themselves, provided the old bolts can be removed and have not completely rusted up. Damaged or broken engine mounts will cause excessive engine vibration, which in turn shakes everything else up and generally makes for an unpleasant experience all round, both for boat and crew.

Realignment of the engine and gearbox on its new mounts with the prop shaft is a more delicate operation that will call for precise adjustments later on.

Step 1

The Beta 14 engine is ready for lifting out. The alternator has been removed, the engine mounts are unbolted, hoses and wires have been disconnected and the engine can now be moved forward before being lifted vertically out of the hatch.

Step 2

The engine only just fits through the hatch. The boat's mainsheet block and tackle is being used to lift the engine out.

Step 3

The badly corroded heat exchanger and header tank needs to be repaired or replaced. In the end, this one was sent to an engineering workshop for repair. The heat exchanger tube stack was descaled and new bronze end caps fitted.

Step 4

The engine is halfway through being stripped back. New engine mounts, hoses and other parts have been ordered from the engine manufacturers. With the engine out of the boat the decision is taken to replace the diesel injectors.

Step 5

Stripping back the old paint and removing all the corrosion is a laborious process. Several coats of engine primer are applied.

Step 6

After the respray is completed, new hoses, belts, bolts and filters are fitted and the engine is now ready to be lifted back into the boat.

Step 7

The engine bay has been repainted and new engine mounts are in place.

Step 8

The boatyard crane has been booked to lift the reconditioned engine back in.

Step 9

The engine is now in the hands of the boatyard team and is lifted up by the crane.

Step 10

Still attached to the crane, the engine is carefully manoeuvred through the hatch.

Step 11

Later the same day, the engine is back in place. All the electrics, hoses, fuel lines and cables are now reattached and all the connections are checked. Finally, the only thing left to do is bleed the fuel system and see if the engine starts. Thankfully, it did.

All boatowners should have a basic knowledge of electrics, both to avoid encountering electrical problems at sea and to stand a chance of solving them should they occur.

It goes without saying that the marine environment is bad news for electric systems and all their components, so maintaining them in good order is one boating essential that should not be overlooked.

Each and every boat has a unique combination of electronics, equipment, batteries and means of generating power. There is no one instruction manual that will talk you through your boat's specific set-up. So, in order to make sense of your specific boat's electrical system,

you need to have a reasonable grasp of how electrics work, especially with regards to boats. Understanding the basics means knowing about current, voltage, resistance and power.

While minor electrical repairs and updates can be carried out when a boat is afloat, major electrical installation work and rewiring are best done when the boat is ashore. Undertaking a major job such as a complete rewire is a time-consuming operation and does require more than a grasp of the basics. Unless

you are confident you have the necessary skills it is best done by a qualified marine electrician or with the help of someone with advanced skills and experience of boat electrics, as has been my experience (thank you Mark!). It also calls for careful planning, problem-solving skills, plenty of patience, dexterity and good eyesight. Being a contortionist can help as well.

As with most boatyard jobs, time spent researching, planning, sourcing parts and having the right tools will pay dividends later on.

BASIC ELECTRICS

Many first-time boatowners have little knowledge and practical experience of electrics, sometimes little more than knowing how to wire a plug, change a fuse or reset a trip switch. So boat electrics can be a little daunting at first, depending on the type and age of the boat, but the good news is that getting started is not that challenging.

The three basic concepts to get your head around are: current (I), voltage (V) and resistance (R).

▲ Key principles are easy enough to grasp, even for the non-technically minded.

Understanding what each means is key to understanding how electricity works:

- **Current:** Electric current is the flow of electrons. The number of electrons flowing through a wire per second is measured in amps (A). When used in a formula the abbreviation (I) is used.
- **Voltage:** Voltage is the force that pushes the current through a wire – it makes the current move. It is measured in volts (V).
- **Resistance:** Electrical resistance is the opposition or obstruction to the flow of an electric current. It is measured in ohms (Ω).

Voltage, current and resistance are closely related to one another and this relationship is known as Ohm's Law where:

- **Current (I)** through a wire can be calculated by dividing the voltage (V) by the resistance (Ω): $I = V/R$.
- **Voltage (V)** through a wire can be calculated by multiplying the current (I) by the resistance (Ω): $V = I \times R$
- **Resistance (Ω)** can be calculated by dividing the voltage (V) by the current (I): $R = V/I$.

There is a fourth basic concept that needs introducing here:

- **Power:** Electrical power is measured in watts (W) and refers to the rate of energy consumed by a component or appliance. For example, in a domestic household a 2500W

electric heater consumes electricity at a far higher rate than a 25W light bulb – 100 times as much. **Power (W)** can be calculated by multiplying the voltage (V) by the current (I): $W = V \times I$.

ESSENTIAL BOAT ELECTRICS

Small yachts and powerboats have 12V DC (direct current) systems, although larger vessels will have 24V electrics. In most cases, the system is split into two parts, one for starting the engine, the other for running all the other electrical equipment on board. There are usually two batteries (or banks of batteries) to ensure there's always a well-charged battery for starting the engine that's never used for anything else. In some cases, there will also be a third system, with another dedicated battery (or bank of batteries) for powering high-current equipment such as electric windlasses, bow thrusters and electric winches.

AC SYSTEMS

Larger boats often have an alternating current (AC) generator to power domestic electrics. The generator can also charge the DC batteries instead of using the main engine.

The more common type of AC system relies on connecting to shore power when the boat is docked. This can be used to run domestic appliances and to charge the batteries. Note that AC and DC systems must be kept separate.

ELECTRICS INSPECTION CHECKLIST

With the boat ashore, here are some recommendations for carrying out a boatowner electrics inspection. Safety is always paramount so remember to do the checks with the batteries off. Wearing a head torch helps. Make notes as you go and only tackle a repair if you are 100 per cent sure you know what you are doing.

WIRING CHECKS

- **Labelling:** The idea of labelling where each wire connects to and from may sound time-consuming but will pay dividends when you or your electrician need to source a component's wiring in a hurry. Being organised here will really be of help and save you money in the long run.
- **Wiring diagram:** Refer to your boat's wiring diagram as you carry out the inspection. If you don't have a schematic of all the boat's equipment and wiring plan, it would be a good idea to sketch one out. This will also be invaluable when troubleshooting faults.
- **Chafing:** Check the condition of the wiring for any signs of chafing, or exposed wires. This can be caused by vibration of wires that are not properly secured rubbing against things or where wires pass through bulkheads. This happens when wire are not properly protected by conduit and suitable grommets or have come into

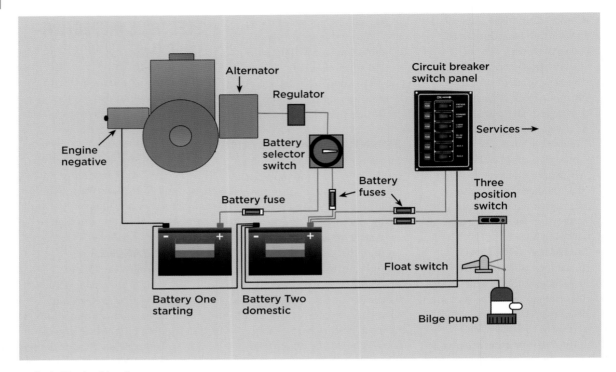

▲ Basic 12 volt wiring diagram.

contact with sharp objects. At very worst, protect with electrical tape, but exposed wiring should be replaced with new marine-grade wire as soon as possible. At the same time you will need to fit suitable conduit, grommets or padding.

- **Melted wires:** Wires that overheat are a serious fire risk and need to be sorted out as a priority. Look for signs of melted wiring insulation, caused either by overloaded wires becoming very hot or from being in contact with a hot engine. Ensuring wires don't come into contact with hot engines is easy enough to fix. However, wires that overheat need some

troubleshooting to determine the cause. This might entail replacing with thicker wire to suit the power draw of the components they connect to and/or protecting with more appropriate fuses (see below). If in any doubt this is the time to call in professional help.

- **Fuses and circuit breakers:** Fuses need to be rated lower than the wires they are protecting and lower than the components they connect to. Check all wires are protected by a fuse or circuit breaker.

- **Connections:** Check the wiring for weak connections, tighten or replace any that are loose and check for corrosion. Poor connections that are not

▲ If an instrument fails, the first thing to do is check if the wiring to the unit is loose.

properly installed or corroded are also fire hazards. Do not use electrical tape to repair a connection.

BATTERY CHECKS

- **Battery connections:** Check the condition of the battery connections. Check for tightness. Clean and coat with petroleum jelly.
- **Battery straps:** Check the batteries have remained secure and the retaining straps are in good condition and have not become weakened.
- **Battery top-up:** Unless they are maintenance-free type, check battery levels and top up with distilled water if necessary.
- **Battery condition:** Test batteries to confirm capacity. Check batteries are kept clean and dry. If the boat is ashore over the winter, consider taking the batteries home for storage as they will last longer. I have done this for the past seven years with my current batteries and they are still in good condition.

ALTERNATOR CHECKS

See page 192.

EQUIPMENT CHECKS

Navigation lights

- Check all navigation lights are working correctly. Make a note of any bulbs that need replacing. The most likely causes of a bulb failure are either that it is blown or that the contacts have become corroded.
- Masthead lights can suffer from voltage drop as there is a long cable run from the battery to the top of the mast and resistance in the wire can

become excessive. Consider replacing with thicker wire if this is the case.
- Corrosion of the bulb contacts and connections need to be checked and cleaned up first, using fine emery paper.
- Check that deck connectors are in good condition.
- Check that lens seals are in good condition and are not allowing ingress of water into the light.

Exterior bulbs

- Clean exterior bulb contact points, including deck lights.
- Spray with anti-corrosion spray.

Interior lights

- Check all interior lights are working.
- Make a note of any bulbs that need replacing.

Bilge pumps

- Check the float switch and manual override switch of the bilge pumps are working correctly.
- If not, check the connections and fuse leading from the battery to the pump. A bilge pump is one of the few pieces of equipment that should be wired directly to a battery via its own fuse to ensure it will work if the batteries are turned off.

Instruments

- Test all the instruments are working satisfactorily and carry out any annual maintenance recommended

by the manufacturer's operator manual.
- Clean instrument screens with plasma screen cleaner.

Solar panels

- Check electrical connections are in good order and secure.

BATTERIES

An automotive-type battery, of a similar specification to those used in cars, can be used to supply the starter motor with the very high loads for the few seconds it takes to start the engine. This type of battery, however, is not suitable for powering the boat's other systems, which will typically draw a relatively small amount of power for many hours, or even days, at a stretch.

▲ Good maintenance helps to prolong battery life.

▲ Keep battery terminals free of corrosion and clean to avoid loss of power.

▲ A well-secured battery bank in a purpose-built battery box.

Deep-discharge (or traction) batteries are designed for slow discharge over a period of time, before being recharged when the engine is running or via shore-power chargers, or solar or wind generators. This type of use would quickly destroy an automotive battery, but a good leisure battery will withstand several hundred such cycles.

There are various grades of such battery – the cheaper ones are not sealed and will need topping up with distilled water from time to time and are likely to have a shorter life span than more expensive models. Gel- and AGM-type batteries cannot spill battery acid and don't produce potentially explosive hydrogen gas when charging. They can withstand many more charge/discharge cycles than conventional deep-discharge batteries and so have many advantages for use on boats, despite their higher

initial purchase price. Some are also capable of being used for both starting and deep-cycling applications.

All batteries lose some of their charge over time. When storing them over the winter, ensure they are fully charged at the start of the storage period and, if possible, charge once a month to maintain the charge

Strategic reserve

Some boatowners always keep a fully charged reserve battery for engine starting.

level. Modern three-stage and four-stage mains-powered chargers may be left connected permanently.

Examples of power usage	
Navigation light	1A (boats up to 12m)
Navigation light	2.5A (boats over 12m)
Interior lights (each)	1A
LED lights (each)	0.2A
Laptop	3–6A
Instruments	1A
Chart plotter	1–2A
Stereo	1–3A
Autopilot	3–6A
Fridge	4A

DETERMINING BATTERY CAPACITY

Undersized battery banks are one of the key factors behind power failure at sea, as well as the premature failure of batteries. It's therefore worth analysing the set-up on your boat when it's ashore in the boatyard to see whether it measures up to the use you put it to.

Deep-discharge batteries are rated in Amp-hours (Ah) – a fully charged 100Ah battery, for instance, will deliver 5A for 20 hours before becoming completely discharged. However, discharging even the best deep-discharge batteries below 50 per cent of their rated capacity will dramatically shorten their life.

Calculating your estimated daily power usage, by multiplying the current in amps of each device by the length of time for which you expect to use each it, will help determine the size of the batteries needed for the boat. If you aim to charge once a day and don't plan to discharge the batteries to more than 50 per cent of their total capacity, your battery bank should in theory be at least twice the size of your estimated daily power usage.

However, even with good battery-charging technologies it becomes increasingly difficult to cram the last 20 per cent of charge into a battery. It's therefore best to size battery banks at around three times the expected daily power usage. Even then, this gives little scope for adding new power-hungry devices such as a fridge or electric autopilot.

Even with correctly sized batteries, it's important to maintain a watch over the battery state throughout a voyage.

CARE OF BATTERIES

Having decided on an optimally sized battery, it must also be kept properly charged, which means never allowing the batteries to discharge below 50 per cent of their total charge.

Optimising charging systems will also help to keep batteries topped up to a higher level of charge. The output of standard alternators can drop to as little as one-third of the alternator's rated output after only 15 minutes or so of engine running. However, a smart charging regulator will keep the charging rate close to the initial figure, thus recharging the batteries in minimum time. This has a further advantage in that it charges batteries to as much as 95 per cent of capacity – compared with less than 80 per cent for a standard alternator regulator.

In addition to improving charging systems, minimising the power drawn from batteries will also extend their lifespan. This need not involve major inconveniences – changing to LED lighting, for instance, will significantly reduce daily current drain and costs significantly less than replacing a battery bank that prematurely runs out of puff. It's also worth ensuring the fridge has at least four inches of insulation all round. Unfortunately, many are lacking in this respect, which can put a huge strain on batteries.

AVOIDING AND IDENTIFYING ELECTRICAL PROBLEMS

The diagnosis of many boating electrical problems is within the grasp of anyone with basic knowledge of electrical systems and a few key skills.

BATTERY STATE

At a basic level, one of the most useful diagnostic tools is a simple digital voltmeter. The voltage produced by a battery, when no load is being drawn from it, is a good guide to its state of charge. When fully charged, a 12V battery can theoretically hold up to 13.2V, although in practice 12.8V or 12.9V is a more likely maximum. At 12.5V, the battery has 75 per cent of its maximum charge remaining, and at 12.2V there's 50 per cent of the battery's total capacity left – the point at which the battery should be recharged.

If the reading drops to 12.0V, there's only 20 per cent of the battery's capacity remaining, and the battery will be (almost) fully discharged at 11.8V.

A battery that's nearing the end of its life may still give reasonable voltage readings when fully charged, but only if no load is being drawn. Switching a couple of lights on will create a large voltage drop in a weak battery, whereas an example in good condition will show a drop of only 0.1 or 0.2V in these conditions.

The voltmeter can also be used to check that the alternator

is producing charge. Standard alternators have their output capped at around 14.2–14.4V, although there may be a voltage drop of 0.5V and occasionally more by the time the charge reaches the batteries. If there is little or no increase in voltage across the battery when the engine is running, then it's very likely that there's a problem with the charging system that will need further investigation.

BATTERY MONITORS

Unfortunately, it takes a long time for battery voltages to settle when load is removed, or after charging, and while a reasonably stable voltage may be seen after a few minutes, it takes several hours for the voltage to completely stabilise. This is one of the benefits of more sophisticated battery monitors that give a precise indication at any time of how much charge there is left in the batteries.

When properly calibrated, battery monitors can account for all factors that affect battery state, including calculating the total charge delivered to the batteries and subtracting the total charge used by the boat's systems. In addition to battery voltage, these monitors can display battery charge/discharge current, state of charge of the battery in amp hours (Ah) or in percentage of total capacity and time to go until the battery needs to be recharged.

Additional information available includes the average depth of discharge, depth of deepest discharge, number of charge/discharge cycles and number of occasions on which an under-voltage alarm has been triggered.

ALTERNATIVE CHARGING INPUTS

With many boats running numerous electrical devices, keeping the batteries topped up on a long passage, or during a period at anchor, can be a challenge. However, there are now many options that mean there should be no need to rely on the engine for this. In the past, wind generators were the mainstay for the power needs of many long-term cruisers and still have their fans today. However, they also have a number of drawbacks: when sailing downwind, for instance, the reduction in the apparent wind speed means their output is quite low.

The cost of solar panels has fallen rapidly and they are increasingly becoming the primary means of charging on many boats. On passage this can be supplemented by further inputs from a towed generator or from the type of hydro-generator that's increasingly common to see on long-distance racing yachts.

COMMON ELECTRICAL PROBLEMS

Most problems with marine electrical systems arise from four possible sources: a lack of maintenance, a poor standard of initial installation, insufficient battery capacity or ineffective charging systems.

Water ingress is a frequent issue – salt water can corrode contacts very quickly. If connections are not scrupulously clean – or are loose – resistance will be increased, resulting in progressively reduced power. Contacts should be cleaned with wet and dry paper until the surface is shiny. Investigate any evidence of water ingress and eliminate the source.

Also make sure you don't confuse a battery that's almost at the end of its life with one that is simply flat. The old battery may give reasonable voltage readings after charging, but these will fall rapidly when even a small load is drawn and the battery will soon be flat again.

▲ This explained why the engine did not start.

FAULT FINDING

This is essentially a case of using logic to eliminate as many potential causes of failure as possible. Occasionally a large dose of perseverance is needed to identify an obscure problem, but equally it's really easy to overlook an obvious problem, so always start with the basics.

In the case of a non-functioning navigation light, for example, the first action should be to check the fuse or circuit breaker. If not the fuse or breaker, the problem is likely to be a defective bulb, so examine the old one. If it's blown – shown by a break in the thin filaments within the glass case – it can easily be replaced.

If the bulb appears to be intact, a voltmeter can be used to measure the voltage at the contacts in the lamp unit. If there's power at the switch panel, but not at the unit, you'll need to trace the wiring and attempt to locate the break in the circuit. How easy this is to find will depend on the individual boat – some boats may have a number of joins in the wire. In any case, a boat with separate red and green pulpit lights will have a junction box somewhere near the bow, where the single supply from the distribution panel divides to take power to the two separate lamps. There will similarly be a junction somewhere for the feed to the stern light.

A meter can also be used on its resistance (Ω) setting to check whether or not a component is damaged. At the most basic

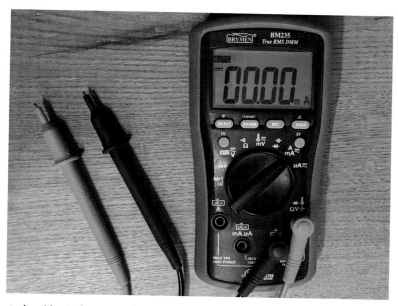

▲ A multimeter is an essential tool for circuit testing and maintenance of electrics.

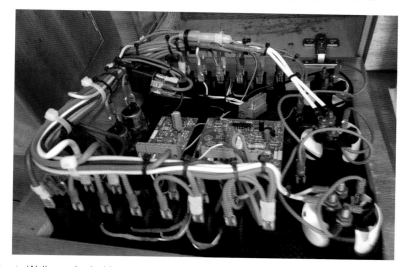

▲ Well organised wiring here all looks in good order.

level, electrical current must flow through the component in order for it to work. The resistance function of the meter passes a small current through the device being tested. If no current flows, it records infinite resistance (often shown as a figure 1 on the left-hand side of a digital meter display), telling us the component doesn't work. Note that components must be isolated from the boat's 12V supply before testing for resistance.

▲ Using a lever to hold the alternator in place while the belt is tightened.

ALTERNATORS

Most marine engines are fitted with a belt-driven alternator with an output normally ranging from 40 to 60A. The same belt often drives the fresh-water circulating pump. The condition of this belt and the alternator itself are both critical to keeping the batteries charged.

Alternators themselves need very little maintenance, but correct belt tension is important in order for the batteries to be charged properly when the engine is running.

Adjusting belt tension

Alternators normally have a support bolt and link adjust bolt. Belt tension is adjusted by loosening these two bolts. The alternator can then be swung outboard as it pivots on its support bolt. The link adjust bolt is tightened first and then the support bolt. The belt should be tightened enough so that it can be depressed by 12mm or so when pushed down by your thumb.

Worn belt

Alternator belts need to be replaced when they can no longer be tightened sufficiently. Always keep a spare, if not two.

Charging test

To test whether the alternator is charging correctly, follow these steps using the instrument panel voltmeter or a digital voltmeter connected to the battery terminals:

Step 1

Check the battery voltage without the engine running. This should read in the region of 12.5V.

Step 2

Start the engine and check the voltage at idle. It should remain the same.

Step 3

Increase engine speed to 2000rpm. The reading should now be somewhere between 13.8 and 14.4V.

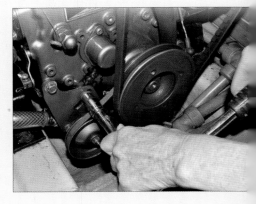

▲ A second bolt is retightened after the adjustment has been made.

Alternator problems

The electronic components of alternators can quickly burn out if the electricity they generate is not being channelled to a battery. This would happen if the battery isolator switch has been turned off, which should never be done when the engine is running.

Like all components, alternators can become worn and ineffective. This will need some troubleshooting to determine if the problem is a problem with the wiring, batteries, regulator or the alternator:

- **Batteries not charging:** If the batteries are not charging this could be either a wiring problem, battery failure, a faulty regulator or a fault in the alternator.
- **Batteries not charging enough:** This could also be a wiring problem, loose alternator belt or the alternator.
- **Batteries overcharging:** This could be a battery problem or a faulty regulator.

In my experience, having an alternator serviced and repaired professionally is the preferred option after identifying that it has a problem.

REWIRING A SMALL YACHT

When I bought my present boat, the wiring was in very poor condition. Although the 35-year-old Contessa had two nearly new batteries, the wiring itself was in a dismal state, with many exposed and corroded connections. It was also in a disorganised tangle made worse by the fact that a succession of instruments and electronics had been added, replaced or removed over the years.

I made some temporary repairs to get the nav lights working when I bought the boat but knew that the rewiring was a top priority and that this would need to be done hauled out in a boatyard.

I was in a bit of a dilemma as I had limited electrical knowledge and hiring a marine electrician to do the job was going to be costly. I needed to learn more about boat electrics. I bought a copy of Pat Manley's *Essential Boat Electrics,* which

proved very useful and helped to demystify the subject. (See **Further Reading** on page 218.) Even so, reading this book made me realise that doing the whole job by myself was going to be challenging, if not foolhardy. Luckily I have a good friend who is much more knowledgeable about electrics than me and

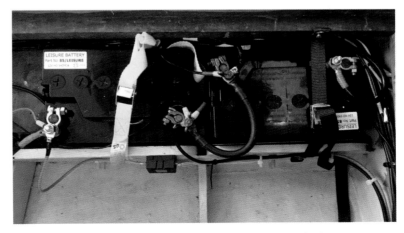

▲ We replaced all the battery wiring and added a battery fuse and voltmeter.

he very kindly helped me out, teaching me a great deal in the process. Here's how we went about the task:

1. Thorough inspection
We made a thorough inspection of the existing system, labelling each wire and checking what it was connected to. At the same time we tested connections using a multimeter, making notes as we went. There were signs of overheated wiring in places, which could have resulted in a serious fire and many of the connections were corroded. Corroded electrical connections have high resistance which causes voltage loss. It soon became clear that doing this job was an absolute necessity.

The assessment took some time, but it was worth doing as it made things much easier later on when we came to replace the wiring.

2. Drawing up a wiring diagram
We made a wiring diagram plan for the new system, showing instruments, location of new equipment, including LED lights plus a new circuit breaker switch panel, busbars, voltmeter and an inverter. The two batteries were in good condition and did not need replacing. We then calculated approximately how much cabling we would need.

3. Removing redundant wiring
Next we removed the dead and redundant wiring, filling a large bin bag in the process. This left the wiring that was still serving a purpose, to be replaced later on. Getting access to some of the wiring was a major challenge, for instance the wiring to the navigation light at the bow had been glassed in beneath the stainless steel pulpit and then threaded through it. We had to

grind the old wire out and then unbolt the pulpit in order to replace with new, which proved a major job in itself.

4. Materials needed
We made a list of all the materials we would need and then bought most of the items from UK marine electrical specialist Furneaux Riddall (see www.furneauxriddall.com). It was definitely worth making the effort and travelling to their shop in Portsmouth. They proved very helpful and are highly recommended.

We bought a 30-metre reel of 21A tinned marine-grade two-core wire, which would be used mainly for the lighting and instruments, and shorter lengths of higher capacity 50 and 70A cable for the starter and battery cables. Tinned marine-grade wire is essential as it is resistant to corrosion and vibration, which can cause chafe and damage.

Other purchases included a circuit breaker switch panel, busbars, an inverter, LED navigation lights, specialist tools, terminals, gauges and some new instruments.

With everything planned and the replacement parts purchased we ordered a Perspex instrument panel with specially cut holes for the circuit breaker, instruments and gauges to fit above the chart table.

◄ My friend Mark was a huge help and we did not need to call in the professionals.

▲ Once you have grasped the basics, replacing instruments is not too daunting.

5. Running cables

Now began the long task of running and labelling the wires and making the connections. We used a cable threader to run wires through some awkward places. Wire cables should be supported in order not to come under strain, which could pull the connections apart. We used corrugated trunking and cable ties to protect the cables.

Eventually, everything came together and after testing all the circuits and tidying up we declared the job done. It is hard to estimate exactly how long it took us as we spread the work over two or three weeks, when other commitments and the weather allowed, but I would say approximately three to four days in total. I certainly learned a lot in the process and am glad to say that the electrics have behaved well since the work was done.

Rewiring: tools and tips TiP

• Doing a rewire afloat would definitely not be advisable, as it is best to empty the boat completely to gain access to all the nooks and crannies. We did the job with the boat hauled out in a boatyard where we had access to shore power and a local chandlery.

• Aside from standard power tools, screwdrivers, spanners, saws, knives and torches, you will need specialist electrical tools, including a multimeter, wire cutters, long-nosed pliers, wire strippers, crimping tool, soldering iron and a cable threader.

• Do not skimp on the materials. Only use electrical gear designed for the marine environment. The cabling should be tinned copper multistrand wiring which is less susceptible to the corrosion, vibration and movement that a boat is subjected to at sea.

• Choosing the correct size, or grade, of wiring is important as undersized wiring is likely to overheat and will become a fire risk. To be on the safe side, it is better to fit high-grade all round.

• Remember to use colour-coded wire with red for positive and black for negative.

• Make a wiring diagram and keep notes of the work you have done. Having a record for any future updates or repairs will be very useful.

• It is definitely worth installing a circuit breaker switch panel, as these are easily reset if one of the circuits is tripped as opposed to having to replace fuses.

• Crimp-type connections are better than soldered connections, which have a tendency to break due to vibration caused by engines and a boat's motion through waves.

• It helps to make a list of all your boat's electrical equipment and the current draw of each item. You can then calculate your boat's electrical requirements over a given period of time by adding up the total number of amp hours all of the equipment will consume (see table on page 188).

• We sent the alternator away to be serviced, cleaned and tested to ensure that the batteries were charged as quickly and as efficiently as possible.

13 INTERIOR

While most interior maintenance work can be done when a boat is afloat, some jobs such as servicing the sea cocks have to be done ashore. It makes sense to do any major interior repairs and improvements with the boat hauled out in the boatyard.

A boat that is ashore for the winter should be kept as clean and dry as possible to prevent the growth of mould, which thrives in damp conditions. The more equipment, provisions and soft furnishings that can be taken off the boat and kept at home the better, which may mean lugging several car loads to and fro. This is not so easy for boatowners who live hundreds of miles from their boat but well worth doing if they are only half an hour away. Emptying the boat will make cleaning and servicing easier and is strongly advised for those planning to do any work on their boat's interior.

It helps to make a plan of what needs doing in the interior after it has been emptied, cleaned and you have been able to do a thorough inspection. You should give priority to the essential maintenance and repair work that can only be done with the boat ashore, estimating how much time this is going to take and the materials that will be required. I then tend to limit myself to one major project per winter – for example, rewiring, engine overhaul, interior painting and varnishing. It all depends on how much time, help and resources you have available.

CLEANING

It is important to get the rubber gloves on and thoroughly clean a boat's interior once it is ashore and emptied – a chore that will be certainly worth the effort. Failure to do so will inevitably result in unpleasant smells and mould developing while the boat is ashore in the boatyard.

A fresh-water clean with a mild detergent or a white vinegar and fresh-water mix will get rid of salt residues on all interior surfaces in the cabin that have been exposed to sea water. If they are left, the salt crystals will absorb moisture as the weather cools and encourage damp and mildew. These are the areas to focus on:

▲ After rewiring the boat, the following winter I spruced up the interior.

HEADS

- Cleaning the heads should be done before haul out. The cause of bad odours can come from the pipework as well as the marine toilet itself, which is why always flushing the system really well is so necessary to ensure no foul water is left standing in the pipes for long periods.
- If this was not done effectively enough when afloat then flushing a mix of white vinegar and fresh water through the system (to remove scale) works well and is also environmentally friendly – but no one is going to thank you for pumping anything through your marine toilet system when the boat is ashore unless you have a holding tank.
- Bicarbonate of soda is also good for cleaning. Alternatively, a more pricey option is to use a purpose-designed product such as Ecoworks Marine toilet cleaner. Remember not to use domestic toilet cleaners, drain cleaner or bleach as they can damage marine toilet pipework and kill aerobic bacteria, as well as harm the environment (see more on **Marine toilets** on page 203).

GALLEY

- Clean inside the galley cupboards, the cooker and the fridge or cool box.
- Check the drains of fridges and coolers are clear as bacteria can gather in them.

Environmentally friendly cleaning products — TiP

The use of non-toxic cleaning products are widely recommended for boat use. Deciding which cleaning product to use can be daunting, not helped by the fact that some are very expensive. Low-cost alternatives have been in use for generations, are readily available and won't break the bank:

- **General cleaner:** Make a cleaning paste by mixing bicarbonate of soda and white vinegar.
- **Bleach substitute:** hydrogen peroxide.
- **Scouring powder:** bicarbonate of soda.
- **Floor cleaner:** 125ml white vinegar in 5 litres of water.
- **Window cleaner:** 250ml white vinegar in 2.5 litres of warm water.
- **Varnish cleaner:** 50:50 white vinegar and water mix
- **Shower cleaner:** On a wet surface, sprinkle with bicarbonate of soda and rub with a scouring cloth.
- **Heads cleaner:** Pour in bicarbonate of soda and scrub with a brush.
- **Chrome cleaner/polish:** Use apple cider vinegar to clean and baby oil to polish.
- **Fibreglass stain remover:** Clean with bicarbonate of soda.
- **Mildew remover:** Mix a paste using equal parts of lemon juice and salt.
- **Wood polish:** Mix three parts olive oil with one part vinegar.

Source: *American Sailing Association*

BILGES

- Clean the bilges, again an unpleasant chore but well worth the effort.
- If the bilges are in a poor and smelly state because of leaking engine oil or fuel, start by mopping up with old absorbent rags and dispose of these in a waste oil bin.
- If there are persistent leaks coming from the engine, then putting a drip tray in the bilge under the engine will at least contain the oil until the leak can be fixed.
- Then use a biodegradable bilge cleaner product such as Starbrite Heavy Duty Bilge Cleaner or Bilgex. Such products are not cheap but they will save a lot of elbow grease. Rinse well with fresh water and dry.

VENTILATION

- Lift the cabin sole boards and leave cupboard doors open to encourage air circulation.

KEEPING THE INTERIOR DRY

Boat interiors that suffer from damp will benefit from having a mains-powered dehumidifier to keep the cabin dry. These are very effective if you have access to power in the boatyard. If no power is available it is worth buying some disposable dehumidifier packs which use calcium chloride crystals that absorb moisture. These last up to two months and then need replacing.

INTERIOR INSPECTION AND CHECKS

With the boat ashore, the most critical interior checks to carry out are those that concern the safety of the boat. This entails the integrity of all through-hull fittings and sea cocks, the gas system and the electrical system (see **Chapter 12**).

▲ A bronze sea cock with two stainless steel jubilee clips holding the pipe in place.

CRITICAL CHECKS

- Check all the through-hull fittings and sea cocks are sound and that there are no signs of leakage such as salt crystals around the fitting. They should all be free of corrosion. If they are in good order and the sea cocks open and close without problem a routine service is all that is required. Make a note of any that are seized or in poor condition as they will require extra work and may need replacing.
- Check the raw-water intakes are not clogged with debris.
- Check hose connections fit well and jubilee clips are in good condition. Remember that poorly fitting hose can easily come loose and potentially sink a boat.
- Check the condition of the hoses leading to and from the sea cocks. If these show signs of cracking, distortion or general deterioration, they will need to be replaced.
- Check the transducer and log skin fittings are in good condition and there are no stains around the fittings, which could be caused by a leaking seal.
- Check the gas system for leaks, following all the hoses carefully from the gas bottles to the appliances. Turn the gas on and brush the pipes and valves with soapy water – any bubbles will indicate there is a leak. Remember that gas is heavier than air and even a small gas leak can build up in the bilges and lead to a catastrophic explosion – all boats should be fitted with gas detectors for this reason.
- Check the gas detector is working.
- Check the condition of the gas regulator and replace if it shows signs of corrosion.
- Check that flexible gas hose is in date and replace if it is out of date.

OTHER INTERIOR CHECKS

Other problems that are less critical but nonetheless important to sort out are any issues with bilge pumps, plumbing, heads, leaks and more cosmetic things like paintwork, varnishing and furnishing.

- Check for leaks in the water system before draining down the system for the winter. Water leaks can be difficult to detect and may be due to a badly joined fitting or pipe.
- Check the condition of both electric and manual bilge pumps. Check float switches are working correctly and that the outlet hoses are clear of debris that could cause a blockage. An outlet hose can be cleaned by back-flushing – you cannot always rely on the strainer preventing debris getting into the outlet hose and causing a blockage. Also check manually operated bilge pumps are working and that their bellows are in good condition and don't need replacing.
- Check for leaks that may be staining woodwork, upholstery

or head linings. These may be coming from poorly sealed fittings, windows, hatches or hull–deck joints (see **Chapter 8**). You need to ascertain how serious these leaks are and if you are unable to trace what is causing them, this may be the time to ask your surveyor for advice.

- Check the condition of the bulkheads and make sure there is no delamination of veneer panels or moulding, which could be early signs of rot beginning beneath. This may not appear too serious at first sight but left unchecked could develop into a nasty problem. Make a note that this will need sorting out in due course. The issue here is that if nothing is done and the problem gets steadily worse you could be looking at a major interior rebuild, which will be both time-consuming and expensive.

PLUMBING

A boat's fresh-water system needs annual maintenance to keep it in good condition.

Some boats have far more complex systems than others, with pressurised hot and cold water, associated pumps, an accumulator, calorifier and pressure valves, all to keep a boatowner busy. On the other hand, smaller boats usually have unpressurised systems, which means they are much less complex, therefore easier to maintain, with less to go wrong.

▲ Yacht interiors can benefit from an interior varnish every few years.

Surveyor's sea cock tips

- I would always suggest that two jubilee clips are used to connect any sea cock to its corresponding pipe.

- Always check the four mounting bolts on older Blake sea cocks. If these are showing signs of corrosion, it may be worth remounting the sea cock.

- Through-hull depth and speed fittings normally have a rubber seal. These can dry out and perish if the vessel is out of the water for a long period of time. It's always worth checking these fittings for leaks as soon as the vessel is lifted back into the water.

- Flexible orange gas hose should not be used behind a gas cooker. Marine gas engineers will recommend a braided hose instead, as this is better protected from chafing and damage.

WATER SYSTEM MAINTENANCE AND TROUBLESHOOTING

Water pumps tend to be robust devices capable of operating for many years without trouble, particularly if there's a filter in the system ahead of the pump. However, they are not immune from wiring and other electrical supply problems and ultimately have a finite lifespan.

Leaks from a tank, or another part of the system, however, are more commonly found. These can be caused in a number of ways, the most obvious being a flexible tank that wears a hole due to chafe, although even stainless steel tanks have the potential to develop pinholes that can be difficult to track down.

WATER TANKS

I have to confess that I'm always a bit wary of fresh-water tanks on boats. The water is usually fine for boiling a kettle and making tea or coffee, but I like to keep bottled water aboard for drinking and have five-litre reusable water carriers for the purpose. I also have a UV Steripen for purifying water on longer trips, which is a brilliant way to disinfect water and leaves no aftertaste.

Fresh-water tanks can be made from stainless steel, fibreglass or plastic, some of which are flexible and therefore able to adapt to the shape of hull where they are installed.

Fresh-water tanks and all pipework should be cleaned annually, which involves draining down the system and then filling with a water sterilising mixture. I normally use Milton sterilising fluid, best known for sterilising baby bottles but also used by boaters. Add 30ml of fluid per 5 litres of fresh water. Leave for a couple of days, then drain the system again. Then either refill with fresh water if the boat is in use or leave the system empty until the boat is returned to the water in the spring.

Other options include adding filters to the water system such as activated carbon filters and sub-micron filters. People also use additives such as Aqua Clean or even lemon juice.

CONTAMINATED WATER SYSTEM

If a water system has become severely contaminated the time may have come to replace all the pipes and possibly the tank as well. Pipes can become contaminated with very unpleasant fungal or algal growth which can be harmful to health. Making a decision is up to the individual boatowner, but if things get that bad and the regular sterilising and system cleaning has been forgotten or has not worked, then I would choose to replace the contaminated pipes. Your boatyard manager should be able to advise on the best course of action.

SEA COCKS

Sea cocks are often awkward to get at, awkward to open and close, and often ignored. Should they fail, the results can prove disastrous as most are sited well below the waterline, so they

▲ A ball valve sea cock made of glass reinforced plastic.

cannot be ignored if your vessel is to remain safe. If sea cocks are always left open and neglected they can eventually seize, which will prove a serious threat to boat safety should a connecting hose fail and the sea cock refuse to close. There are three main types of sea cock: ball valves, cone valves and gate valves.

Servicing sea cocks

All through-hull fittings, including sea cocks, should be serviced at least once a year. As well as cleaning and regreasing the sea cocks themselves, the condition of the hoses and stainless steel clips need to be checked and replaced as necessary. Make sure two hose clips are used at each end of the hoses connected to sea cocks.

BALL VALVES
• Ball valves are hard-wearing but can stiffen and seize if they are not kept greased, which will also make them more likely to corrode. If a ball valve has become very stiff or seized, the first thing to do is use penetrating oil to try to loosen it.

- Even if the valve is moving reasonably satisfactorily, it will still pay to take it apart and check it for corrosion, give it a clean and apply fresh waterproof grease to help keep it in good working condition.
- If on inspection the valve looks seriously corroded, be prepared to replace it with a new one, even if it is still working, as trouble could be brewing. Remember to order a marine-grade valve as they are also made for domestic systems.

CONE VALVES

- Cone valves are usually made of bronze. They have a conical tube or plug that fits inside a cylindrical body which connects to a hose. The plug has a hole in one side and as it is turned by a handle the sea cock is opened and closed. Although bronze is hard-wearing the plug needs to be kept greased so that it can turn smoothly and also to prevent corrosion. The plug is held in place by a keeper plate with two bolts and locking nuts which need careful adjustment to allow the valve to operate smoothly.
- To service the valve, undo the keeper and remove the plug.
- Clean the plug and housing using a degreasing agent.
- Check the condition of the plug. Use grinding paste or fine wet and dry paper to polish the plug smooth before adding fresh sea cock grease – note that any old grease is not recommended: it is best to use the manufacturer's recommended waterproof grease, even if this is pricey.
- If the plug is badly pitted it might need replacing.

GATE VALVES

- Gate valves should also be greased and inspected annually. They are usually made of brass with a circular handle connected to a threaded rod which moves up and down to open and close a gate in the valve. They are more prone to failure than cone and ball valves, being very susceptible to corrosion in the marine environment.

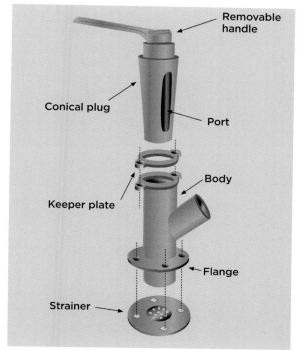

▲ A cone valve.

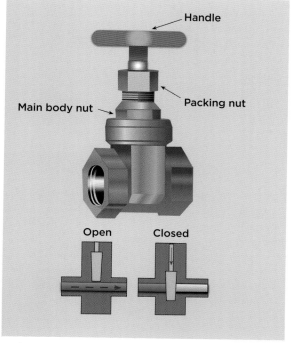

▲ A gate valve.

- The handles can get very stiff to operate and if they seize they will most likely need to be replaced. If so, it would be best to replace with a ball or cone valve, which are considered more reliable. A big drawback with gate valves is there is no way of knowing whether the valve is open or closed when it is seized.
- To service a gate valve, remove the valve body and dismantle it.

- Check for corrosion, clean and regrease.
- Also check for damage to the bottom part of the gate which is quite common.

JAMMED SEA COCKS
- Sea cocks can seize through lack of maintenance, corrosion or through lack of use. If a sea cock is seized, start by spraying it with penetrating oil and leave it for an hour or two.

Applying heat from a hot air gun also works. Resorting to a hammer is not a good idea.

International standard
The international standard for metal sea cocks and through-hull fittings is ISO 9093-1:1998. When replacing a sea cock check the replacement complies with this standard. Sub-standard fittings are more likely to corrode and fail.

Through-hull tips

TiP

Make a note of where all sea cocks and through-hull fittings are located.

- Ensure all hoses attached to sea cocks and through-hull fittings have two stainless steel hose clips.

- Tie a tapered softwood plug to each sea cock and fitting. Plugs can be hammered into a hole in case of a fitting failure.

Replacing a sea cock.
Top left Disconnect the pipe. Remove the sea cock and through-hull fitting.
Top right Thoroughly clean around the hole, removing all the old sealant.
Bottom left Fix the new through-hull fitting and attach the new sea cock.
Bottom right Double-check for leaks and warn the crane operators when relaunching.

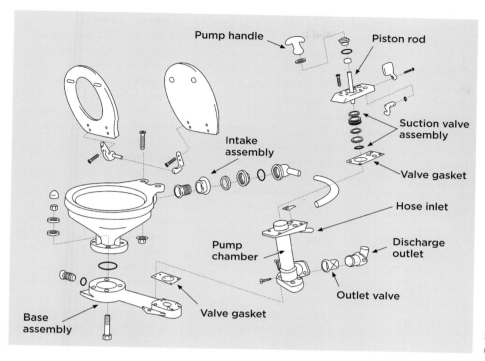

▲ Marine toilets need regular maintenance. Most manufacturers sell service kits with everything you need.

MARINE TOILETS

There are a number of different types of marine toilet or heads. They fall into one of three categories – manual, electric and vacuum, the most common being the manual, hand-pumped type. These have double-acting piston-pumps which both discharge the waste and flush the toilet with sea water. Composting toilets are also becoming more commonly used on boats. These are very effective and work by separating out the solids from the liquid waste and storing the solids in small holding tanks that can be emptied ashore, while liquid waste is pumped overboard.

Marine toilets have an inlet hose and outlet hose connected to sea cocks, which need regular servicing. Toilets below the waterline must have a vented loop fitting to prevent water from being siphoned into the boat via a leaking inlet valve. The vented loop should be fitted above the level of the waterline according to the manufacturer's instructions. Allowance should be made for sailing boats where the angle of heel will change the level of the waterline.

The main issues that cause problems with the heads through the boating season are scale deposits, blockage and unpleasant odours.

Scale deposits

A build-up of scale deposits in the hoses and toilet system causes the heads to become harder and harder to flush and the valves no longer function either.

The easiest way to avoid this happening is to flush the system with white vinegar from time to time. The vinegar dissolves the scale and will keep the problem under control.

A stronger acid such as hydrochloric acid is used by some boatowners to deal with more established build-up of scale, but then the issue is that such acids are harmful to the environment and sending hydrochloric acid to a holding tank is not desirable either. Regular flushing with white vinegar is preferable as it does not harm the environment. However, if the problem is well advanced sometimes the decision made is to replace the hoses, which is quite a costly solution.

One technique used is to remove the clogged pipes from the boat when it is in the boatyard and bash them against a wall or hard surface, which breaks down the calcium and this then falls out of the pipe.

Blockage

At some time or other most boatowners have had to deal with a marine toilet blockage or malfunction which they would rather forget about. This is seldom the fault of the system but more often than not is because an object other than human waste has been put in the toilet. Clear instructions need to be given to all those who come aboard how to use a marine toilet and these instructions should be provided in the heads also, to remind users and avoid embarrassment. Keeping a small waste bin in the heads is also advised.

Clearing a blockage in a manual toilet is done as follows:

- Close both sea cocks.
- Follow instructions for servicing the pump.
- Remove the pump and non-return valve in the discharge pipe, which will cause a leakage, so be ready with a bucket and sponge.
- Clear any debris between the bowl and the non-return valve.
- Check the pump for any debris.
- If no debris has been found, the problem lies in the pipework to the sea cock or holding tank if fitted.

Bad odours

The main source of bad odours comes from anaerobic bacteria, which break down sewage. These bacteria do not need oxygen to live while aerobic bacteria, which also break down raw sewage, do. Keeping the system aerated is therefore desirable as non-smelly aerobic bacteria will thrive. This can be done by ensuring that holding tanks have proper air vents fitted and that stagnant effluent is not allowed to remain trapped in hoses. Chemical treatments are available as are fresh-water flush systems.

Poor-quality outlet hoses that are not of a recommended sanitary grade should not be fitted to a toilet system as odours can find their way through the piping, even if liquid does not. To check if a hose is the culprit, the easiest way is to rub a clean cloth along it and then smell the cloth. The remedy here is to replace such permeable hoses with the correct grade, which may be expensive but necessary. If your boat does not have sanitary-grade piping this might be a boatyard job worth considering.

Leaks are another cause of bad smells, so it is worth keeping a check of all the joints in the sanitary system through the season, as the smallest leak will need to be dealt with.

Other causes of bad smells come from rotting organic matter such as seaweed and small marine organisms becoming trapped in the water inlet system or even in the toilet itself.

One remedy for this is to fit a raw-water strainer, similar to the strainers used for engines. Another is to get into the habit of doing fresh-water flushes of the heads, which entails closing the sea cocks and connecting to fresh water in order to do so.

Winterisation

Marine toilets should be drained completely, both as protection against frost damage and to prevent anaerobic bacteria from growing in the pipework. Follow the manufacturer's instructions on how to drain the system ashore, which typically include the following steps:

- Open any secondary valves.
- Remove the base drain plug.
- Disconnect the discharge flange from the pump.
- Loosen hose clips and disconnect the hose end from both sea cock hose tails. Pump the handle to drain the toilet pump and ensure all water is drained from the toilet system.

The use of antifreeze is not recommended as it is impossible to ensure that it penetrates the complete toilet system. If it is used, it must be glycol-based.

Holding tanks

Holding tanks should always be pumped out in a marina prior to lift out. They should also be flushed out with clean water regularly. If you decide to clean the inside of an empty tank out when ashore, most have inspection panels which can be removed to provide access.

SERVICING

Servicing the heads or replacing worn parts is not too horrendous a job when done ashore. Service kits and replacement parts are readily available and comparatively easy to install – though with boats we all know that is easier said than done.

Manual heads have a pump with a system of valves and seals which need replacing periodically as they become worn or damaged by calcification. When this happens they begin to leak. A service every year or two, depending on usage, is advisable. Make sure you have the correct service kit for your model of toilet, together with the manufacturer's instructions. Here is a very abbreviated list of instructions to give an idea of what is involved:

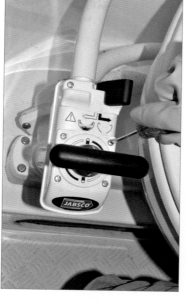

- Remove the pump assembly.
- Dismantle the pump assembly.
- Clean and disinfect all parts.
- Remove scale.
- Replace the piston O-ring and pump seals.
- Replace top and bottom valve gaskets and the joker valve, unless in perfect condition.
- Reassemble the pump, lubricating the cylinder bore with petroleum jelly.
- Vent loop valves can sometimes become blocked by salt crystals in the line. It is therefore a good idea to unscrew the valve and wash it in warm water.

GAS SYSTEM

There are correct types of hose for plumbing, sewerage, exhaust, cooling and gas. All hoses should be checked regularly for wear and deterioration. Hose clips should also be checked for corrosion. Nowhere is this more important than with the gas system, so it is important to check on the

▲ A gimballed gas stove with oven.

condition of the piping and clips. If there are any signs of corrosion, cracking or leaking in the pipes or flexible hose, these should be replaced as a top priority.

Gas bottles should be well secured in their lockers and gas drains left unobstructed. Don't be tempted to use the gas locker for extra stowage, as this could result in a blocked gas drain. The gas stove should have no signs of corrosion and burners need to be in full working order, including their safety cut outs.

GAS REGULATOR

Bottled gas is stored in gas bottles under very high pressure. A gas regulator is required to reduce the pressure before it enters the gas system. The regulator also incorporates an on/off control.

A regulator has a small air hole which is needed in order for a diaphragm inside it to work.

Safety first TiP

Gas systems should be installed by qualified engineers and in some countries this is compulsory. It is important for a boatowner to understand their boat's gas system and to be able to troubleshoot any potential problems. However, if an owner chooses to do their own maintenance work, then hiring an engineer to do a final check of the system is advised to ensure their boat is safe.

If this becomes blocked the gas will not flow properly, so this needs to be checked. If the regulator is corroded or has passed its expiry date it should be replaced.

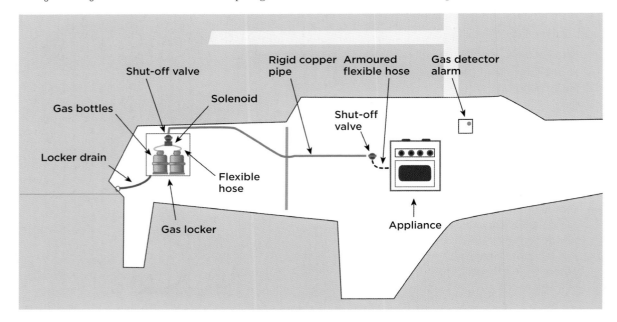

Gas bottles — Shut-off valve — Solenoid — Rigid copper pipe — Armoured flexible hose — Gas detector alarm — Shut-off valve — Locker drain — Flexible hose — Gas locker — Appliance

VARNISHING

Boat interiors on the whole are pretty resilient, but over time bulkheads, doors, the cabin sole and surfaces become scuffed, stained and suffer general wear and tear due to the marine environment. With the boat ashore and emptied, now is the time to think about giving the bilges a coat of paint and/or varnishing the interior over the winter months.

These are not quick jobs, at least in my experience. However, if other parts of the boat are under control and you can spare the time, brightening up the interior can prove to be a very rewarding boat improvement, especially of an older boat.

In an ideal world, the best location to undertake such a project is inside a heated boatshed, well protected from the winter weather and with access to power for decent lighting. Unfortunately, this was not my recent experience two winters ago, with the boat exposed to the elements and no access to power, but with perseverance I nonetheless achieved some satisfactory results.

Most boat interiors have a combination of varnished and painted surfaces, including solid wooden joinery, plywood laminates with thin hardwood veneers and glass reinforced plastic. When making your assessment of what you are going to do, bear in mind that the varnishing process consumes a lot of time, especially if the

▲ If you are going to varnish the interior, get everything out of the boat beforehand.

existing surfaces are in poor shape. This is because, in order to do a decent job, the preparation takes much longer than the brush work itself.

PREPARATION

Stripping and refinishing interior woodwork is best approached with some caution. Veneered surfaces are usually very thin and it is possible to sand right through a veneer.

Cleaning

- Start by cleaning surfaces with a mild bleach such as a hydrogen peroxide and water solution to remove any traces of mould. Bicarbonate of soda is good for removing oil and grease and a Scotch Brite-type pad soaked in ammonia works well.
- Bleached and darkened timber can be restored with oxalic acid in order to achieve a uniform timber surface. Trial and error works best as it all depends on

the actual state of the surfaces and whether the wood has been treated with varnish or oil over the years. Solid teak will often have been treated with oil, while a veneer will more likely have been varnished.
- Allow everything to dry before sanding.

Stripping

- If areas of old varnish are cracked and flaking, this will need to be scraped off using a paint scraper. Care needs to be taken not to damage the wood so a plastic scraper is preferable to a stainless steel one – either way proceed with caution.
- The decision then is whether to use a chemical stripper or proceed to sanding. I chose to use a gel-type paint stripper and although this proved a slow, messy process, in the end it worked out fine. I wore rubber gloves and a breathing mask to be on the safe side.

Filling

- Some of the bulkheads on my boat had had screw holes drilled into them in the past, presumably for securing instruments, fittings or shelving. I filled these with a teak-coloured wood filler before sanding.

Sanding

- Some people just launch straight in with the sanding, which may be fine with timber in good condition, but for those who have been cleaning, stripping and filling you are about halfway through the process. Somewhere between an 80- and 320-grit aluminium oxide paper is recommended for sanding, depending on the surface condition. It is best to use a sanding block to get an even finish and to finish with a 320-grit paper.
- Remember to sand along the grain of the wood to avoid scratches showing through the varnish.
- Once satisfied with the finish, some hours or even days later, remove all sanding dust, which is easier said than done in a confined space. This will most likely entail removing overalls and giving them a good shake outside.

Thinners

- Back inside and with dust removed, now brush the sanded surfaces with thinners and wipe with a clean soft cloth. This will remove traces of dust and any oil residue on the surface of the wood.

APPLYING THE VARNISH
Preparing to brush on

Good-quality brushes are a must with at least two sizes – for fine work and larger areas. Decant the varnish into an old jam jar and seal the lid of the tin to prevent any dust from getting in. I chose International's Goldspar Satin varnish, which is recommended for interior use. This can be thinned if necessary using thinners and is easy to apply.

Application

- When applying varnish on a vertical surface such as a door, brush in a vertical direction. For the first coat, thin the varnish a little as recommended on the instructions label on the tin.
- Work quickly in a controlled manner, taking care not to leave

▲ Emptying the boat was a good idea as tools soon take over. The cabin sole was taken home to allow the bilges to be painted.

▲ Putting dustsheets down is a must. Remember to wear a respirator when sanding. Apply the varnish on a dry sunny day with the hatches open. Two or three coats are best.

a build-up of varnish along the edges. Once you have worked over an area do not be tempted to brush over it again until it is completely dry. If there are any imperfections you notice these are best left until the varnish is dry. Only then can you sand the edges back before applying another coat.

- Be prepared to apply several coats of varnish to get a good finish, sanding in between coats with 220- to 320-grit wet and dry paper. Much depends on how much of a perfectionist you are.

If your objective is to restore your interior to pristine condition and to do the work yourself, then rather than sanding back and revarnishing old veneered surfaces in poor condition it may make more sense to consider replacing the veneered surface altogether.

INTERIOR PAINTING

If you have invested considerable time and effort varnishing your boat's interior, set aside a little extra time to paint the bilges, lockers, galley and heads with a fresh coat of paint. I recommend Danboline bilge paint for this, which is tough, durable and finishes to a thick, hard-wearing gloss. After all that varnishing, doing this is a piece of cake by comparison and almost as rewarding as the varnishing.

Prepare and paint the surfaces as follows:
- Remove any flaky paint with a wire brush.
- Remove debris with a vacuum cleaner or dustpan and brush.
- Use duct tape or other sticky tape to pull debris and grit out of inaccessible corners.
- Make sure the limber holes (waterways) in the bilges and bottom of lockers are clear of any blockages.
- Wash the surfaces with a degreaser to remove traces of oil, then a mild detergent. Rinse and dry thoroughly using old rags.
- Apply one or two coats of Danboline, following the instructions on the tin.

As spring approaches boatyards get busier and busier as owners prepare to get their boats launched. Most yard managers know only too well that this is the time they are going to be most in demand and are used to bending over backwards to help accommodate boatowners' requests to help with last-minute jobs.

It is worth talking to the yard well in advance and agreeing an approximate date for the launch day. Then the challenge is to work towards that date and have all the essentials done in time – we all benefit from a bit of pressure from time to time, but this is where some advance planning really helps.

ESSENTIALS

If jobs still need doing or completing, you need to prioritise which of these have to be done before the boat is back in the water. Here are some of the essential jobs to remember about well in advance of launch date:

- **Hull work:** Finish off all hull work such as antifouling, hull polishing, prop servicing and replacing anodes. Allow two or three days to do this work.

- **Bearings:** Check the cutless bearings and rudder bearings are all OK. If these have been forgotten remember that replacements need to be done with the boat out of the water. Talk to the yard as soon as possible if these need doing.
- **Through-hull fittings:** Are all the through-hull fittings checked and serviced? Allow at least half a day to do this work.

- **Rig inspection:** Sailing boats should have annual rig inspections. Has this been overlooked? Hopefully you did this months ago. If not, riggers are in much demand at this time of year so don't delay. Make sure that you do your own inspection if it is too late to book a rigger. Remember to grease the furling gear.

▲ A last-minute polish of the topsides prior to an early spring launch.

OTHER JOBS

It is easy to get sidetracked by non-essential jobs that can be done when the boat is afloat. However, if things are well under control then doing or finishing off the following tasks is a good idea with the boat in the boatyard:

- **Engine service:** The engine can be serviced afloat, but in my experience it is more convenient to do this in the boatyard.
- **Outboard service:** It is best to service the tender's outboard before launch day and check it is running OK.
- **Varnishing:** The problem with varnishing is that you need some warm weather to do this and it is not a winter job. If spring comes early, then take advantage of good weather to do some varnishing when the boat is ashore.

- **Winch servicing:** A good job to get done ashore if possible as you are less likely to lose springs and pawls over the side.
- **Running rigging:** This can be done once the boat is afloat, but if time allows it is a good idea to fit all the running rigging in the days before launch.

Preparing for the launch day

- Replace any of the spares that you may have used with the boat ashore.
- Take all the gear down to the boat the week before launch day.

▲ One day to launch, almost there.

◄ Finish off any varnishing before launch day if time and weather allows.

SAFETY EQUIPMENT CHECKS

- Check all safety equipment is in date and serviceable, including liferaft, fire extinguishers, man overboard equipment, flares, EPIRB and PLBs. Replace any safety equipment that is out of date.
- Check lifejackets for wear and tear of straps, belts, harnesses and stitching. Test the lifejackets for leaks by manually inflating them. They should retain air pressure for a minimum of 24 hours. Also check the lifejacket gas cylinders for corrosion and replace where necessary.

▲ The sun comes out and all the spruced up boats are itching to get in the water.

LAUNCH DAY

This year, everything went according to plan on launch day until I stepped on to the boat when it was afloat and still in the slings. Before removing the slings, the yard likes the owners to go aboard their boats to check the sea cocks and that the engine is all OK. The sea cocks were fine, but the engine was dead as a dodo. A certain amount of panic set in.

To cut a long story short, I was towed to the quayside and eventually traced the problem to an engine wiring fault. I was able to get on my way without having to call in outside help – very satisfying. As I set off under motor to my mooring a few miles from the yard, it felt very good to be back afloat. It didn't take long for me to decide to raise the sails and head off in the opposite direction for a couple of hours. Job done.

▲ That is me below the boat touching up the underneath of the keel with antifouling.

GLOSSARY

Adhesive sealant A gel-like sealant with adhesive qualities added. Used to seal joints on wood, fibreglass, metal and plastics. Cures to form a firm, rubbery, waterproof seal.

AIS The Automatic Identification System used to identify and track shipping and to exchange data with nearby ships.

Algaecide A biocide used for killing and preventing the growth of algae.

Alternator A belt-driven device connected to an engine that converts mechanical energy from the engine into electrical energy in the form of alternating current. Electronic components called diodes inside the alternator convert the alternating current into direct current for the purpose of battery charging.

Amp The Standard International (SI) unit (symbol A) that measures electric current.

Anode Also known as sacrificial anode, a metal object normally made of zinc that is attached to the hull and protects a marine engine, or propeller, shaft and other metal components from corrosion through electrolysis.

Antifouling A type of paint or coating designed to prevent the growth of barnacles and other marine organisms on the underwater surfaces of a boat's hull.

Backstay Part of the standing rigging that runs from the top of the mast to the stern of a sailing vessel, to give fore and aft support to the mast.

Ballast A heavy material placed in the bilge or purpose-made tanks below the waterline of a vessel to provide stability. Ballast counteracts the effects of weight above the waterline. A yacht's keel provides ballast to resist the lateral forces on the sails which cause heeling.

Batten A sail batten is a thin, flexible strip of fibreglass, carbon fibre or wood that is inserted into a pocket sewn into a sail. This helps to improve the sail's aerodynamic shape and performance.

Bilge The lowest parts inside a boat where water and other liquids collect.

Biocide A substance or microorganism that is used to deter, render harmless and kill living organisms by chemical or biological means.

Bleeding A process which rids a diesel engine's fuel lines of air, to enable the engine to start. Air trapped in a fuel line prevents the supply of fuel to the cylinders. Bleeding the air involves opening and closing a series of valves in the system.

Boom vang A device for pulling the boom down in order to flatten the mainsail and prevent the boom from rising.

Bottle-screw A screw fitting on guardrails, shrouds and stays, used to adjust their tension.

Bulkhead A vertical panel or partition within the hull of a vessel, often designed to provide structural rigidity and used to create watertight compartments to reduce the risk of flooding if a hull is breached.

Butyl A synthetic rubber used widely as a flexible sealant, also commonly used for gasket materials when an airtight seal is required. Butyl is often found in the form of tape and has the consistency of chewing gum.

Cap shroud Part of a sailing boat's standing rigging that holds the mast in place from side to side and is adjusted to centre the masthead over the centre of the boat. Cap shrouds, also known as upper shrouds, are attached at the masthead and run down to deck level where they are attached to a chain plate.

Carvel A method used in wooden boat building where hull planks are laid edge to edge and fastened to a strong frame, resulting in a smooth hull surface. Carvel planks are joined to each other with a caulking sealant to keep the hull waterproof.

Caulking A material used to seal joints or seams to prevent leakage between planks of wood, commonly used on wooden vessels. Traditional materials used for caulking include cotton fibres and oakum, which are driven into the hull and deck seams using a caulking iron, and then covered with mastic. Modern materials used for caulking include marine sealants.

Chain plate A metal fitting on each side of the hull to which the shrouds are attached.

Clevis pin A pin similar to a bolt, either threaded or unthreaded, that fastens through a U-shaped piece or clevis to form a shackle.

Clinker A method used in wooden boat building where the lower edge of a hull plank overlaps the upper edge of the plank below it. The planks are riveted together using copper nails. Clinker construction requires no caulking.

Collet Part of a winch used to hold the shaft in place in the casing. A collet has a tongue that projects through a hole in the casing into a groove in the shaft, thereby holding the mechanism in place while it is rotated.

Composite A term commonly applied to describe structures incorporating a combination of fibres and materials. A composite material is produced from two or more different constituent materials that may be combined for various reasons including saving weight, strength and efficiency.

Compressor A mechanical device similar to a pump that increases the pressure of a gas or fluid by reducing its volume.

Cotter pin A stainless steel pin used for securing items such as turnbuckles, rigging screws and pulley blocks.

Crevice corrosion A type of metal corrosion occurring in confined spaces, found, for example, in the gap or crevice between two joining surfaces where salt water has penetrated, causing corrosion to take place.

Cringle A small reinforced hole or eye in a sail through which a rope can pass.

Cunningham A sail control line used to adjust the tension of a sail's luff.

Cutless bearing A type of bearing that is used at the outer end of a propeller shaft to help hold it in place and lubricate the shaft. The bearing has an inner sleeve made of rubber and an outer case made of metal or composite material.

Dacron A type of polyester fibre commonly used in sailcloth.

Deck collar Also known as a mast collar, a deck collar is used on a rig with a keel-stepped mast to prevent deck level chafe and minimise wear between the mast and the hull.

Delamination A failure in a laminated material, which results in the separation of the layers caused by cracking, bending, flexing and adhesion failure.

Displacement hull A hull designed to always remain in the water and push through it rather than skim or plane across the surface.

Dremel A rotary tool, which can be used for grinding, cutting, buffing and sanding.

Dye testing An inspection method used to locate defects such as hairline and fatigue cracks in non-porous materials.

Dyneema A very lightweight strong synthetic rope often used for halyards and backstays.

Electrolytic action Corrosion that is caused by stray currents from a power source via faulty wiring, a faulty device leaking current or via a shore power connection with no galvanic isolation.

Epoxy resin A type of strong compound glue used as an adhesive or coating made by converting liquid polyethers into infusible solids through a process called curing.

Eroding antifouling see **Soft antifouling**.

Exhaust elbow The part of a marine engine where the raw-water cooling mixes with and cools the exhaust gases from the exhaust manifold before they are forced to the exhaust outlet.

Eye splice A permanent loop or eye in the end of a rope.

Foot The lower edge of a sail.

Forestay The stay that runs from the masthead to the bow to give fore-and-aft support to the mast.

Fractional rig A type of sailing boat rig where the forestay is attached to the mast between the spreaders and the top of the mast.

Galvanic corrosion An electrochemical action between two metals in which one metal causes the other to corrode when in contact with each other or in the presence of an electrolyte, for example stainless steel causes aluminium to corrode in the presence of sea water.

Gate valve A valve that shuts off the flow of liquid through a pipe by lowering a barrier to close the valve and raising the barrier to open it; operated by turning a wheel on top of the valve.

Gelcoat A material used to give a high quality, smooth gloss outer layer finish to a GRP-moulded hull.

Gelshield A quick-drying epoxy primer that protects GRP hulls against osmosis by reducing the level of water penetration into a hull.

Genoa A large headsail that overlaps the mainsail.

Gimbal A pivoted support that allows the rotation of an object about a single axis and so remain horizontal, for example as used to stabilise a compass or a galley stove when a boat pitches and rolls.

Gland A seal on a rotating shaft used to prevent leakage of oil or water.

GMDSS Global Maritime Distress and Safety System.

Gooseneck A universal joint fitting on a mast that secures the boom to the mast.

GRP Glass reinforced plastic.

Gudgeon The cylindrical female part of a rudder fitting normally attached to a transom of a boat into which a pivoting hinge or pintle fits.

Guy Rope running aft connected to a spinnaker pole used to pull the pole backwards; also a rope running forward from a boom to prevent an unexpected gybe.

Halyard Rope used to haul a sail up a mast.

Hard antifouling The basic type of antifouling which withstands regular wiping down and does not erode much. Biocide is released from the surface of the coating to deter microorganisms but over time the leaching rate reduces and after a few seasons the antifouling needs to be scraped off the hull and replaced.

Head The top corner of a sail.

Heads A nautical term used for a boat's toilet compartment. In old sailing vessels the toilet was in the bows or head, hence the name.

Heat exchanger A system used to transfer heat between two fluids which pass close to each other through a system of pipes or tubes for both cooling and heating purposes.

Holding tank Storage tank for holding toilet waste.

Hull-to-deck joint The joint that holds the deck and hull of a boat together. A number of methods are used to attach a deck to a hull, including a glassed joint, bolting the deck and hull together, and simply attaching the deck by means of screws, which is considered less reliable and more prone to leakage.

Hydro-generator A device that uses the speed of a boat to turn a propeller that produces electricity.

Impeller A rotor connected to a motor-driven shaft used to increase the flow and pressure of a fluid, as found in a marine engine's cooling system.

Inhibitor A fuel additive used to protect against corrosion in diesel engine fuel systems.

Injector A system that uses an atomising nozzle and a valve to direct high pressure fuel into an engine evenly, for optimum combustion and efficiency.

Inner forestay A stay attached to the mast above the spreader and made fast at deck level aft of the main forestay and parallel to it.

Inverter A device that converts DC to AC current to power electrical appliances.

Jackstay A tightly stretched wire along which something can slide. Term commonly used for the safety webbing or wire running along the deck for crew to attach their lifelines to.

Kedge anchor A light anchor, often kept in a cockpit locker, used to anchor for a short time.

Keel bolt Fastener used to attach a bolted-on keel to a hull. The majority of keel bolts are made from stainless steel studs that are cast into the keel and secured with nuts. The studs and nuts should be inspected annually for signs of rust or staining.

Knuckle A sharp curve in a frame or in the contour of a hull.

Laminate A laminate sail has multiple layers of materials with different characteristics, which are combined to help resist stretching.

Leech The after edge of a sail.

Lift pump A low-pressure pump that moves diesel fuel from the fuel tank to the high pressure injection pump of an engine. Lift pumps often have a lever that allows the pump to be operated by hand.

Liquid penetrant inspection An inspection test using a highly fluid liquid that is applied to a surface and penetrates fissures and voids open to the surface.

Log A device, also known as a speed log, fitted with a paddlewheel or small propeller that measures the speed and distance a vessel travels through the water.

Luff The front edge of a sail.

Mast tang A fitting used for fastening rigging externally to a mast.

Masthead rig A type of sailing boat rig where the forestay is attached to the top of the mast.

Mastic 1: a generic term used to describe flexible sealant and adhesive that may be made from a variety of substances. 2: a natural plant resin that comes from mastic trees and is traditionally used in varnishes.

Mizzen The mast furthest aft in a yawl or ketch.

Moisture meter An instrument that detects excessive moisture in GRP and hardwood hulls. Specifically used to identify the presence of osmosis in GRP hulls.

Multimeter An electronic measuring instrument used to measure voltage, current and resistance.

NAVTEX (Navigational Telex) delivers navigation, meteorological and safety information to shipping up to 200 nautical miles offshore.

Osmosis Term describing the blistering found on GRP boat hulls. This occurs as water molecules pass into a hull and condense within small air pockets, voids and tiny cracks in the layers of polyester resin reinforced glass fibres that make up the hull. The water reacts with water soluble components, the voids increase in size and the rate of water absorption increases, resulting in a pressure build up that causes blistering. As the process continues more blistering forms and treatment may be required as the structural integrity of the hull is affected.

Outdrive See: **Sterndrive**.

Pawl A spring-loaded mechanical component pivoted at one end and used in the winch mechanism. This allows the winch to turn one way only and prevents it from recoiling.

Pintle A rudder pintle is a metal fitting onto which a hanging rudder is hung.

PLB Personal Locator Beacon.

Polyester resin A synthetic plastic or polymer that bonds well with glass fibres and once cured is weather and water resistant. In fluid form it is known as 'unsaturated' and in fibre form is known as 'saturated'. Unsaturated resin is normally a solution of polyester in styrene. This requires a catalyst to be added in order for the resin to harden, or cure.

Polyurethane A synthetic plastic or polymer material used in various forms for manufacturing purposes, including adhesives, coatings, composites and building materials. As an adhesive polyurethane creates a permanent bond.

Preventer A line rigged to secure the boom and prevent an accidental gybe.

Pulpit A protective rail at the bow of a boat.

Pushpit A protective rail at the stern of a boat.

Quadrant A fan-shaped fitting mounted on a rudder post around which cables are attached that connect via sheaves to the pedestal of a wheeled steering system. Quadrants are usually made from cast aluminium or bronze.

Raw-water cooling system An engine cooling system that sucks water from outside a boat (sea water or fresh) through a sea cock to a filter, circulates it via a pump through a network of pipes in the engine to cool it, then pumps it out of the boat via the exhaust system.

Regulator A governor mechanism that may control or limit something, for example the flow of fuel, voltage or gas pressure.

Resistance Is a measure of the opposition to the flow of current in an electrical circuit. Resistance is measured in ohms (Ω).

Running rigging Ropes used for raising, lowering, shaping and adjusting the sails and spars of a sailing boat – as opposed to the standing rigging.

Saildrive A propulsion system that incorporates a series of gears, which enable a vertical shaft to extend downwards from a gearbox aft of the inboard engine through the hull. This connects to a short horizontal output shaft to which the propeller is attached.

Sandwich construction A form of boat construction used for hulls and decks where two outer skins of resin saturated fibreglass are held apart by a lightweight inner core of balsa, foamed plastic or similar. This method saves weight, achieves stiffness and improves buoyancy compared with traditional GRP hull construction.

SART Search And Rescue Transponder.

Scarf joint A joint that enables two lengths of timber to be joined end to end. The two ends are cut at a shallow angle to allow the glued joint to be at least eight times the width of the timbers.

Scope The length of anchor cable.

Sea cock A through-hull fitting with a valve that allows the ingress or egress of water.

Sealant Material used to seal a joint so as to make it airtight or watertight. Sealants are designed to retain flexibility after they have cured.

Shaft drive A conventional propulsion system where power is transmitted from an inboard engine to a propeller shaft which exits the hull at a slight angle near the stern of a boat.

Sheave The wheel part of a pulley block.

Shroud A stay, usually made of wire, that supports each side of a mast. Cap shrouds reach the top of the mast.

Lowers reach an intermediate point, often below the spreaders.

Silicone A synthetic polymer, derived from silicon metal. It is available in the form of rubbers, greases and fluids. It has excellent resistance to UV and ozone degradation.

Skeg A vertical blade beneath the hull, used to support and protect the rudder.

Skin fitting A term which refers to a variety of metal or plastic components which involve going through the hull fittings, the sea cock being an example.

Slab reefing A system used to reduce sail area where the sail is partially lowered and folded along the boom in layers or slabs. Cringles (eyes) on the luff and leach of the sail form the new tack and clew, allowing the shortened sail to be controlled.

Snatch block A block which can be hinged open at the side to allow a rope to be easily inserted through it.

Soda blasting A form of abrasive blasting where sodium bicarbonate particles are blasted against a surface using compressed air. It is less abrasive than sandblasting.

Soft antifouling A type of antifouling that erodes slowly as a vessel moves through the water in order that a fresh film of antifouling is always present on a hull's surface.

Solenoid A device that converts an electrical signal into mechanical motion using an electromagnet. A solenoid is an important component of an engine's starter motor.

Spar A general term used for masts, booms, gaffs, yards and spinnaker poles.

Spline A thin strip of wood inserted into a seam of a wooden hull to seal it.

Split pin Also known as a cotter pin, is a metal fastener often used to secure a clevis pin. Split pins are normally made from a piece of wire or metal (usually stainless steel) that is folded in half. They have two tines or prongs with an eyelet at the bend. The pin can be inserted through a hole in a clevis pin and the two prongs folded back to hold it securely in place.

Spreader A strut, normally used in pairs, attached horizontally to a mast. The spreaders hold the shrouds equidistantly away from the mast in order to widen the angle between the shrouds and the mast, so ensuring they support it effectively.

Stanchion Metal poles that support the guard rail lines.

Standing rigging The fixed lines, wires or rods which support the masts of a sailing vessel.

Stay A wire that runs either forward or aft of the mast, to help support it.

Stern gear General term for the propeller, the propeller shaft plus supporting brackets and bearings.

Stern gland A collar made of either brass or rubber that prevents the ingress of water where a propeller shaft exits a boat's hull.

Stern tube A hollow tube which holds the bearings, seals and propeller shaft. The stern tube is filled with grease, oil or water and forms a barrier between the water outside the hull and the engine room of a vessel.

Sterndrive A form of propulsion which combines an inboard engine connected to an outboard drive unit outside the stern of the hull.

Stringer In wooden boat construction, fore-and-aft timbers running the length of a hull. In GRP hulls wooden stringers may be bonded into the laminate for extra stiffness.

Swaging A method of securing wire rope or cable with a permanently applied fitting or sleeve. A swaged terminal is a fitting attached to the end of a rigging wire using great force. The wire is inserted into a hollow terminal and pulled through a set of roller dies under great pressure.

Tack The lower, forward corner of a sail.

Tang A metal strip, riveted or bolted to a spar to provide an attachment point for running rigging.

Thimble A metal or plastic eye which fits inside an eye formed in a rope to prevent chafe.

Through-hull fitting A fitting with a hole that passes through the hull of a boat. A through-hull fitting can be used to allow sea water in for cooling purposes, to expel waste water or to allow sensors such as depth gauges and speed logs to be fitted.

Topsides The sides of a hull between the deck and the waterline.

Transceiver A device that combines both a transmitter and receiver in one housing.

Transducer The unit of an instrument system that converts depth, speed, etc. into electrical signals.

Transponder A device used in search and rescue that emits a signal in response to a rescue ship's radar.

Trim tab An underwater plate fitted at the stern of a motorboat designed to lift the stern. This lessens the drag through the water as the boat builds up speed and prevents the bow from rising. Trim tabs are adjustable to achieve maximum performance and efficiency.

Trysail A small, heavy sail used to replace the mainsail in very strong winds**.**

Vang See: **Boom vang**.

Volt The Standard International (SI) unit (symbol V) that measures electromotive force or the potential difference required to carry 1 ampere or amp (symbol A) of current through a resistance of 1 Ohm (Ω).

Watt The Standard International (SI) unit of power, corresponding to the rate of consumption of energy in an electric current where the potential difference is one volt (V) and the current one ampere (A).

Yawl A two-masted yacht where the aft mast is aft of the rudder post.

FURTHER READING

The Adlard Coles Book of Diesel Engines
by Mel Bartlett
ISBN 978-1-4729-5540-1

The Adlard Coles Book of Hull & Deck Repair
by Don Casey
ISBN 978-1-4081-0002-8

The Adlard Coles Book of Maintenance and Repair for Diesel Engines
by Jean-Luc Pallas
ISBN 978-1-4729-0120-0

The Adlard Coles Book of Maintenance and Repair for Outboard Motors
by Jean-Luc Pallas
ISBN 978-1-4729-0122-4

Boat Building Techniques Illustrated
by Richard Birmingham
ISBN 978-0-7136-7621-1

The Boat Maintenance Bible
by Pat Manley and Rupert Holmes
ISBN 978-1-4081-5609-4

The Boat Repair Bible
by Rupert Holmes, Richard Johnstone-Bryden and Jake Kavanagh
ISBN 978-1-4081-5917-0

Boatowner's Mechanical and Electrical Manual
by Nigel Calder
ISBN 978-1-4729-4667-6

Clinker Boatbuilding
by John Leather
ISBN 978-0-7136-3643-7

The Complete Book of Yacht Care
by Michael Verney
ISBN 978-0-7136-4658-0

The Complete Guide to Metal Boats
by Bruce Robert-Goodson
ISBN 978-0-7136-6951-0

Essential Boat Electrics
by Pat Manley
Fernhurst Books Ltd
ISBN 978-1-9099-1110-9

Fibreglass Boats
by Hugo Du Plessis
ISBN 978-1-4081-2274-7

Fitting Out Your Boat – Fibreglass or Wood
by Michael Naujok
ISBN 978-0-7136-6806-3

Metal Corrosion in Boats
by Nigel Warren
ISBN 978-0-7136-7817-8

Upgrading Your Boat's Interior
by Mike Westin
ISBN 978-1-4081-3295-1

Wooden Boatbuilding
by Jean-Francois Garry
ISBN 978-1-4081-2853-4

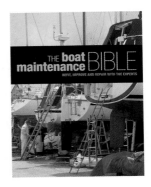

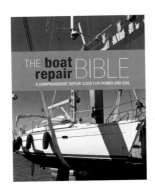

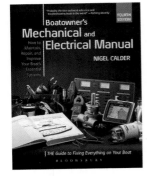

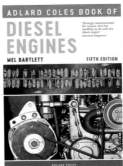

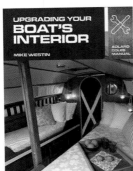

PHOTO CREDITS & ACKNOWLEDGEMENTS

(Top/centre/bottom = t/c/b,
left/right = l/r)

All photographs © the author and
Bloomsbury Publishing except:

Amnat jomjun/Getty Images: 76.
Beta Marine Limited: 146c.
Henry Bettle: 68, 69c, 69b, 98,
99t, 119tr, 126tr, 158, 159, 167,
177tl, 177tc, 177b, 180t.
Mark Bowden: 57tr, 199.
Niki Cath: 8t, 12t, 12b, 43tr, 43b,
44t, 46, 54–55, 56, 64, 111tc,
138, 142, 211l, 212, 213.
Freya Lister: 43tl, 43tc.
Viki Moore: 17, 19, 24, 25t, 25b.
Shutterstock 140.

AUTHOR'S ACKNOWLEDGEMENTS

Henry Bettle BEng (Hons) AMRINA
AMSCMS AMIMarEST for providing
the Surveyor's Tips – see pages 22,
68, 111, 135, 173, 174 and 199.

Mark Bowden for providing his
expert advice and encouragement.

Tim Cath, owner of The Bosham
Yacht Company for providing his
advice and Niki Cath for providing
photographs (see photo credits).

Viki Moore, for her permission to
reproduce her maintenance log
on pages 26–33 and for providing
photographs (see photo credits).

I am immensely grateful to the staff
at Adlard Coles who have been
very supportive throughout the
book's development, especially to
Sarah Jones and Elizabeth Multon.

Lastly to my wife Clara for
her constant support and
encouragement during the writing
and illustrating of this book.

INDEX

SPECIFICATIONS AND INVENTORY

Name:	Builder:	Model:	Year:

Length overall	m/ft	Engine	
Length waterline	m/ft	Engine power	kw/hp
Beam	m/ft	Cruising speed	kts
Draft	m/ft	Fuel capacity	lit /gal (uk)
Sail area with jib	sq m/ft	Drive type	
Sail area with genoa	sq m/ft	Propeller	
Displacement	kg/lb	Gas installation	
Ballast	kg/lb	Electrical circuit	
Keel type		Batteries	
Hull type		Navigation lights	
Rudder		Nav equipment	
Steering		Water capacity	lit /gal (uk)
Deck fittings		Galley	
Hatches		Heads	
Rig		Sea cocks	
Standing rigging		Holding tank capacity	lit / gal (uk)
Running rigging		Other equipment	
Sails		Other equipment	
Anchors		Other equipment	
Chain and warp		Other equipment	